Sweetness

CHRISTY JORDAN

Sweetness

SOUTHERN RECIPES
TO CELEBRATE THE WARMTH, THE LOVE, AND THE BLESSINGS OF A FULL LIFE

Workman Publishing · New York

Library of Congress Cataloging-in-Publication Data is available.

ISBN 978-0-7611-8942-8

DESIGN by Jean-Marc Troadec
PHOTOGRAPHY by Lucy Schaeffer
AUTHOR PHOTO courtesy of Hoffman Media copyright © 2013
FOOD STYLING by Nora Singley
PROP STYLING by Sara Abalan
ILLUSTRATIONS by James Williamson

All family photos appear courtesy of the Jordan family.

Workman books are available at special discounts when purchased in bulk for premiums and sales promotions as well as for fund-raising or educational use. Special editions or book excerpts can also be created to specification. For details, contact the Special Sales Director at the address below, or send an email to specialmarkets@workman.com.

Workman Publishing Company, Inc.
225 Varick Street
New York, NY 10014-4381
workman.com

Printed in the United States of America
First printing September 2016

10 9 8 7 6 5 4 3 2 1

This book is dedicated to that golden generation: your grandparents, my grandparents. The people who blazed the trail for us and taught us how to cook, snap beans, ice cakes, and set the table. This is dedicated to the strong arms that all too soon became frail and still managed to love us like no one else ever could. To the folks who seemed to know a little bit about everything and had the biggest hearts we will ever know. You are missed, but the sweetness you brought to our lives still remains.

To Grandmama, Granddaddy, and Lela:
I sure do miss you.

Contents

A cookie jar is meant to be filled with handmade treats, and these cookie recipes will ensure that it's never empty! There's something for everyone here: Graham Cracker Praline Cookies, Milk Dunkin' Peanut Butter Cookies, Monster Cookies, Easy Coconut Macaroons, Flop Cookies, Candy Cane Cookies, Chewy Cranberry Zingers, and more.

There is something supremely satisfying about baking up a pan of brownies or bars and cutting them into squares for everyone to enjoy. Please a crowd with Peanut Butter Cheesecake Bars, Easiest S'mores Brownies, Chewy Pear Bars, Chocolate Chip Dream Bars, and Cranberry Bliss Bars.

A homemade cake makes any occasion special, especially when frosted with the perfect icing or topped with a decadent drizzle of glaze. Choose from all manner of cakes, like Mama Reed's Jam Cake, Red Velvet Cupcakes, Hummingbird Cake, Lemon Custard Poke Cake, Buttermilk Lime Pound Cake, Dark Chocolate Mousse Cake, and Peanut Butter Cup Trifle.

No matter the reason or occasion, a slice of pie is always a welcome treat. Here you'll find some of my family's favorite recipes plus tried-and-true classics, like Peach Buttermilk Pie, Chocolate Chess Pie, Faux Apple Pie, Frozen Oreo Pie, Strawberry Cream Pie, Fruit Cocktail Pie, and Old-Fashioned Coconut Pie.

Remarkably delicious but simple enough to whip up at a moment's notice, dense cobblers and creamy puddings are a great addition to any gathering. You can't go wrong with recipes like Mimi's Peach Cobbler, Old-Fashioned Banana Pudding, Lemon Syllabub, Sweet Potato Crème Brûlée, Old-Fashioned Butter Rolls (think cinnamon buns in a rich custard sauce), and Vanilla Wafer Pineapple Pudding.

No matter the time of day, homemade breads and muffins are the perfect treat to satisfy any sweet tooth. Fill up a breakfast basket with Mom's Banana Bread, Strawberry Pecan Bread, and Amazing Pineapple Bread, or bake up some Apple Oat Muffins, Hot Cocoa Muffins, and Bake Shop Blueberry Muffins and tuck them, still warm, into lunch boxes or snack bags.

These classic dishes are staples of the Southern dessert table. They're refreshing, versatile, and have nearly endless variations—and you'll find my favorites here: Peach Buttermilk Congealed Salad, Aunt Tina's Dr Pepper Salad, Raspberry Salad, Five-Cup Fruit Salad, Guilt-Free Orange Dream Salad, Ambrosia, and more.

These super easy crowd-pleasers are ideal for holidays and celebrations, easily transportable and even easier to devour! Make the party with a batch of Cream Cheese Mints, Cornetha's Strawberry Candy, Chocolate Chip Meringues, Peanut Butter Cups, Cinnamon Cashews, and 3 kinds of fudge.

Nothing's more inviting than an icy cold beverage on a hot summer day—or a warm mug that takes the chill off a cold one. Serve up Daddy's Milkshakes, Old-Fashioned Egg Creams, Fresh Strawberry-ade, Southern Sweet Tea, and a whole host of simple, delectable drinks both cold and hot.

Missing something? There's no need to make a special trip to the store when you can whip up simple basics like Cookie Crumb Crust, Mix-in-Pan Pie Crust, Meringue, Homemade Whipped Cream, and other pantry staples.

Preface

My entire life has been lived hand in hand with memories. First as a child, hearing the stories of folks long since gone, told amid laughter in rooms where there were so many assembled it was standing room only. Often, the more tender memories were shared at my mother's elbow in the kitchen, when she gave me a glimpse into her life when she had been my age. As I grew, the stories began to include me from time to time, my life becoming its own thread in the tapestry of family and friends. One of the great joys in my life now involves watching how my children, Brady and Katy, add their own threads to this ever-growing work of life.

Life is not always easy. Sometimes the hardships seem almost insurmountable. Stories of times in which my ancestors didn't know how they would make it through have, over time, been woven in with similar experiences from my parents and eventually people in my own generation.

I am reminded of my grandmama, Lucille, who always had a smile when a smile was needed most. Being that she was a Southern woman, many of my memories of her are in the kitchen. She had lived a hard life by anyone's standards, but she managed to come to a point where food was plentiful—and her cooking followed suit.

My grandmama never lacked appreciation for any dish that was set upon the table, and that genuine gratitude came from living in a place where food was scarce. She didn't dwell on that, though, as she placed bowls of vegetables and tender cuts of meat on a table that welcomed all. The final dish always brought a particular twinkle to her eye and made her usual smile all the more bright: dessert.

"We've got to have a little something sweet to finish it off," she'd say. To someone who didn't know her life, they would think she was talking about the meal, and she was in a way. But when you sat back and listened to stories she told, the tales of hardship always ended on a good note, because no matter what trial the family had faced, they had grown closer, stronger, and more aware of the magnitude of blessings they possessed.

Grandmama taught me that life is going to present challenges, storms to weather, and great losses. We are going to fall down and it may take some time to stand up again. But amid all of this, the blessings rise up around us in friends, experiences, and moments of warmth and tenderness that our hearts capture and hold dear as if they were precious photographs, enclosed in a gilded frame.

And at the end of the day and at the end of a life, what we remember most is that special touch, the memories and laughter, the warmth and the love: the sweetness.

Why Is It That We Cook?

Do you ever pause to think about why we cook? Beyond the old Southern expression "Well, we've gotta eat!" and past the utility of meals and the physical purpose that they serve. When you put that off to the side and really take a look at the underlying picture, why is it that we cook?

For me, I don't necessarily cook because I am hungry. If it is just me, I grab a sandwich or make a salad. But when I cook for my family, that's different. I cook for them not just to feed them, but because I love them. And for me, cooking is a way to show that. I cook delicious food and take extra time beyond sandwiches and salads because I want to sit across from them and see them enjoy their meal while I hear about their day.

Why do we cook the old-fashioned dishes, though? Think about the recipes we grew up with. The handwritten ones, from old cookbooks with broken spines and pencil notes written in the margins. The ones where our heart leaps at finding a decades-old speck of flour that remains long after the cook has been gone from our lives.

We cook those recipes because we miss the people we have lost.

We miss the way their house smelled when we walked in to find them in the kitchen, pulling out a pan of cookies or stirring a pot of something special they made because they knew it was one of our favorites. We miss the smile of satisfaction as they fixed us a plate and sat across from us to watch us enjoy it. We miss that first bite, which, no matter what it was, tasted better than anything else in the world because it was made for us with such love. We miss the flavors, but mostly we miss the people, the ones who used to sit across from us at the end of our day.

Making those dishes again renews that connection, just like visiting their resting place does, only in a more real, tangible way. By following the same steps they did, reading notes they made, and remembering them measuring, mixing, and rolling, it is like they are really there with us all along when we sit down to the finished dishes and take that first bite.

We cook for a variety of reasons, but the best meals are the ones where we take time to reach through the generations and bring to life once more the moments from our past. We cook their recipes because we miss them. And cooking these dishes, in the old-fashioned ways, in our hearts and in our memories, brings them back in a very real way.

There you are, Grandmama. I sure have missed you.

From the Cookie Jar

WE DIDN'T HAVE much money growing up. My dad was a police officer and he worked extra jobs on the weekends so Mama could stay home and care for the three of us because that was important to them. Like most families I know (then and now) there was very little wiggle room in Mama's grocery budget. She managed to set a fine table despite that, but it still bothered her that she couldn't afford to buy us treats from time to time like many of our friends had.

Did we feel bad? No sir, not for one minute, because Mama worked hard to provide us with other treats, and one of those was homemade cookies. She usually made cookies twice a week, sometimes more if the neighborhood kids showed up in larger numbers than usual. Everyone knew Mama was always good for a homemade cookie and a glass of Kool-Aid whenever they were over. I have so many memories of the wonderful things my mother baked for us growing up, but at the top of the list has to be those countless pans of fresh-baked comfort.

Monster Cookies

If you want to make a cookie that everyone will fall in love with, start here. Peanut butter, chocolate chips, M&M's, oats for the oat lover, butter for the butter lover—there is so much to love in this chewy cookie that I don't even know where to begin! These are some of my favorite cookies to tuck into lunch boxes and briefcases as little surprises. *Makes 5 to 6 dozen cookies*

Nonstick cooking spray,
    for coating the baking sheets
1½ cups chunky peanut butter
    (see Note)
1 cup dark brown sugar
1 cup granulated sugar
½ cup (1 stick) butter,
    at room temperature
3 large eggs
4 cups quick-cooking or
    old-fashioned oats
2½ teaspoons baking soda
1 teaspoon vanilla extract
½ teaspoon salt
1 cup peanut butter chips
1 cup semisweet or milk
    chocolate chips
1 cup mini M&M's

1 Preheat the oven to 350°F. Lightly coat 2 baking sheets with cooking spray.

2 Combine the peanut butter, sugars, butter, eggs, oats, baking soda, vanilla, and salt in a large mixing bowl. Beat with an electric mixer at medium speed until well combined, 1 to 2 minutes. Add the peanut butter chips, chocolate chips, and M&M's and beat again until well blended.

3 Form the dough into golf ball-size balls and place them 2 inches apart on the cookie sheets.

4 Bake until lightly browned, 10 to 12 minutes. Remove from the oven and let them cool for 5 minutes before removing from the pans.

Monster Cookies will keep, in an airtight container at room temperature, for up to 1 week.

NOTE: If you have only creamy peanut butter in your pantry, use that. No need to make a special trip and spend extra money.

Monster Cookies, page 3

All-American Oatmeal Chocolate Chip Cookies

My son's favorite cookie is the good old classic chocolate chip, and this has become our standard recipe. The addition of oats helps keep the cookie moist and chewy (even if my teenage son leaves the lid off the cookie jar overnight), while the dark brown sugar and morsels of semisweet chocolate balance it out to make it nothing short of all-around amazing. *Makes about 4 dozen cookies*

Nonstick cooking spray,
   for coating the baking sheets
1 cup (2 sticks) butter,
   at room temperature
1 cup dark brown sugar
1/2 cup granulated sugar
2 large eggs
2 teaspoons vanilla extract
2 cups all-purpose flour
1 cup quick-cooking oats
1 teaspoon baking powder
1 teaspoon baking soda
1 teaspoon salt
2 1/2 cups semisweet
   chocolate chips

1 Preheat the oven to 325°F. Lightly coat 2 large baking sheets with cooking spray and set aside.

2 Place the butter and sugars in a large mixing bowl and beat with an electric mixer at medium speed until fluffy, about 1 minute. Add the eggs and vanilla and beat again until blended.

3 Add the flour, oats, baking powder, baking soda, and salt. Beat until smooth and blended, scraping down the side of the bowl as needed, about 1 minute. Stir in the chocolate chips just until incorporated.

4 Using a cookie scoop or tablespoon, shape the dough into 1-inch balls and place on the prepared baking sheets 2 inches apart.

5 Bake until lightly browned at the edges, 12 to 15 minutes. Allow to cool slightly on the baking sheets before transferring to a waxed paper-lined countertop or cooling rack to cool completely. Enjoy!

All-American Oatmeal Chocolate Chip Cookies will keep, in an airtight container at room temperature, for up to 1 week.

Chocolate Chocolate Chip Cookies (and How to Be the Best Mama Ever)

My Katy has loved chocolate since she was a toddler. I let her have a tiny taste one day and she was hooked. Before she could even walk she'd crawl over to me, pull herself up by grabbing on to my pants leg, and say, "I need chocwat." So whenever I make a deeply chocolaty recipe, I know she's going to be thrilled.

These wonderfully chewy double chocolate chip cookies are her all-time favorite. They taste like they require a good bit of fuss, so let's just keep how easy they are to make between us. The first time I made them for her, she declared me to be the best mom ever. Whenever I feel like we're running a little low in the "Mama Appreciation" department, I just mix up a batch of these and my cup runneth over! *Makes about 3 dozen cookies*

1 package (12 ounces) plus 1 cup
   semisweet chocolate chips
2 cups baking mix
   (such as Bisquick)
1 can (14 ounces) sweetened
   condensed milk
1 large egg
1 teaspoon vanilla extract
¼ cup (½ stick) butter, melted

1 Preheat the oven to 325°F.

2 Pour the package of chocolate chips into a medium-size microwave-safe bowl and heat in the microwave at 30-second intervals, stirring after each, until smooth.

3 Transfer the melted chocolate to a large mixing bowl and add the baking mix, milk, egg, vanilla, and melted butter. Beat with an electric mixer at medium speed until well blended, about 2 minutes. Add the remaining chocolate chips and beat again on low speed until they are incorporated.

4 Using a tablespoon, drop the dough 2 inches apart onto ungreased baking sheets. Bake until lightly browned, 10 to 12 minutes.

5 Let cool on the baking sheets for 4 to 5 minutes, then remove to a wire rack to continue cooling.

Chocolate Chocolate Chip Cookies will keep, in an airtight container at room temperature, for up to 1 week.

Choosing Cookie Baking Sheets

The pans you choose for baking cookies have a greater effect on the cookies than most people realize: Too thin and your cookies burn easily; too thick and they may need extra time in the oven. More often than not, when folks have burned cookies, a too thin, old baking sheet is to blame.

When it comes to baking sheets, I prefer stainless steel, preferably commercial grade. You can find these in department stores, but I purchase mine at less than half the cost by checking the restaurant supply section in warehouse stores such as Sam's or Costco. I've been using these baking sheets for over a decade now, ever since I first happened upon them, and they still look like new.

Avoid baking sheets with nonstick coating if possible, mainly because it really isn't necessary. Cookies that don't require it won't stick anyway due to their butter content. Cookies that require greased baking sheets will come right off after a simple application of cooking spray or a light swiping of vegetable shortening. Nonstick baking sheets are also more difficult to clean: Residue left from oils tends to form a sticky film rather than wash right off as it does on stainless ones.

If possible, every kitchen should have at least two half-sheet–size (18 x 13-inch) stainless-steel commercial-grade baking sheets. I prefer to have four on hand, since I bake in large quantities and use them for so many things.

Flop Cookies

We all make mistakes in life. Everyone. Those folks who seem cool as a cucumber, like they have it all together? Yup, them, too. The difference between success and failure lies in how we handle our mistakes. Do we kick the dirt, plop down, and sag our shoulders in defeat, or do we look at it as Thomas Edison did: "I have not failed. I've just found ten thousand ways that won't work."

It's our spirit that defines, in many ways, how our lives play out. What some choose to view as defeat, others choose to use as a stepping stone. The hope, of course, is that as we grow older we will make fewer mistakes. But the good news is that continuing to make mistakes as we grow older means that our knowledge is growing at a pretty rapid pace. Everything we do that doesn't work out as planned makes another huge deposit into

Don't Forget to Linger

It's hard to believe that my son is in eleventh grade this year. Another year and he'll be graduating high school and off to college. Not long after that my daughter will follow suit, and my days of watching them begin new grades will be behind me. No more scavenger hunts for school supplies, no more class parties to bake treats for, no more homework to help with, and no more field trips. I miss them already!

It seems like just yesterday I was holding my babies and anticipating their first steps. We tend to think this perception is only in our minds, but my friend Maralee McKee pointed out something in her book, *The Gracious Mom's Guide to Authentic Manners*, that floored me, and I'm sure it will do the same to you. "Children only live under our roofs for about 20 percent of our lives . . . which means about 80 percent of our lives will be spent without daily contact with our kids."

Oh, my heart! No wonder it seems as if they've grown from babies to teenagers overnight. In the grand picture of life, they almost have. After reading that, I felt a renewal in my commitment to really be present when we're together, to remind myself to look in their eyes when they speak to me and take the time to listen—even when I truly have no idea what my tech-savvy son is talking about. The truth is that I am so deeply interested in and fascinated by their lives, but it's easy for me to become preoccupied and forget to show them that.

So now, when I send my kids off to another year of school and know I'll do this only a few more times (not like I'm counting though, right?), I am determined to live in the moment. Twenty percent of our lives. Ask your grandparents how quickly it passed and take that to heart.

This evening, knowing that we have only this small percentage, I'll sit down and hold out my hand, grasping the others to form a circle around our table as we give thanks, making sure the kids hear that one of the things I am most thankful for is them.

Tonight, when we have supper, I'm going to remind myself to eat a little slower, ask a few more questions, and take time to linger with the people I cherish most. Because if there is one thing my grandparents taught me, it is that at the end of the day, happiness isn't found in our schedules or to-do lists—it's found in what we choose to linger over.

The sweetness of life is in the lingering.

that bank of knowledge. That's how you get to be a wise old person, which is my ultimate goal. (Actually, my goal is to be a wise old person living on top of a mountain somewhere in Tennessee, but I digress. . . .)

Sometimes, though, what we view as a mistake others will consider a success, and so we just stand off to the side, scratching our heads and looking at them like they're crazy. And that is where this cookie recipe enters the picture. I found it in one of my mama's old cookbooks and decided to tweak it to make it easier and more streamlined. The result was a soft, chewy cookie that tasted great but didn't rise as much as I'd like.

I took one bite and thought they were delicious but still—they weren't "pretty." So I chalked it up to an experiment with plans to remake the recipe and get it right later that evening.

And then my kids and husband walked in the door. I didn't have time to tell them the cookies were a flop before the smell had them grabbing cookies off the plate. Their eyes rolled back in their heads. The kids pronounced the cookies "one of the all-time best" and told me I had to make them more often (and why hadn't I made them before?).

I looked at them in utter confusion and told my husband they were flops and I was going to remake them. *He looked at me like I'd grown two heads and decided to shave one of them into a mohawk.*

"Are you crazy? These are amazing! Don't you dare change these cookies!" he said.

They were gone by that evening, and the next morning, my son, Brady, woke up asking if we had more. It quickly became apparent that I had to give up on improving the recipe because, as fate would have it, my family liked my mistake just as it was. So here ya go. One of the best-tasting flops you ever had. *Makes about 4 dozen cookies*

3 cups cornflakes, crushed
3/4 cup (1 1/2 sticks) butter,
    at room temperature
1 package (8 ounces) cream cheese,
    at room temperature
2 1/2 cups brown sugar
    (light or dark)
2 1/2 cups self-rising flour
    (see page 276)
1 1/2 cups sweetened shredded
    coconut (unsweetened will
    work)
1/4 cup milk
Nonstick cooking spray,
    for coating the baking sheets

1 Place the cornflake crumbs in a small bowl and set aside.

Real or Imitation?

I often use imitation vanilla instead of pure vanilla extract. The primary reason for this is cost. I can purchase a large bottle of imitation vanilla for only a fraction of the price of real vanilla, and no one in my family is able to tell the difference. I know a lot of my readers prefer real vanilla and many even make their own. Occasionally, I will pick up a bottle of the "real stuff" and enjoy it until it runs out. That is when my handy imitation vanilla is always waiting in the wings. I applaud using what works best for you either way!

2 Combine the butter, cream cheese, and brown sugar in a large mixing bowl and beat with an electric mixer at medium speed until blended and creamy, about 2 minutes. Add the flour, coconut, and milk and beat again until well blended. Cover and chill in the refrigerator until cold, 2 to 3 hours.

3 Preheat the oven to 350°F. Lightly coat 2 baking sheets with cooking spray.

4 Form the dough into 1-inch balls and roll them in the crushed cornflakes to coat, placing them 2 inches apart on the prepared baking sheets.

5 Bake until lightly browned on top, being careful not to burn them, 15 to 20 minutes. Let cool completely on the baking sheets.

Flop Cookies will keep, covered at room temperature, for up to 3 days, or in the refrigerator for up to 1 week.

Milk-Dunkin' Peanut Butter Cookies

Before my husband and I met, he used to keep a jar of peanut butter and a loaf of bread at his desk to make peanut butter sandwiches for lunch—every single day! You would think that he would get tired of peanut butter sandwiches, but to this day, even though I cook supper every night, my night-owl husband just can't resist the allure of a peanut butter sandwich once in a while before bedtime. I try to help satisfy his craving in other ways as often as I can, so these soft peanut butter cookies come in handy! They are especially good to have on hand for road trips. In fact, my kids will likely remember these as the cookies that I always gave them from the front seat of the car during our many travels as a family. *Makes about 4 dozen cookies*

Nonstick cooking spray,
   for coating the baking sheets
1 cup vegetable shortening
1 cup plus 2 tablespoons
   granulated sugar
1 cup brown sugar
   (preferably dark)
2 large eggs
2 teaspoons vanilla extract
2 teaspoons baking soda
1/2 teaspoon salt
1 cup creamy peanut butter
3 cups all-purpose flour
1 cup peanut butter chips
   (optional)

1 Preheat the oven to 350°F. Lightly coat 2 baking sheets with cooking spray and set aside.

2 Place the shortening, the 1 cup of granulated sugar, the brown sugar, eggs, vanilla, baking soda, salt, and peanut butter in a large bowl. Beat with an electric mixer at medium speed until smooth and creamy, about 2 minutes. Add the flour and chips, if using, and mix until incorporated, about 2 minutes. The dough will look a little crumbly.

3 Form or scoop the dough into 1/2-inch balls and place them 2 inches apart on the prepared baking sheets.

4 Place the remaining granulated sugar in a small bowl. Dip a fork into the sugar and press into each cookie to form a crisscross design.

5 Bake until lightly browned around the edges, 10 to 15 minutes.

Milk-Dunkin' Peanut Butter Cookies will keep, in an airtight container at room temperature, for up to 2 weeks.

Busy Week Cake Mix Cookies

Sometimes, when life is extra busy, I just get a hankering to do some baking. It's a stress reliever for me. I love to get into the kitchen and surprise my kids (or their friends) with something warm from the oven. But during those crazy times, I don't love dirtying up a sink full of dishes or spending more than half an hour piddling around when I have other work needing my attention. These cookies are the perfect solution. Cake mix makes an excellent starting point, and these delicately crisp cookies stay fresh for over a week. The options are limited only by your imagination; you'll find a few of my favorites in the Variations. *Makes about 2 dozen cookies*

1 box (15 to 18 ounces) cake mix
(see Variations for flavors)
2 large eggs
½ cup vegetable oil

1 Preheat the oven to 350°F.

2 Combine the cake mix, eggs, and oil in a large mixing bowl and beat with an electric mixer at medium speed until well blended, about 2 minutes.

3 Form the dough into balls a little smaller than golf-ball size and place them 2 inches apart on 2 ungreased baking sheets.

4 Bake until very lightly browned at the edges, 10 to 12 minutes. Allow to cool completely before removing from the baking sheets.

Busy Week Cake Mix Cookies will keep, in an airtight container at room temperature, for up to 1 week.

VARIATIONS

RED VELVET COOKIES: Use red velvet cake mix and stir in 1 cup white chocolate morsels after mixing.

CHOCOLATE CHIPPERS: Use chocolate cake mix and stir in 1 cup semisweet chocolate chips after mixing.

STRAWBERRY CRINKLES: Use strawberry cake mix and stir in 1 cup white chocolate morsels after mixing. Roll the dough balls in confectioners' sugar before placing on the baking sheets for a pretty snow-capped crinkle.

BUTTER PECAN CRINKLES: Use butter pecan cake mix and stir in ½ to 1 cup pecan pieces after mixing. Roll the dough balls in confectioners' sugar before placing on the baking sheets.

Busy Week Cake Mix Cookies

How to Freeze Cookie Dough

Method 1: Line baking sheets with waxed or parchment paper (I use waxed paper because it is cheaper and works just as well). Form the cookie dough into individual balls and place them on the sheets just as you would if you were going to bake them. Place these sheets, uncovered, in the freezer until the cookie dough is just hard to the touch. This method is called "flash freezing." Remove the dough from the sheets and place in a zip-top bag before returning to the freezer. When it comes time to bake these, simply take out the frozen dough balls, place them on prepared baking sheets, and bake as usual, adding 2 to 3 minutes to the baking time (no temperature adjustment needed).

Method 2: Another way to freeze cookie dough, and what I most often do, is to transfer it directly from the mixing bowl to gallon-size zip-top freezer bags. Press the bags flat and squeeze as much air out as possible before freezing. The night before I want to bake the cookies, I simply place the bag of dough in the refrigerator to thaw, then form and bake as I would freshly made dough.

No matter how you choose to freeze your cookies, always label the bag with the type of dough, baking instructions, and the date the dough was prepared. Cookie dough will keep in the freezer for about 3 months.

Easy Coconut Macaroons

For those of us who love coconut, these macaroons are an amazing treat. Really and truly, this recipe is one of those that almost seems too easy, but I love that it takes away the excuse of not making them since it's only three ingredients stirred together in a bowl! The result is a wonderfully moist and chewy pillow of coconutty goodness. *Makes about 4 dozen cookies*

Nonstick cooking spray,
   for coating the baking sheets
5 cups (about two 5-ounce bags)
   sweetened shredded coconut
1 can (14 ounces) sweetened
   condensed milk
2 teaspoons vanilla extract

1 Preheat the oven to 350°F. Line a large baking sheet with aluminum foil and lightly coat the foil with cooking spray. Set aside.

2 Place the coconut, condensed milk, and vanilla in a large bowl. Stir together with a large spoon until combined. (This may take a while, but as you keep stirring it will come together!)

3 Using a cookie dough scoop or large spoon, form the dough into 1-inch balls and drop them 2 inches apart onto the prepared baking sheet.

4 Bake until lightly browned, being careful not to burn, 12 to 14 minutes.

5 Allow the macaroons to cool completely on the baking sheet. Use your fingers to peel each macaroon off the foil.

Easy Coconut Macaroons will keep, in an airtight container at room temperature, for up to 1 week, or in the refrigerator for up to 2 weeks.

Sunshine Lemon Blossoms

Lemon is one of my favorite flavors when it comes to sweets—it tastes like sunshine and happiness. (How can you not love a dessert that brings sunshine and happiness?) These delicate glazed shortbread cookies with a citrusy topping are one of my special delights to bake for folks who may need a little cheering up, including myself.

Feel free to make a double batch of glaze if you like. *Makes about 5 dozen cookies*

For the cookies
1 cup (2 sticks) unsalted butter or
    margarine, at room temperature
1 cup granulated sugar
3 cups all-purpose flour, plus extra
    for rolling out the dough
1 teaspoon baking powder
1/2 teaspoon baking soda
1/4 teaspoon salt
1/3 cup lemon juice

For the glaze
1 1/2 cups confectioners' sugar
3 tablespoons lemon juice
Yellow food coloring (optional)

1 Make the cookies: Cream together the butter and granulated sugar in a large mixing bowl and beat with an electric mixer at medium speed until combined and creamy, about 1 minute.

2 In a separate bowl, stir together the flour, baking powder, baking soda, and salt.

3 Add the lemon juice to the butter mixture, then dump in the flour mixture. Beat at medium speed until the dough comes together and forms a ball, 2 minutes. Cover and refrigerate for 1 hour.

4 Preheat the oven to 400°F. On a floured surface and with a lightly floured rolling pin, roll out the dough to ¼-inch thickness. Using a small circle cutter (I use a 1½-inch cutter), cut out rounds of dough. The scraps can be rerolled and used to make additional cookies. Place the rounds 2 inches apart on ungreased baking sheets and bake until set and very lightly browned at the edges, 8 to 10 minutes. Let cool on the baking sheets.

5 Meanwhile, make the glaze: Combine the confectioners' sugar, lemon juice, and 2 or 3 drops food coloring, if using, in a small mixing bowl and stir with a spoon until the lumps disappear and the mixture is thick.

6 Spoon about a teaspoonful of the glaze into the center of each cookie, spread it around with the back of the spoon, and let set, about 1 hour.

Sunshine Lemon Blossoms will keep, in an airtight container at room temperature, for up to 1 week.

Memom's Chocolate Oatmeal No-Bakes

from LAURA GRIFFIN

"Some of my earliest childhood memories are of making these no-bake cookies with my memom. This recipe has always been a hit in our house: Every time the pot starts to boil, family members begin hovering in the kitchen, praying the cookies will cool quickly. Most of us have burned our fingers and tongues more than once through the years trying to devour these treats before they cool!

"My memom taught me how to make these delicious cookies when I was just two years old. She would sit me on the kitchen countertop and give me little toddler tasks. I would wait with anticipation until she said those magic words, 'Hey Laura, do you want to make our cookies?' Our cookies. I can still taste the love, the memories, and, of course, the goodness every time I make them. Today I can manage the recipe on my own, but I would still rather make these cookies with my memom than with anyone else in the world."

Makes 2 dozen cookies

CHRISTY'S NOTE: These are the same cookies that I grew up eating. They are quick, easy, and made of ingredients that you usually have in your pantry. They are great after they cool, but as a kid I usually ate them in a bowl with a spoon while they were warm. Their chocolaty goodness cannot be beat—especially with a big glass of milk.

2 cups granulated sugar

1 can (5 ounces) evaporated milk (or 1/2 cup whole milk)

1/2 cup (1 stick) butter

1/3 cup unsweetened cocoa powder (I use Hershey's)

2 1/2 cups quick-cooking oats

1/3 cup creamy peanut butter

1 teaspoon vanilla extract

1 Combine the sugar, milk, butter, and cocoa in a medium-size saucepan over medium-high heat. Bring to a boil and cook,

stirring constantly. Once the mixture comes to a boil, stop stirring and allow to boil for exactly 1 minute, then remove from the heat.

2 Add the oats, peanut butter, and vanilla and stir well to combine.

3 Lay a sheet of waxed paper on a heatproof surface and drop the oatmeal mixture onto it by the tablespoonful, spacing them about 1 inch apart.

4 Let cool completely and enjoy.

Memom's Chocolate Oatmeal No-Bakes will keep, in an airtight container in the refrigerator, for up to 2 weeks (if they last that long!).

Chewy Cranberry Zingers

Folks often ask me what my favorite recipe is, but I've never been able to call out just one that I love more than all of the others. Well, now that I'm publishing this cookie recipe, that is about to change. This is my personal all-time favorite cookie. Filled with oats and sliced almonds for even more chew, studded with bright spots of cranberry, and spiced

Chewy Cranberry Zingers

with just a hint of a gingery zing—yes, this cookie is everything for me. *Makes 2 dozen cookies*

Nonstick cooking spray,
   for coating the baking sheets
1/2 cup packed dark brown sugar
1/4 cup granulated sugar
1/2 cup (1 stick) butter, at room
   temperature
1 teaspoon ground cinnamon
1 teaspoon ground ginger
1 large egg
1/2 cup self-rising flour
   (see page 276)
1 1/2 cups old-fashioned oats
1 cup dried cranberries
1 teaspoon vanilla extract
1/2 cup chopped almonds, pecans,
   walnuts, or other nuts

1 Preheat the oven to 350°F. Lightly coat 2 baking sheets with cooking spray and set aside.

2 Combine the sugars, butter, cinnamon, ginger, and egg in a large mixing bowl with an electric mixer at medium speed, about 2 minutes. Add the flour and mix thoroughly.

3 Add the oats, cranberries, vanilla, and nuts and beat at medium speed until combined into a stiff dough.

4 Form the dough into golf ball–size balls using a cookie scoop or tablespoon and place them 2 inches apart on the prepared baking sheets.

5 Bake until lightly golden at the edges, 12 to 15 minutes. Allow to cool for a few minutes on the baking sheets, then transfer to a platter or wire rack to cool completely.

Chewy Cranberry Zingers will keep, in an airtight container at room temperature, for up to 1 week.

Icebox Oatmeal Cookies

from WAYNE LAMMERS

66 Just this morning I saw an oatmeal cookie recipe on a box of oatmeal and was instantly taken back to a time when I was the oldest of six little stair-step kids enraptured by the aroma of Aunt Polly's icebox oatmeal cookies wafting through the old boarding house where I grew up in the late 1940s and '50s. I could see my grandmother—'Mammaw' to us kids—standing over that big ten-burner stove in the back kitchen with my mother right beside her. Aunt Polly was cutting more cookies while

Uncle Robert, back from touring some sea islands with the United States Marine Corps, placed them on the baking pans.

"The baking we do today is like making a tiny time capsule that will live forever in the hearts of those we love enough to bake for. Recipes are the reminders that trigger the memories we've made, allowing us to once again share the love of those who have gone on before us.

"My years have been long, but my time grows short now. Soon I will go to rejoin the Old Ones, and I am certain Aunt Polly will have a plate of her oatmeal cookies to welcome me home. I can hardly wait." *Makes 2 dozen cookies*

CHRISTY'S NOTE: As an oatmeal cookie lover, I just had to make these. I was not disappointed! These are the kind of cookies I can see sitting in a cookie jar on Grandmama's counter, steadily disappearing as little hands lift the lid over and over for just one more. The old-fashioned oatmeal gives them a little more texture than normal oatmeal cookies. They will almost melt in your mouth. I don't think it is possible to eat just one.

If you would like to make more cookies, just mix up two batches instead of doubling ingredients into one batch. For some reason, these do not turn out well when doubled.

1 cup light brown sugar
1 cup granulated sugar
1 cup vegetable shortening
2 large eggs, beaten
1/2 cup all-purpose flour
1 teaspoon baking soda
1 teaspoon salt
3 cups old-fashioned oats
1 teaspoon vanilla extract

1 Cream the sugars and shortening in a large mixing bowl with an electric mixer at medium speed until well combined and creamy, about 1 minute. Add the eggs and mix again until they are fully incorporated.

2 In a separate medium-size bowl, sift together the flour, baking soda, and salt. Add to the sugar mixture and mix at medium speed, scraping down the side of the bowl as needed, until the dough is fully combined, about 2 minutes.

3 Add the oats and vanilla and mix well until combined. The dough will be very thick.

4 Divide the dough in half and form each piece into a log about 12 inches long and 1 1/2 to 2 inches thick. Wrap each log in waxed paper and refrigerate for at least 4 hours or, ideally, overnight.

5 Preheat the oven to 300°F. Line 2 baking sheets with parchment paper.

6 Remove the dough logs from the refrigerator, unwrap each, and use a sharp knife to slice them into 1-inch rounds. Place the rounds 2 inches apart on the prepared baking sheets (the cookies will spread during baking).

7 Bake until the cookies are lightly browned, 20 to 25 minutes. Let the cookies cool completely on the baking sheets.

Icebox Oatmeal Cookies will keep, in an airtight container at room temperature, for about 1 week.

Peanut Butter Cream Sandwiches

This is one of those recipes that I started out doubling, and quickly learned that I needed to triple whenever I made it. Chewy soft peanut butter cookies with a lightly sweet peanut butter marshmallow filling make a delicious snack or anytime treat. I make them up and then wrap each sandwich individually in plastic wrap. Once I'm done with all of that, I usually stack them on my kitchen counter and watch them magically disappear. My son is the main culprit. He has been known to take twenty or thirty at a time.

A Bit About Butter

Most of my recipes that don't specify salted or unsalted butter are generally intended for unsalted. However, I pretty much go to the fridge and grab the first stick of butter I find. Salt helps to balance a recipe's sweetness, so using salted butter generally adds about 1/2 teaspoon of additional salt to your entire batch of cookies or bars or cake—not enough for most people to notice. But if your taste buds are especially sensitive to salt, you will want to use unsalted butter in all recipes unless the recipe specifies otherwise.

There are countless valid points in favor of using butter over margarine, but if margarine is what you are able to afford or what is readily available to you, feel free to substitute it for butter in my recipes. Butter will lend a richer flavor and is certainly better for you, but margarine will work just fine. Make sure you stay away from "light" versions, as they will yield flat baked goods and cookies that spread more than they rise.

Peanut Butter Cream Sandwiches

In his defense, though, he likes to pass them out to his friends at lunchtime. These would be an excellent entry for a bake sale. *Makes 15 sandwich cookies*

For the cookies
2 cups creamy peanut butter
2 cups granulated sugar
2 large eggs

For the filling
1 cup creamy peanut butter
1 cup marshmallow cream
  (such as Fluff)
1 teaspoon vanilla extract

1 Preheat the oven to 350°F.

2 Make the cookies: Combine the 2 cups of the peanut butter, the sugar, and eggs in a large mixing bowl and beat with an electric mixer at medium speed, scraping down the side of the bowl as needed, until blended and creamy, about 2 minutes.

3 Using a 1-inch cookie dough scoop or tablespoon, drop the dough 2 inches apart onto 2 ungreased baking sheets. You should have 30 dollops of dough. If you wish, gently press the tines of a fork into the top of each dollop to make a crosshatch.

4 Bake until lightly browned just around the edges, 10 to 12 minutes. Allow to cool completely on the baking sheets.

5 Make the filling: Place the 1 cup peanut butter, marshmallow cream, and vanilla in a medium-size mixing bowl and beat with an electric mixer at medium speed until fluffy, 2 minutes.

6 To assemble: Spread the filling on the bottoms of half of the cookies. Top with the other cookies and press together lightly.

Peanut Butter Cream Sandwiches will keep, individually wrapped in plastic wrap or stored in an airtight container at room temperature, for up to 1 week.

Graham Cracker Praline Cookies

This is a cookie confection found in two of my granny's hand-scrawled cookbooks. It's as easy to make as laying graham crackers out on a baking sheet, boiling up a sauce, and pouring it over the crackers before popping everything in the oven. Once the cookies cool, they become a graham cracker wrapped in a light coating of crunchy praline. The recipe almost seems too simple, but sometimes the simplest treats are the best! *Makes 28 cookies*

14 whole graham cracker sheets

3/4 cup (1½ sticks) butter
(salted or unsalted)

1/2 cup granulated sugar

1 teaspoon vanilla extract

1 cup chopped pecans (optional)

1 Preheat the oven to 350°F. Carefully break the graham cracker sheets into squares and arrange them in a single layer on a rimmed baking sheet.

2 Heat the butter in a small saucepan over medium heat until just melted. Add the sugar and stir until dissolved. Remove from the heat and stir in the vanilla.

3 If using the pecans, sprinkle them evenly over the graham crackers. Spoon the butter mixture over the crackers and pecans.

4 Bake until golden brown, 12 to 15 minutes. Allow to cool for a few minutes, then run a spatula underneath the cookies to prevent them from sticking. Allow them to cool completely before removing from the pan.

Graham Cracker Praline Cookies will keep, in an airtight container at room temperature, for up to 1 week.

Pecan Thumbprints

When my mother was little, her mother occasionally hosted showers for expectant mothers or brides to be. She always bought these cookies from a bakery and served them with punch. They have the taste of a pecan sandy with just a little extra oomph provided by the icing.

My mother looked for this recipe for years. It is kind of hard to find a recipe when you have no idea what the cookie is called or any of the ingredients needed to make it! Finally, she was at a bakery with her best friend, Sue, and spied these cookies for sale. She explained to Sue how she had always wanted the recipe but couldn't find it. Sue immediately said that they were called thumbprint cookies and she had the recipe.

The next time Sue came to visit, she brought these cookies. They were everything my mother remembered, and now we all can enjoy them.

When making the indentations in the cookies, dip your thumb into flour periodically to prevent it from sticking to the dough. I know the cooking time may seem long for these cookies, but bear in mind that they bake at a relatively low temperature. *Makes 3 dozen cookies*

For the cookies

1 cup (2 sticks) butter or
    margarine, at room temperature

¼ cup granulated sugar

2 cups all-purpose flour

¼ teaspoon salt

1 teaspoon vanilla extract

1 cup finely chopped pecans

For the glaze

1 cup confectioners' sugar

1/2 teaspoon almond extract

1 teaspoon milk or water

Food coloring of your choice
    (optional)

1 Preheat the oven to 300°F.

2 Make the cookies: Place the butter and granulated sugar in a large mixing bowl and cream together with an electric mixer at medium speed until fluffy, 1 to 2 minutes. Add the flour, salt, and vanilla and mix again, scraping down the side of the bowl as needed, until well incorporated. Add the pecans and mix again until combined.

3 Drop the dough by teaspoonfuls 2 inches apart onto 2 ungreased baking sheets. Make an indentation in each cookie with your thumb.

Cookies: Chewy or Crunchy?

When it comes to cookies, most folks fall into one of two camps: chewy or crunchy. While many recipes will always yield one or the other, some are capable of yielding both, simply by altering the cooking time or adding an ingredient.

There are a few ways to modify your favorite crunchy cookie recipe, if you'd care to experiment, to come up with a chewy cookie:

- Try substituting brown sugar for white. Brown sugar has more moisture content than white sugar and also adds a deeper flavor.
- Add ¼ cup honey or corn syrup. I often add honey to my Basic Baking Mix Bar Cookies (page 45) to make them chewier.
- Add both oats and honey for more texture and moisture. This is kind of a one-two-punch approach for me because I love what both of those ingredients bring to the table: 1/2 cup oats combined with 1/2 cup honey can transform a standard cookie into a whole other animal.
- Keep in mind that these additions will work for many recipes, but you will have to experiment to see if they work as well in your own.

Pimento Jar Heirlooms

After my grandmother Lucille passed way, my cousin and I went to her house to get a little something to remember her by. I wanted a coffee cup, one that she used often so I could use it, too, in remembrance of her and all of our phone conversations over coffee in the wee hours of the morning.

As I opened her cabinets, I came upon a stash of pimento jars, all neatly cleaned and stored away. It was like finding a stash of gold! (Some folks may not know this but pimento jars are just about the finest storage containers there are.)

Grandmama was never one to waste things, and I can hear her now saying, "Those are good little jars to have! If you ever need any, you let me know."

That's how her generation worked. They used things the first time around and then found another use for them, never wasting something that could help in some way.

Grandmama would wash those jars out by hand, dry them real well, and tuck them away until one of her great-grandkids needed a home for a family of roly-polies or for safekeeping of a lost baby tooth.

I reached in for two, handing one to my cousin and keeping one for myself. I put mine up on a shelf in my kitchen. If you happen to catch a glimpse of it in photos from time to time, it may look empty, but I see a whole lot of sweetness when I look at that jar.

Grandmama had just taken a bite of a pimento cheese sandwich I made for her! You can see the light and joy in her face.

4 Bake until lightly browned, 20 to 25 minutes. Allow the cookies to cool on the baking sheets for 2 minutes, then remove to a wire rack to cool completely.

5 Meanwhile, make the glaze: Place the confectioners' sugar, almond extract, and milk in a small bowl and stir until there are no lumps. Add a few drops of food coloring, if using, and stir until blended.

6 Spoon a small amount of glaze into each thumbprint. Allow the glaze to set, uncovered, for about 1 hour.

Pecan Thumbprints will keep, in an airtight container at room temperature, for up to 1 week, or in the freezer for up to 3 months.

Old-Fashioned Butter Cookies

This recipe is as old as the hills and was often served in cafeterias and Sunday schools back in the day. It's been loved for generations, and one bite transports me to slower days and greener times. Mixing in some rainbow sprinkles (nonpareils) brings them up to date for today's kids while still keeping that deliciously simple butter flavor we all know and love.

These cookies come out flatter than most, with a delicious crunch that packs a wallop of flavor! *Makes about 3 dozen cookies*

1 cup (2 sticks) butter,
   at room temperature
1 cup granulated sugar
2¼ cups all-purpose flour
2 teaspoons vanilla extract
2 tablespoons rainbow sprinkles
   (nonpareils)

1 Combine the butter and sugar in a large mixing bowl and beat with an electric mixer at medium speed until fluffy, 1 minute.

2 Add the flour, vanilla, and sprinkles and mix again at medium speed until well combined and the dough is formed. Place the dough in a zip-top plastic bag or airtight container and refrigerate for at least 30 minutes or up to 2 days.

3 Preheat the oven to 350°F.

4 Form the dough into 1-inch balls and place them 2 inches apart on 2 ungreased baking sheets. Bake until lightly golden around the edges, 12 to 15 minutes. Allow to cool on the pans for a few minutes before removing.

Old-Fashioned Butter Cookies will keep, in an airtight container at room temperature, for 1 to 2 weeks.

Chocolate-Tipped Butter Cookies

A Recipe to Cure the Grumpies

Ever need a cure for the grumpies? We've all been there! Feeling disgruntled and unfulfilled is the result of not having a purpose, so try asking yourself this question: "What can I do to make the world a little better for as many people as possible this week?"

That one question creates a goal . . .

That goal creates a purpose . . .

That purpose removes the focus from ourselves and puts it on others. . . . And breeds joy for you and all around you. Most of all, it just makes life plain FUN!

Wanna change the world? It's not a matter of how, it's a matter of how many times you can do it in a single day!

Wake up with a purpose and wake up EXCITED!

Chocolate-Tipped Butter Cookies

These extra-special cookies came to me by way of an extra-special friend, Karen Branscum. Karen is one of those people who spends her life loving on others. She volunteers for Meals on Wheels, at her local church, and any other place where she finds a need she can fill. On top of this, she takes care of her family to an extent that the fiercest matriarch would nod to in approval.

Whenever I travel for a book tour, my stops are usually a little hectic. I land at an airport, get a rental car, go straight to a few television stations, then radio stations, find my hotel at some point, and try to grab a quick bite of supper before my book signing that night. This is not the case when I go to a stop within driving distance of Karen, though. She meets me at the airport, usually with a fun sign, whisks me away in her car, and manages to turn the entire day into a fun girls' outing. Karen is just the epitome of sweetness, so you know she had to be included in this book.

Makes about 2 dozen cookies

Tend Your Garden

My granddaddy was a masterful gardener. Whenever we went to visit in the springtime we'd find him out behind his house, turning the soil or checking on his newly sprouted crops. I loved to help him. We'd spend hours out in the garden together, talking about everything under the sun while I watered plants and he pulled up weeds. I often begged to spend the night on weekends, and we'd head out early in the morning to see how the plants had grown overnight while Grandmama cooked up breakfast. When we were ready to head back to the house, I'd be rewarded with a morning ride in his trusty wheelbarrow.

He's been gone more than a decade now, but each spring I find myself itching to get my hands in some soil and help coax new plants to life. I'll never be the gardener he was, but I grow the obligatory tomatoes (a requirement for all Southerners) and assorted peppers, and the wild bunnies let me keep the occasional carrot or two.

Even though my garden is not on the same scale as Granddaddy's was, I still find my youngest dropping whatever she's doing to follow me whenever I'm headed that way, and we both enjoy the early morning surprise of seeing what new leaves and fruits sprouted up overnight. Most days she has the fun of watering while I look for weeds, and I'm proud to say I do have a wheelbarrow for rides.

There is a satisfaction in helping something grow, and I enjoy passing that on to my kids. Through the years they've helped me put up jams and jellies, freeze and can tomatoes, make pickles, and simmer the most delicious marinara sauces from food that we have grown on our own soil with our own hands. This teaches them to respect where food comes from. I don't want my kids growing up thinking it magically appears on grocery store shelves.

Even though we aren't dependent on gardening like our ancestors were, this is one of those practical life skills that helps us understand and respect the old ways of life—one more bridge that connects us to our past in order to have a better footing in our future.

When I step out onto the back porch and hear those footsteps following closely behind me, I realize that Granddaddy knew full well he was cultivating more than earth and seeds. It's taken me some time to learn a few of my granddaddy's tricks when it comes to helping things bloom and grow, but one thing he taught me well was that gardening is very much like life. Things grow best when given plenty of love and attention.

Nonstick cooking spray, for coating
the baking sheets

1 cup (2 sticks) butter,
at room temperature

1/2 cup confectioners' sugar

1 teaspoon vanilla extract

2 cups all-purpose flour

1 tablespoon vegetable shortening

1 package (6 ounces) semisweet
chocolate chips

1/2 cup pecans, finely chopped, or
crushed peppermint or other
candies

1 Preheat the oven to 350°F. Lightly coat 2 baking sheets with cooking spray.

2 Cream together the butter and confectioners' sugar in a large mixing bowl with an electric mixer at medium speed until light and fluffy, about 2 minutes. Add the vanilla and flour and continue mixing, scraping down the side of the bowl as needed, until well combined and a dough forms, 1 to 2 minutes.

3 Shape the dough into 2½-inch by ½-inch logs (or into small mounds for round cookies) and place them 2 inches apart on the baking sheets. Flatten three quarters of each log slightly with the tines of a fork, leaving the tip unflattened.

4 Bake until lightly browned, 12 to 14 minutes. Allow to cool on a wire rack.

Christmas Baking in October!

The holidays bring out the baker in just about everyone I know. We head into the kitchen and spend hours making up cookie trays to gift and enjoy. No other time of year has such delicious smells wafting out of kitchens across the country. Still, amid all of this baking, there are so many other activities that I like to do with my kids! So, beginning as early as October, I like to mix up batches of cookie dough to freeze. If I make just one or two batches a week, I'll easily have enough for all of my Christmas needs.

5 Meanwhile, combine the shortening and chocolate chips in a microwave-safe bowl and heat in the microwave at 45-second intervals, stirring between each, until melted and smooth. Dip the unflattened end of each cookie into the melted chocolate and place on a plate. Sprinkle with chopped pecans and let cool.

Chocolate-Tipped Butter Cookies will keep, in an airtight container at room temperature, for up to 1 week.

Candy Cane Cookies

These cookies will always make me smile as I look back on what a fun childhood I had. My mother, who has a great sense of humor and a fun spirit, used to buy the inch-thick, twelve-inch-long candy cane sticks to make these cookies. She'd place the candy inside a plastic bag and then put it under the tire of her car. My brother, sister, and I would stand on the front porch and watch as she fired up the engine and repeatedly backed over the candy canes until they were thoroughly crushed.

Looking back, I can surely come up with easier ways to crush a candy cane, but they wouldn't have made memories nearly as sweet! *Makes about 4 dozen cookies*

1/2 cup (1 stick) butter or
    margarine, at room temperature
1/2 cup vegetable shortening
1 1/2 cups granulated sugar
1 large egg
1 teaspoon vanilla extract
1/2 teaspoon peppermint extract
2 1/2 cups all-purpose flour
1 teaspoon salt
3/4 teaspoon red food coloring
1/2 cup crushed peppermint
    candies (see Note)

1 Preheat the oven to 375°F.

2 Cream together the butter, shortening, and 1 cup of the sugar in a large mixing bowl and beat with an electric mixer at medium speed until light and fluffy, about 2 minutes. Add the egg, vanilla, and peppermint extract and mix again until incorporated. Add the flour and salt and beat again at medium speed, scraping down the side of the bowl as needed, until incorporated, about 2 minutes.

3 Remove half of the dough from the bowl and place it in a separate bowl. Add the food coloring to the remaining dough and mix at low speed until blended, about 1 minute.

4 Roll 1 teaspoonful each of the red and white doughs into 4-inch-long ropes. Place the two ropes side by side, press them lightly together, and twist. Place the twist on an ungreased baking sheet and curve the top to make the handle of the candy cane. Repeat with the remaining dough.

5 Bake until lightly browned, 8 to 10 minutes.

6 Meanwhile, place the peppermint candy in a small bowl and stir in the remaining 1/2 cup sugar until well combined.

7 While the cookies are still warm, sprinkle them with the candy mixture; it will melt just enough to adhere.

Candy Cane Cookies will keep, in a covered container at room temperature, for up to 1 week.

NOTE: If you don't want to use your car to crush the candies, you can place them in a heavy-duty zip-top bag and bash-roll them with a rolling pin several times.

Shipping Cookies

Whether sending a care package to a hero who is deployed, a child away at college, or a long-distance friend, you'd be hard-pressed to find a store-bought gift that can make someone feel as loved as something home-baked can.

Here are my tips for sending sweets—and sweetness—to the ones you love.

PACKAGING

When shipping, it is best to choose multiple small containers. For bar cookies and brownies, I prefer the sandwich-size containers, which give my cookies less room to move around. A 9 × 13-inch pan generally holds 5 or 6 sandwich-size containers. With less air in the containers, cookies will also stay fresh longer.

I wrap each container in bubble wrap and then place them in a box. You can also use packaging peanuts or shredded newspapers. If going the route of loose packaging, tape or tie containers together before placing them inside and pack filling all around them.

SHIPPING

Traditionally, the postal service offered fast and affordable shipping options and while they still do, you might want to check on rates from UPS and FedEx, as they have both become much more affordable in recent years and may be able to get your package to its destination more rapidly.

RECIPES

The distance a package has to go should be considered when choosing recipes and slight recipe modification may need to come into play as well. Packages sent overseas may take 3 to 4 weeks (sometimes longer) to reach their destination. I have shipped my Basic Baking Mix Bar Cookies (page 45) overseas numerous times and they have always arrived in good shape, still moist and delicious. There are six main variations I use, but with this base recipe, the options are as endless as your imagination.

When shipping a great distance, keep in mind that the baked goods will have the shelf life of their least stable ingredient. For this reason, I usually bake with margarine rather than butter to help increase the shelf life. Although I understand that many folks are butter purists, having a package that you know could be in transit for over a month is a special case that might call for an exception.

2

Deeply Delicious Brownies and Bars

BEING A MAMA, for me, has meant an awful lot of baking for an awful lot of people. My kids love to bring treats to parties, teachers, classrooms, and even entire schools! Many of my go-to recipes for traveling and feeding a crowd are in this chapter. I love brownies and bars because they are so easy to tote, but also because the recipes run the gamut from chocolaty to gooey, filling, fruity, and downright decadent. When I bake for others, I want to deliver the ultimate treat—that's what you'll find in this chapter.

Rich and Fudgy One-Bowl Brownies

This is my go-to brownie recipe, because it dirties up only one bowl and uses ingredients I always have on hand. I make these two ways—milk chocolate or dark chocolate—so go with the level of chocolate you find yourself needing at any given moment! These are loved by old and young alike. *Makes 9 brownies*

Nonstick cooking spray,
 for coating the pan
3/4 cup (1 1/2 sticks) butter
1 cup granulated sugar
3/4 cup dark brown sugar
2 teaspoons vanilla extract
1/3 cup all-purpose flour
1/2 teaspoon salt
1 cup unsweetened cocoa powder
 (I use Hershey's)
3 large eggs
1 cup semisweet chocolate chips
 (see Note)

1 Preheat the oven to 350°F. Lightly coat the bottom and sides of an 8 x 8-inch baking pan with cooking spray and set aside.

2 Place the butter in a medium-size microwave-safe bowl and heat at 45-second intervals, just until melted (be careful not to let it get so hot that it pops). Alternatively, you can melt the butter in a saucepan on the stove over low heat.

3 Add the sugars, vanilla, flour, salt, and cocoa powder to the melted butter. Stir with a large spoon until the ingredients are just moistened. Add the eggs and stir again until well incorporated and no lumps remain. Stir in the chocolate chips.

4 Spread the batter into the prepared pan and bake until set, 30 to 35 minutes, being careful not to overbake. Allow to cool in the pan before cutting into bars.

Rich and Fudgy One-Bowl Brownies will keep, in an airtight container at room temperature, for 2 to 3 days.

NOTE: Any type of chip will work: milk chocolate, butterscotch, peanut butter, white chocolate, and so on—choose your favorite!

VARIATION

DARK CHOCOLATE BROWNIES: Substitute Dutch-process cocoa powder for the unsweetened cocoa and light brown sugar for the dark brown sugar.

Sometimes Castles Look Like Mobile Homes

Did you ever dream of living a fairy-tale life? Movies, books, and television shows set this ideal that is usually achieved only in fairy tales. But you know what? The folks who came before you can testify that sometimes castles look like mobile homes. Sometimes dragons look like bills to pay and laundry piles. Sometimes riches look like smiles and feel like hugs. And I happen to know that the best princes and princesses often wear T-shirts, drink coffee, and drive used cars.

Life, just like fairy tales, has highs and lows. I don't know what part you're at right now, but the truth is, in order to live your fairy tale, in order to truly appreciate the richness of your own life, you've got to get your nose out of everyone else's storybook to see it.

Life is good. And if you let it, it gets even better.

Amazing Brownie Bars

These bars boast a chocolate bottom and top with a layer of gooey chocolate goodness in the center. It's one of those recipes that travel really well, and folks can't ever figure out just how you made them! *Makes 12 bars*

Nonstick cooking spray, for coating the pan
1 box (15 to 18 ounces) chocolate cake mix
1/4 cup vegetable oil
1 large egg
1 cup chopped pecans or walnuts (optional)
1 can (14 ounces) sweetened condensed milk
1 1/2 cups semisweet chocolate chips
2 teaspoons vanilla extract

1 Preheat the oven to 350°F. Lightly coat a 9 x 13-inch pan with cooking spray and set aside.

2 Place the cake mix, oil, and egg in a large bowl. Beat with an electric mixer at medium speed until crumbly, about 1 minute. Stir in the nuts, if using.

3 Transfer 1½ cups of the crumb mixture to a small bowl and set aside. Press the remaining mixture into the bottom of the prepared pan to form a crust.

4 Place the condensed milk and chocolate chips in a small microwave-safe bowl or a saucepan. If microwaving, heat at 45-second intervals, stirring between each, until the chocolate chips are melted and the mixture is smooth and well combined. If heating in a saucepan, stir over medium-low heat until the same result is achieved. Once the mixture is smooth, stir in the vanilla until well incorporated.

5 Pour the chocolate mixture over the crust in the pan and carefully spread it to cover the crust. Sprinkle with the reserved crumb mixture. Bake until set, 25 to 30 minutes. Allow to cool in the pan before cutting into bars.

Amazing Brownie Bars will keep, in an airtight container at room temperature, for up to 1 week.

Easiest S'mores Brownies

I wanted a graham crust without the fuss, so I tried out an idea and it worked just as I hoped it would. Spend five minutes whipping up these beauties and remind some loved ones (or yourself) that life is sweet today. It will bring back memories of eating s'mores by the campfire when you were a child.

This recipe calls for packaged brownie mix, so be sure to have on hand whatever additional ingredients are needed to make the batter—usually eggs and vegetable oil or melted butter. *Makes 9 brownies*

About 5 whole graham cracker
    sheets (enough to cover the
    bottom of the baking dish)
¼ cup (½ stick) butter, melted
1 box (8 x 8-inch size) brownie
    mix, plus the ingredients called
    for on the package
1 cup semisweet chocolate chips
7 ounces marshmallow cream
    (such as Fluff) or 1 bag
    (8 ounces) marshmallows

Easiest S'mores Brownies

1 Preheat the oven as directed on the package of brownie mix.

2 Line the bottom of an 8 x 8-inch baking dish with the graham crackers, breaking them apart as needed to fit. Brush them evenly with the melted butter.

3 Prepare the brownie mix according to the package directions. Pour the batter over the graham crackers and use a rubber spatula to spread it out. Sprinkle the chocolate chips on top of the batter. Bake as directed.

4 Remove the brownies from the oven and immediately top with the marshmallow cream or marshmallows.

5 Turn the broiler on low. Place the baking dish under the broiler (at least 6 inches away from the heat) until lightly browned on top, 1 to 2 minutes. Watch carefully and do not leave unattended while the topping is browning because it happens quickly. Allow to cool slightly in the baking dish. Cut into bars and enjoy!

Easiest S'mores Brownies will keep, in an airtight container at room temperature, for 2 days.

A Note About Cake and Brownie Mix Sizes

In recent years, cake mix companies have changed the amount of product in their boxes. These changes are minor, ranging anywhere from 1 to 2 ounces in difference. For the recipes in this book that call for a cake mix, I am referring to the kind without pudding in the mix, and the size that will make a 9 x 13-inch cake. You'll notice a sliding scale when I list the size (15 to 18 ounces) and that is just to let you know that you can use different brands and sizes just fine in my recipes, as long as you get the mix that is large enough to make a 9 x 13-inch cake (even if the recipe is making a 2-layer, 8-inch round cake).

Brownie mixes also come in multiple sizes these days, and there are so many different flavors—some with chocolate chunks, some with fudge packets—that the weights can vary quite a bit. So when I call for brownie mix, I describe it by the pan size noted on the box: either 8 x 8-inch size or family size (9 x 13-inch).

Tie-Dyed Cheesecake Brownies

1 package (8 ounces) cream cheese,
    at room temperature
1 large egg
1/2 teaspoon clear vanilla extract
1/4 cup granulated sugar
Two colors of gel food coloring
    (optional)

This is the recipe my son requests the most whenever he takes goodies to school for his friends. Cheesecake and brownies—what a perfect partnership! At Christmastime, I divide the cheesecake topping into three parts, dye one part red and one green, and leave the other white. Then I put dollops on top of the brownies and swirl them with a butter knife for a pretty Christmasy effect. Any other time of the year, I just add the cheesecake topping and swirl.

I usually make these for Christmas, but you can easily swap out the red and green for school colors or other holiday colors. Gel food coloring is the key to good, rich colors. You can find it in the cake decorating aisle in most craft stores. *Makes 12 rectangular brownies*

Nonstick cooking spray,
    for coating the baking dish
1 box (family-size) brownie mix,
    plus the ingredients called for
    on the package

1 Preheat the oven to 350°F. Lightly coat a 9 x 13-inch baking dish with cooking spray and set aside.

2 Prepare the brownie mix according to the package directions. Spread the batter evenly into the prepared baking dish.

3 Combine the cream cheese, egg, vanilla, and sugar in a large mixing bowl. Beat with an electric mixer at medium speed until smooth and creamy, about 2 minutes.

4 If you're adding color, divide the cream cheese batter into three bowls. Set one aside for your white color and tint the remaining two bowls a different color by adding a few drops of food coloring to each and stirring until fully mixed.

5 Using a tablespoon, drop dollops of each color cream cheese batter over the brownie batter, being careful not to let the colors overlap. Use a butter knife to gently swirl the colors until they resemble tie-dye (it's okay

Basic Baking Pantry List

The secret to being able to whip up treats whenever the occasion calls for it is the same secret to being able to put supper on the table every night without having to make emergency trips to the grocery store: a well-stocked pantry. Here are the things that I make sure to always keep on hand.

DRY GOODS
- All-purpose flour
- Self-rising flour
- Sugar
- Baking mix (such as Bisquick)
- Brown sugar (dark or light)
- Brownie mix
- Solid vegetable shortening
- Cooking oil
- Honey
- Old-fashioned and quick-cooking oats
- Confectioners' sugar
- Cocoa powder (such as Hershey's Natural)

- Shredded or flaked coconut (sweetened or unsweetened)
- Vanilla extract
- Butter flavoring
- Ground cinnamon, ground nutmeg, and other spices
- Cornstarch (can use flour in a pinch)
- Baking soda (replace once a year)
- Baking powder (replace once a year)
- Shelf-stable milk
- Canned evaporated milk
- Sweetened condensed milk
- Semisweet chocolate chips
- Canned pineapple and other canned fruits
- Raisins

REFRIGERATED GOODS
- Milk
- Eggs
- Butter
- Lemon juice

if the cream cheese batters don't cover the brownie batter completely; they will spread during baking).

6 Bake until set in the center, 30 minutes. Allow to cool completely in the dish before cutting into bars.

Tie-Dyed Cheesecake Brownies will keep, in an airtight container at room temperature, for 3 to 5 days.

Peanut Butter Cheesecake Bars

This recipe can also be baked in 2 standard muffin tins to make 24 individual brownies. Place 24 paper liners in the cups of the tins and divide the brownie batter evenly among them (the cups will not be filled all the way). Spoon a small dollop of each color of the cream cheese batter on top of the brownie batter in each cup. Gently swirl the colors with a butter knife. Bake until set in the center, 20 to 25 minutes.

Peanut Butter Cheesecake Bars

If you're a peanut butter and cheesecake lover, get ready to sing "Glory!" Here is a cookie bar that combines soft peanut butter cookies with a cheesecake filling studded with peanut butter morsels. It's an easy recipe to throw together, even at the end of a long day, and the bars travel well, too! *Makes 9 bars*

Nonstick cooking spray, for coating the pan
1 package (8 ounces) cream cheese, at room temperature
1 large egg
1 teaspoon vanilla extract
1/3 cup sweetened condensed milk
1 cup peanut butter chips
1 package (16 ounces) peanut butter cookie dough (such as Pillsbury), refrigerated

1 Preheat the oven to 350°F. Lightly coat an 8 x 8-inch pan with cooking spray and set aside.

2 Place the cream cheese, egg, vanilla, and milk in a large mixing bowl. Beat with an electric mixer at medium speed until smooth and creamy, 2 to 3 minutes. Stir in the peanut butter chips.

3 With damp hands pat half of the cookie dough into the bottom of the pan. Pour the cheesecake mixture over the dough and spread it to cover.

4 Break up the remaining cookie dough into pea-size pieces and scatter on top of the cheesecake mixture.

5 Bake until lightly browned on top, 35 to 40 minutes. Allow to cool in the pan before cutting into bars (or eat warm if you prefer!).

Peanut Butter Cheesecake Bars will keep, in an airtight container at room temperature, for up to 3 days, or in the refrigerator for 1 to 2 weeks.

Bake Sale Tips and Tricks

In an age of store-bought cakes and fast-food snacks, bake sales call us back to a simpler time when communities and groups pulled together to lend their talents in the kitchen to a good cause. Should you be asked to participate in one, here are some of my tried-and-true tips.

SMALLER SERVINGS MEAN MORE SALES

Large cakes are fine, but individual servings will sell faster and bring a higher profit margin for the organization. I usually include one full-size pie or cake in bake sales to use in the cake walk, but I focus my efforts on slices, individual bar cookies, and brownies. While a cake may bring in $10 to $20, slices at $3 to $4 each will almost always be your best bet. Plus, there will undoubtedly be many wonderful desserts on display, and smaller portions allow folks to sample more of the delights from some of their favorite people.

YOU CAN'T GO WRONG WITH BROWNIES

Brownies are always one of the first items to sell out. Bake them in paper-lined muffin cups rather than a pan. These are easy to transport as well as sell. I generally leave them in the papers and package them in twos in clear zip-top sandwich bags for the perfect portion.

CONSIDER COOKIES AND BARS

I am always looking for cute ways to package my cookies. They can be individually wrapped in plastic wrap or grouped in small party favor bags. While any kind of cookie is great for a bake sale, I have found that bar cookies sell better and are faster to make with less of a mess to clean up afterward.

PRICE EVERYTHING

As a shopper, don't you just hate not being able to find a price on an item you're interested in? People will be reluctant to ask because if it is more than they wish to pay, they will be put on the spot. So I cut large labels out of paper and tape them prominently to the package with the name of the dish beneath the price so no one has to play "guess that dessert."

PAY ATTENTION TO INGREDIENTS

If your bake sale is catering to a younger crowd, note the ingredients on the packaging whenever possible. While older generations tend to expect nuts and eggs in certain dishes, some folks in younger generations have developed very dangerous allergies to these ingredients. To be on the safe side, I list "nuts" or "no nuts" and try to be on hand for questions about ingredients. If I know there is a child who has specific dietary needs and I am able to easily modify a recipe just for them, it always makes a nice treat.

Basic Baking Mix Bar Cookies

I have more variations to this cookie than I can count and they are all one-bowl easy and bake in no time flat. The fact that they are a bar cookie means no scooping out dough onto multiple sheets. Just spread it in a baking dish, bake, and cut after they are cool. Don't let yourself overlook these just because they are so simple to make. These tender brown sugar- and butter-flavored bars are every bit as much the showstopper as much fussier cookies! *Makes 12 to 16 cookies*

Nonstick cooking spray, for coating
   the baking dish
1 cup packed brown sugar
   (light or dark)
2 cups baking mix
   (such as Bisquick)
1 large egg
1/2 cup (1 stick) butter, melted
1 teaspoon vanilla extract
Add-ins of your choice (optional;
   see Variations, page 46)

1 Preheat the oven to 350°F. Lightly coat an 8 x 8-inch baking dish with cooking spray.

2 Combine the brown sugar, baking mix, eggs, butter, and vanilla in a large mixing bowl and stir with a large spoon until well blended.

3 Stir in the add-ins of your choice (if using candy, reserve a small handful to place on top).

4 Pat the dough into the prepared baking dish, sprinkle with reserved candies, if using, and bake until lightly browned on top, about 20 minutes. (These may look undercooked, but resist the urge to overbake them—they set after they cool.) Allow to cool completely and cut into bars.

Basic Baking Mix Bar Cookies will keep, in an airtight container at room temperature, for up to 1 week.

CLASSIC CHOCOLATE CHIP BARS: Add 1 cup chocolate chips to the dough.

FRUITCAKE COOKIE BARS: Add 1½ cups diced fruitcake mix (or diced candied fruit of your choice), ½ cup raisins, ½ cup sliced almonds, and ½ cup chopped walnuts or pecans to the dough.

M&M'S COOKIE BARS: Add 1 to 2 cups M&M's to the dough.

OATMEAL SCOTCHIES: Add ½ cup old-fashioned oats, ½ cup raisins, and ½ cup butterscotch chips to the dough.

SNICKERDOODLE BARS: Add 1 tablespoon ground cinnamon to the dough. While the cookies bake, stir together 1 tablespoon ground cinnamon and ¼ cup sugar in a small bowl. When the cookies are done baking, brush them lightly with 1 tablespoon melted butter and sprinkle with the cinnamon-sugar mixture.

HARVEST CANDY CORN BARS: Add 1 cup chocolate chips or butterscotch chips to the dough. When the cookies are done baking, immediately sprinkle them lightly with candy corn. Return the cookies to the oven and bake until the candy sticks but does not melt, 2 to 3 minutes.

Honey Nut Bars

These bars marry the fun of a candy bar with the decadence of a cookie. With a shortbread-like bottom and a PayDay-style top, they are a step above your average cookie bar! I use peanuts when I make them, just to cut down on the expense, but you can use whichever nuts you prefer. *Makes 12 bars*

Nonstick cooking spray, for coating
   the baking dish
3 cups all-purpose flour
1½ cups packed dark brown sugar
1 cup (2 sticks) plus 3 tablespoons
   butter, melted
1 teaspoon salt
2 cups coarsely chopped pecans,
   walnuts, or whole peanuts, or a
   combination
½ cup honey
1 cup butterscotch chips

❶ Preheat the oven to 350°F. Lightly coat a 9 x 13-inch baking dish with cooking spray.

❷ Combine the flour, brown sugar, 1 cup of the melted butter, and the salt in a large mixing bowl and stir with a spoon until it forms a dough.

3 Press the dough into the bottom of the prepared baking dish. Bake until lightly golden, 12 to 15 minutes. Sprinkle the nuts evenly over the top and set aside.

4 Stir together the honey, butterscotch chips, and the remaining melted butter, in a small saucepan over medium heat. Bring to a boil and allow to boil for 2 minutes, stirring constantly. Remove from the heat.

5 Pour the honey mixture over the nuts. Return the baking dish to the oven and bake until set, an additional 12 to 15 minutes. Allow to cool completely in the baking dish before cutting into bars.

Honey Nut Bars will keep, in an airtight container at room temperature, for up to 2 weeks.

Pecan Chewies

During the signing for my first book, a man and his wife stood in line for a good bit of time holding a big basket. Once they got up to the front, the man smiled from ear to ear, introduced himself as Stacey Little, and presented me with a basket of Pecan Chewies. At that very first meeting, we became lifelong friends. I opened up the basket and shared the Pecan Chewies with everyone there. Just like back then, wherever these bars make an appearance, they bring the party!

Stacey writes a blog called Southern Bite, and I was honored to write the foreword to his first book. He has become like a brother to me, which makes this recipe all the more special. *Makes 12 bars*

Vegetable shortening and flour, for coating the baking dish
1 cup (2 sticks) butter, melted
1 cup granulated sugar
1 cup packed light brown sugar
2 large eggs, well beaten
2 cups self-rising flour (see page 276)
1 cup pecans, chopped
2 teaspoons vanilla extract

1 Preheat the oven to 300°F. Lightly grease and flour a 9 x 13-inch baking dish and set aside.

2 Place the butter and sugars in a large mixing bowl and stir with a large spoon until smooth. Add the eggs and stir well. Add the flour and stir until all the lumps are gone. Add the pecans and vanilla and stir until well combined.

3 Using your hands or a spatula dipped in water, spread the dough to cover the bottom of the prepared dish.

4 Bake until lightly golden, 40 to 50 minutes; be careful not to overbake. Allow to cool completely in the dish before cutting into bars.

Pecan Chewies will keep, in an airtight container at room temperature, for up to 5 days.

Rocky Road Brownie Mix Cookies

As you've probably guessed by now, I love brownies any way you fix them. And while from-scratch ones are great, I can honestly say that I've never met a brownie mix I didn't like. Given that I have a teenager, parties and events often crop up at a moment's notice, so I always keep a few boxes of brownie mix on hand for any last-minute treats. These wonderful brownie cookies are a creative way to make something a little unexpected. I usually leave out the pecans when making them for kids since so many have nut allergies. *Makes 2 to 3 dozen cookies*

Nonstick cooking spray, for coating
  the baking sheets
1 box (family-size) brownie mix
2 large eggs
1/3 cup vegetable oil
1 1/2 cups semisweet chocolate
  chips
1 1/2 cups miniature marshmallows
1/2 cup chopped pecans (optional)

1 Preheat the oven to 350°F. Lightly coat 2 baking sheets with cooking spray and set aside.

2 Stir together the brownie mix, eggs, and oil in a large bowl until no dry spots remain. Stir in the chocolate chips, marshmallows, and pecans.

3 Drop by rounded spoonfuls 2 inches apart onto the prepared baking sheets. Bake until set, 10 to 12 minutes. Allow to cool completely on the baking sheets.

Rocky Road Brownie Mix Cookies will keep, in an airtight container at room temperature, for up to 1 week.

Chocolate Chip Dream Bars

When I was developing this recipe I brought the bars on a quilt retreat I was attending with my mother. They were devoured on the very first day and I hand-wrote the recipe to pass around to those who asked for it. These moist, tender cookie bars have a layer of decadently soft chocolate—truly dreamy. *Makes 20 bars*

Nonstick cooking spray, for coating
   the baking pan
1 can (14 ounces) sweetened
   condensed milk
2¹/₂ cups semisweet chocolate
   chips
³/₄ cup (1¹/₂ sticks) butter, melted
   and cooled
1¹/₂ cups dark brown sugar
1 teaspoon vanilla extract
2 large eggs
2¹/₂ cups baking mix (such as
   Bisquick)

1 Preheat the oven to 350°F. Lightly coat a 9 x 13-inch baking pan with cooking spray.

Birthdays for Teddy

When my son was little, he loved my birthday cakes and always anxiously awaited the next time I would make one. The waiting must have gotten to him because one day he brought me his teddy bear and told me that it was Teddy's birthday. I immediately acted horrified that I'd forgotten such an important occasion and got to work mixing up cake batter and buttercream icing. Little Brady was so impressed that a few days later, wouldn't you know he found another stuffed animal who was celebrating its entry into this world. We celebrated a lot of birthdays back then!

2 Combine the sweetened condensed milk with 1¹/₂ cups of the chocolate chips in a microwave-safe bowl and heat at 30-second intervals, stirring between each, until melted and smooth. (Alternatively, melt together in a small saucepan over medium heat, stirring constantly until smooth.)

3 Place the melted butter, brown sugar, vanilla, eggs, and baking mix in a medium-size bowl and stir until well combined. Stir in the remaining 1 cup chocolate chips.

4 Spread two-thirds of the batter in the bottom of the prepared pan. Spread the melted chocolate mixture on top and spread to the sides. Drop spoonfuls of the remaining batter over the top.

5 Bake until golden brown on top, 25 to 30 minutes. Allow to cool completely in the pan before cutting into bars.

Chocolate Chip Dream Bars will keep, in an airtight container at room temperature, for up to 5 days.

Love at First Bite Brown Sugar Bars

I love the taste of brown sugar and so does my friend Jyl. When I gave her one of these gooey, buttery bars to try, her first words were, "Oh Christy, they are perfect!" These brown sugar bars are our dear favorites. The texture is something like a gooey brownie. Everyone who tries them falls in love instantly. *Makes 12 bars*

Nonstick cooking spray, for coating the baking dish
2 cups packed light or dark brown sugar

½ cup (1 stick) butter, at room temperature
3 large eggs
2 cups self-rising flour (see page 276)
1 teaspoon vanilla extract
1½ cups pecans, chopped
Homemade Whipped Cream (page 277), for serving (optional)
Ground cinnamon, for garnish (optional)

1 Preheat the oven to 325°F. Lightly coat a 9 x 13-inch baking dish with cooking spray and set aside.

2 Beat together the brown sugar and butter in a large mixing bowl with an electric mixer at medium speed until blended and creamy, about 1 minute. Add the eggs, flour, and vanilla and mix, scraping down the side of the bowl as needed, until well combined, about 2 minutes. Stir in the pecans.

3 Spread the dough into the prepared baking dish and bake until lightly browned on top 20 to 30 minutes. Let cool in the baking dish.

4 Cut into squares just before serving. Serve with a dollop of whipped cream on top and a sprinkling of cinnamon, if desired.

Love at First Bite Brown Sugar Bars will keep, in an airtight container at room temperature, for up to 1 week.

Katy's Birthday Cake Cookie Bars, page 52

Katy's Birthday Cake Cookie Bars

A few years back, I asked Katy, "If you could invent any cookie, what would it be?" Without missing a beat she said, "Birthday cake cookies!" I was intrigued and started running ideas by her—these delicious bars are the result. They are flavored so that the cookie mimics the taste of a homemade birthday cake, and they have a blondie-like texture for extra deliciousness. Top it all off with a generous layer of fluffy buttercream icing and a sprinkling of rainbow candies, and we have a treat fit for the most special of days! These would be great for a class party or birthday celebration where the treat might have to hold up during considerable travel. *Makes 12 bars*

For the bars
Nonstick cooking spray, for coating
    the baking dish
1 cup (2 sticks) butter, melted
1 cup granulated sugar
1 cup brown sugar (light or dark)
2 large eggs
2 cups self-rising flour
    (see page 276)
2 teaspoons vanilla extract

1 teaspoon butter flavoring
1 teaspoon almond extract
4 tablespoons rainbow sprinkles,
    plus extra for finishing
    (optional)

For the icing
1 cup (2 sticks) unsalted butter,
    at room temperature
6 cups confectioners' sugar
4 teaspoons butter flavoring or
    clear vanilla extract
4 to 8 tablespoons milk

1 Preheat the oven to 350°F. Lightly coat a 9 x 13-inch baking dish with cooking spray and set aside.

2 Make the bars: Place the melted butter and the sugars in a large mixing bowl and stir until well blended. Allow to cool for a few minutes.

3 In a separate bowl or measuring cup, beat the eggs well with a fork. Add the eggs, flour, vanilla, butter flavoring, and almond extract to the butter mixture and stir to combine. Stir in the rainbow sprinkles, if using.

4 Pour the batter into the prepared baking dish and bake until golden brown and set but still soft in the center, 40 to 45 minutes. Allow to cool completely in the baking dish.

5 Meanwhile, make the icing: Place the butter and about 1 cup of the confectioners' sugar in a large bowl and beat with an electric mixer at medium speed until light and fluffy, 1 to 2 minutes. Add the butter flavoring, 4 tablespoons of the milk, and the remaining confectioners' sugar and beat again, scraping down the side of the bowl as needed, until smooth and creamy, 2 to 3 minutes. Add a little extra milk if needed.

6 Frost the cooled cookie bars while still in the dish. Top generously with additional sprinkles, if desired, and let the icing set, uncovered, for about 30 minutes before cutting into bars.

Katy's Birthday Cake Cookie Bars will keep, in an airtight container at room temperature, for up to 4 days.

Chewy Pear Bars

These wonderful chewy bars taste of butter, brown sugar, and graham cracker crumbs studded with bits of ripe, juicy pear. Oh my word, are they ever good! You really should make them today, because even if you don't have homegrown pears handy, you have to buy only two pears to make this. *Makes 12 bars*

For the crust
3 cups graham cracker crumbs
3/4 cup (1 1/2 sticks) butter,
    at room temperature
1/4 cup granulated sugar

For the filling
2 1/2 cups dark brown sugar
    (or light if that is what you have)
2/3 cup graham cracker crumbs
2 tablespoons all-purpose flour
1 teaspoon ground cinnamon
1/2 teaspoon ground ginger
3/4 teaspoon salt
1/2 teaspoon baking powder
3 large eggs
1 teaspoon vanilla extract
1 cup peeled and diced pears
    (about 2 pears)

1 Preheat the oven to 350°F.

2 Make the crust: Place the graham cracker crumbs, 3/4 cup butter, and 1/4 cup sugar in a medium-size mixing bowl. Using a long-tined fork or pastry cutter, cut and stir the ingredients together until combined and crumbly. Press the mixture evenly into the bottom of an ungreased 9 x 13-inch baking dish and bake until lightly browned, 10 to 12 minutes.

3 Meanwhile, make the filling: Combine the brown sugar, graham cracker crumbs, and flour in the same bowl used to make the crust.

53

Stir until the flour is well incorporated. Stir in the cinnamon, ginger, salt, and baking powder. Add the eggs and vanilla and stir until a batter is formed. Fold in the diced pears.

4 Pour the filling into the browned crust and spread it to the edges. Bake until the filling is set in the center, 25 to 30 minutes. Allow to cool completely in the baking dish before cutting into bars.

Chewy Pear Bars will keep, in an airtight container at room temperature, for up to 5 days, or in the freezer for up to 3 months. Thaw completely before serving.

Gooey Cherry Bars

These bars are a cherry lover's dream. A shortbread-like crust is topped with a gooey cherry filling. While baking, it forms a delicate layer on top that is perfectly finished with a light sprinkling of confectioners' sugar after the bars cool. When I go to an event with other food bloggers, these are the bars I take most often. Even among that discerning crowd, they get rave reviews. I can pretty much guarantee this will become the dish you're asked to bring again and again. *Makes 12 bars*

For the crust
Nonstick cooking spray, for coating the baking pan
2 cups all-purpose flour
1 cup (2 sticks) butter, at room temperature
1/2 cup confectioners' sugar

For the filling
2 cups granulated sugar
4 large eggs
1/2 cup all-purpose flour
1/2 teaspoon salt
1 teaspoon baking powder
2 teaspoons vanilla extract
1 jar (6 ounces) maraschino cherries, drained and halved (see Note)
1 1/2 cups chopped pecans (optional)
Confectioners' sugar, for finishing (optional)

1 Preheat the oven to 350°F. Lightly coat a 9 x 13-inch baking pan with cooking spray.

2 Make the crust: Place the 2 cups flour, 1 cup butter, and 1/2 cup confectioners' sugar in a medium-size mixing bowl and cut them together with a pastry cutter or long-tined fork until they're well combined and form a crumbly dough. Press the dough evenly into the pan.

3 Bake the crust until just lightly browned around the edges, 20 to 25 minutes. Remove from the oven and set aside. Reduce the oven temperature to 325°F.

4 Make the filling: Place the sugar, eggs, flour, salt, baking powder, and vanilla in the same bowl you used to make the crust (no need to wash it). Stir together using a wooden spoon until smooth and creamy—the batter will be very thick. Stir in the cherries and the pecans, if using, until well combined. Spoon the mixture in large dollops over the crust and gently spread to the edges.

5 Bake until set, about 30 minutes. Allow to cool completely in the pan, then sprinkle the top with a light dusting of confectioners' sugar, if desired, and cut into bars.

Gooey Cherry Bars will keep, in an airtight container at room temperature, for up to 4 days.

NOTE: To cut the cherries, I drain and reserve the juice, pour the cherries onto a plate, and slice each one in half. Even though you don't use the cherry juice in this recipe, I always save it in my refrigerator to add to orange juice or lemon-lime soda for a fun flavor splash.

Cranberry Bliss Bars

I f you ever find yourself anywhere near Belvidere, Tennessee, you simply must stop in at one of my favorite haunts, the Swiss Pantry. My friend Charlotte runs this little shop, and while it features bulk foods, the real star of the show is the bakery. Homemade sourdough breads, doughnuts, cinnamon rolls, cookies, pies, cakes, and more are made from scratch daily in their open-view kitchen. Whenever we stop by (and we often take day trips there just for Charlotte's goodies), the first thing I do is go look in a little basket on the bakery counter to see if there are any Cranberry Bliss Bars left. My husband can always tell if I found one by the huge grin on my face!

If you do stop at the Swiss Pantry, and even if you score a Cranberry Bliss Bar, you'll still miss out on the best part of the place if you don't take time to meet Mrs. Charlotte. Amid all the doughnuts, cakes, and pies, her smile is one of the sweetest offerings they have! *Makes 12 bars*

For the bars

Nonstick cooking spray, for coating
   the baking pan
1 cup (2 sticks) butter,
   at room temperature
1 cup light brown sugar
1/3 cup granulated sugar
3 large eggs
1 tablespoon frozen orange juice
   concentrate, thawed
2 teaspoons vanilla extract
2 cups all-purpose flour
1 1/2 teaspoons baking powder
1/2 teaspoon salt
1 teaspoon ground ginger
1 cup dried cranberries
1 cup white chocolate chips

For the frosting and topping

4 ounces cream cheese,
   at room temperature
2 tablespoons butter,
   at room temperature
3 cups confectioners' sugar
2 tablespoons frozen orange juice
   concentrate, thawed (see Note)
1 teaspoon vanilla extract
1/2 cup dried cranberries
1/2 cup white chocolate chips

1 Preheat the oven to 350°F. Lightly coat a 9 x 13-inch baking pan with cooking spray and set aside.

2 Make the bars: Place the butter, brown sugar, and granulated sugar in a medium-size bowl and mix with an electric mixer at medium speed until creamy, about 1 minute. Add the eggs, orange juice concentrate, and vanilla and beat well.

3 Whisk the flour, baking powder, salt, and ginger together in a medium-size bowl and add gradually to the butter mixture. Stir in the cranberries and white chocolate chips. The batter will be thick.

4 Spread the batter into the prepared pan and bake until lightly browned, 20 minutes. Allow to cool completely.

5 Meanwhile, make the frosting: Beat together the cream cheese, butter, and confectioners' sugar in a medium-size mixing bowl with an electric mixer at medium speed until well blended, 1 to 2 minutes. Add the orange juice concentrate and vanilla and beat until blended.

6 Immediately spread the frosting over the bars and sprinkle with the cranberries.

7 Place the white chocolate chips in a small microwave-safe bowl and microwave at 45-second intervals, stirring intermittently, until melted. Allow to cool for a few minutes, then spoon into a zip-top bag. Cut the tip off one corner and gently squeeze the chocolate in a zigzag pattern over the top of the bars. Allow to cool completely so the topping sets, then cut into bars. Enjoy!

Cranberry Bliss Bars will keep, in an airtight container at room temperature, for 3 to 4 days, or in the refrigerator for up to 1 week.

NOTE: Use the rest of the orange juice concentrate to make Best Ever Orange Meringue Pie on page 140.

Blueberry Crunch Bars

This recipe is from my friend Valerie Holt, who teaches home economics at Woodland High School in Cartersville, Georgia. We met at the National Cornbread Festival and became fast friends. She told me that I was living her dream, which surprised me, because I always intended to use my home ec degree to do exactly what she does now. So in my mind, she is living *my* dream. In the end, the best dreams that come true are always the ones you never planned anyway. There is an amazing sweetness when dreams you never dared to dream come true.

The agriculture teacher at Valerie's school has a father in middle Georgia who raises blueberries. All of the teachers at her school wait eagerly each summer for him to bring gallons of berries back from his visit with his dad. Valerie makes these bars with the berries every time. As a blueberry lover myself, I have to tell you that I made these the moment Valerie shared the recipe with me and have already lost count of how many times I've made them since! *Makes 12 bars*

Blueberry Crunch Bars

Guard Your Light Switch

Have you ever had a conversation that goes something like the following?

"Good morning!"

"Yeah, it might be for you but . . ."

"There is so much to be grateful for!"

"Maybe for you but . . ."

"I'm going to choose a good attitude today!"

"Well, obviously, that is easy for you but . . ."

Oh goodness, some people would argue with a hole in the wall. Maybe they want you to try to convince them otherwise. Maybe they want a little hope and need you to go one step further to convince them it is there. Offer that hope, but if they repeatedly come back with a "but," don't let yourself get sucked out of your joy and into their argument. Some people aren't ready to be convinced of the light just yet. When you encounter people like that (I've been one of them), it's a wonderful thing to be kind and show compassion. . . . Just don't let 'em near your light switch.

For the crust

Nonstick cooking spray, for coating
   the baking dish

1 cup granulated sugar

1 1/2 cups all-purpose flour

1 1/2 cups quick-cooking oats

3/4 cup (1 1/2 sticks) cold butter,
   cubed

1/8 teaspoon salt

1/2 teaspoon baking soda

1/2 teaspoon ground cinnamon

For the filling

3 cups fresh or frozen blueberries

2 tablespoons cornstarch

3 tablespoons lemon juice

3/4 cup granulated sugar

1 Preheat the oven to 375°F. Lightly coat a 9 x 13-inch baking dish with cooking spray.

2 Make the crust: Place the sugar, flour, oats, butter, salt, baking soda, and cinnamon in a food processor and process just until

Contentment

I have contentment. The ability to say you have that is one of the greatest treasures these days. Our entire culture screams at us not to be content, telling us daily that we need more. We need more recognition, more money, bigger houses, nicer clothes, nicer china, manicured lawns, faster cars, bigger diamonds, bigger audiences, bigger hair (okay, I'm not going to argue with that one), artful language, sharper retorts. Everything is "more" or "er." BiggER, bettER. How many people do you think sit back and just breathe and experience contentment on a daily basis?

How about even once a month or even once a year? It must be absolutely exhausting never to be content.

Being content isn't about wanting more—it's about appreciating what you have. It is one of the greatest gifts that you could ever give yourself, and it's one to guard as closely as you can.

I let things like TV, music, and advertising into my life, but when they start messing around with my contentment, it's time for them to go. I gave up television a few years back except for the occasional special that we watch as a family. I listen to only two radio stations. I've gotten rid of most of the music from my phone because I don't want to be

crumbly. Set aside 2 cups for the topping. Press the rest of the crumb mixture into the prepared dish and set aside.

3 Make the filling: Place the blueberries, cornstarch, lemon juice, and sugar in a small saucepan and bring to a boil over medium heat. Boil until the mixture thickens, 2 to 3 minutes. It will look like blueberry jam.

4 Spread the filling over the crust. Sprinkle the reserved topping over the blueberry filling and bake until golden, 25 to 30 minutes. Cool completely before cutting into bars.

Blueberry Crunch Bars will keep, in an airtight container at room temperature, for 2 to 3 days.

walking around singing songs in my head about how hard my life is or how angry I am when I'm not.

I can spend that extra time with the television off sitting on my back porch and watching the birds hop from branch to branch as I drink my coffee. I can keep that radio off and hear my kids' animated voices tell me about their days with the knowledge that all too soon they'll be under their own roofs and I'll have to rely on telephone calls rather than these wonderful daily conversations face-to-face. Without the radio and music blaring, I find myself humming the old songs that my grandmothers hummed while they went about their days, and I hope my kids will someday recall the gentle humming from their mama's kitchen.

Rather than wishing for a bigger house, I enjoy living under this sturdy roof of ours, with walls just tall enough to hold our memories but windows so thin they couldn't possibly hold in the laughter. My cool days are spent in worn flannel shirts and my warmer ones in T-shirts and capris that have seen just enough summers to be well seasoned and soft. And while my younger self used to dream about traveling to distant shores, my older self has been blessed with just enough travel under my belt to know that there is no place I'd rather be than the place where we give tight good-morning hugs and never have to put on shoes.

And while some folks may look at my life and think I'm missing out, I can look back with a smile of understanding knowing that I took the road I was meant to take. I didn't give up anything—I just traded up for the sweetness that can be found only in contentment.

Lela's Fried Peach Pie Bars

There is such a treasure found in recipes that have been passed down through the generations. This recipe is a collaborative effort between my great-grandmother Lela and me. I took the filling for her fried peach

My great-grandmother Lela standing behind the zinnias that she planted every spring.

61

pies and used it as the center of a delicious shortbread bar with streusel topping. The streusel topping spreads and covers the bars with a lightly crisp coating that perfectly sets off the peaches. This simple bar has all of the flavors I love in Lela's fried peach pies, and still brings to mind sweet memories of her. *Makes 12 bars*

For the crust
Nonstick cooking spray, for coating
    the baking pan
2 cups all-purpose flour
1 cup (2 sticks) butter, at room
    temperature
1/2 cup confectioners' sugar

For the fruit filling
6 to 7 ounces dried peaches
    (or apples, apricots, or other
    dried fruit)
1 cup granulated sugar
1/4 cup (1/2 stick) butter
1 tablespoon lemon juice (optional)
1/2 teaspoon ground cinnamon
    (optional)

For the streusel topping
1/2 cup (1 stick) butter, at room
    temperature
1 cup all-purpose flour
1/2 cup confectioners' sugar

1 Preheat the oven to 350°F. Lightly coat a 9 x 13-inch baking pan with cooking spray and set aside.

2 Make the crust: Place the flour, butter, and confectioners' sugar in a medium-size mixing bowl and cut together with a pastry cutter or long-tined fork until they're well combined and form a crumbly dough. Press the dough into the bottom of the prepared pan. Bake until just lightly browned around the edges, 20 to 25 minutes.

3 Meanwhile, make the fruit filling: Place the dried fruit, sugar, butter, lemon juice, if using, and cinnamon, if using, in a medium-size saucepan and cook over medium-high heat. Stir constantly until it comes to a boil, then reduce the heat to medium-low and simmer, stirring every so often, until thick and reduced by about half, 15 to 25 minutes. Spread the fruit mixture over the crust.

Seasonal Treats

Little bits of sweetness sprinkled throughout the year are always welcome, but some treats just seem to herald certain seasons. Here are a few that I like to make during particular seasons to heighten the anticipation of the fun that is to come!

SPRING
Sunshine Lemon Blossoms (page 15)
Katy's Lemon Juice Cake (page 72)
Fresh Strawberry Cake (page 111)
Best Every Orange Meringue Pie
 (page 140)

SUMMER
Easiest S'mores Brownies (page 37)
Lela's Fried Peach Pie Bars (page 61)

Tropical Pig Pickin' Cake (page 85)
Apple Salad (page 225)

FALL
Chewy Cranberry Zingers (page 17)
Chewy Pear Bars (page 53)
Old-Fashioned Butter Rolls (page 177)
Shortcut Amish Friendship Bread
 (page 185)
Slow Cooker Caramel Apple Cider
 (page 269)

WINTER
Candy Cane Cookies (page 32)
Lotsa Crumb Cake (page 83)
Sweet Potato Crème Brûlée (page 173)
Amazing Apple Bread (page 193)
Mulled Pineapple Juice (page 266)

4 Make the streusel: Combine the butter, flour, and confectioners' sugar in a small bowl and cut together with a pastry cutter or long-tined fork until well blended and crumbly. Sprinkle the streusel over the fruit filling.

5 Return the pan to the oven and bake until the top is lightly golden, 15 to 20 minutes. Allow to cool in the pan before cutting into bars. (Oh, go ahead—try one warm!)

Lela's Fried Peach Pie Bars will keep, in an airtight container at room temperature, for up to 3 days.

3

Poke Cakes, Pound Cakes, Layer Cakes, and Love

BACK IN THE day, the Reed family used to have huge reunions each year. Mama Reed would start baking cakes for the event days ahead of time. Without a refrigerator, she'd cover them in a lightweight cloth and set them out in the cool air on her porch to help keep them fresh for the big event. If you were to go back in time and ask those folks, you'd probably be surprised to find many of them were going to the reunion just as much for Mama Reed's cakes as they were for the fellowship. Cakes still make the event now just as much as they did back then.

Small Batch Yellow Cake

This is a simple-to-make 8 x 8-inch yellow cake that is about as versatile as they come. Think of it as a homemade version of a Jiffy cake mix. My husband loves this cake topped with Creamy Chocolate Buttercream (page 122), but I sometimes just serve it with sweetened berries for a summer treat.

This cake bakes up pretty and high in an 8 x 8-inch pan. However, most square cake pans are actually 9 x 9-inch nowadays, which will yield a slightly shorter cake. If you want a more sky-high version, make sure you check the size of your pan. *Serves 9*

Vegetable shortening and flour, for coating the baking dish
1 cup self-rising flour (see page 276)
3/4 cup granulated sugar
1/4 cup vegetable shortening
1/2 cup buttermilk (see page 277)
1 large egg
1 teaspoon vanilla extract or butter flavoring
1/4 teaspoon almond extract (optional)

Frosting of your choice (pages 121–131), for finishing (optional)
Fresh berries, for serving (optional)

1 Preheat the oven to 350°F. Lightly grease and flour an 8 x 8-inch baking dish and set aside.

2 Combine the flour, sugar, and shortening in a large mixing bowl. Beat with an electric mixer at medium speed until well combined, 1 to 2 minutes.

3 Add the buttermilk, egg, vanilla, and almond extract, if using, and beat again at medium speed, scraping down the side of the bowl as needed, until smooth and creamy, 2 to 3 minutes. Pour the batter into the prepared dish.

4 Bake until a toothpick inserted in the center comes out clean, 30 to 35 minutes. Allow to cool on a wire rack. This cake can either be frosted and served straight from the baking dish or turned out onto a serving plate and then frosted. Or serve it topped with fresh berries, if you like.

Small Batch Yellow Cake will keep, covered at room temperature, for up to 3 days, or in the refrigerator for up to 1 week.

Chocolate Snack Cake

When my grandmother passed away, I inherited her well-worn cookbook. I put it to good use when choosing recipes to include in this book because I am of the firm belief that good-hearted people make the best-tasting food. This is a simple chocolate cake that can be dressed up for special occasions, but like a good old friend, I prefer it to come as it is. *Serves 9*

Nonstick cooking spray, for coating
   the baking dish
1/2 cup (1 stick) butter,
   at room temperature
1 cup granulated sugar
4 large eggs
1 cup self-rising flour
   (see page 276)
1 1/2 cups chocolate syrup
   (such as Hershey's)
1 1/2 teaspoons vanilla extract
1 cup semisweet chocolate chips

1 Preheat the oven to 350°F. Lightly coat an 8 x 8-inch baking dish with cooking spray and set aside.

2 Cream the butter and sugar together in a large mixing bowl with an electric mixer at medium speed until light and fluffy, 1 to 2 minutes. Add the eggs and beat again, scraping down the side of the bowl as needed, until incorporated, about 2 minutes.

3 Add the flour, chocolate syrup, and vanilla. Beat again until incorporated, 1 to 2 minutes more. Stir in the chocolate chips.

4 Pour the batter into the prepared dish. Bake until the center springs back when lightly pressed, 40 to 45 minutes.

Chocolate Snack Cake will keep, covered at room temperature, for up to 3 days.

Dark Chocolate Mousse Cake

Chocolate mousse is one of those rare treats in my life. I may have it once or twice a year at most, but whenever I do, I can't help but feel like I'm enjoying one of the most decadent treats life has to offer. This dark chocolate cake is made easy with a cake mix, but the real "icing on the cake" is the quick chocolate mousse frosting that goes on top! *Serves 12*

Dark Chocolate Mousse Cake

Take the Cake!

Life is complicated enough as it is, so I like a good shortcut when time and circumstances allow. With the quality of cake mixes on the market today, I don't hesitate to use one. So while many of the recipes in this chapter are made from scratch, they are also balanced out with shortcut recipes that start with a mix. However, if mixes aren't your thing, feel free to use the homemade cake recipes featured in this chapter in place of the store-bought mixes.

For the cake

Nonstick cooking spray, for coating
   the baking pan
1 box (15 to 18 ounces) chocolate
   cake mix
1 container (8 ounces) sour cream
1/2 cup milk
1/4 cup vegetable oil
3 large eggs
2 heaping tablespoons Dutch
   process cocoa powder
   (or regular)
1/2 cup chocolate syrup
   (such as Hershey's)

For the frosting

1 1/2 cups semisweet chocolate
   chips
2 cups heavy cream, chilled
3 tablespoons confectioners' sugar

1 Preheat the oven to 350°F. Lightly coat a 9 x 13-inch baking pan with cooking spray and set aside.

2 Make the cake: Place the cake mix, sour cream, milk, oil, eggs, and cocoa powder in a large mixing bowl. Beat with an electric mixer at medium speed until well combined and smooth, scraping down the side of the bowl as needed, about 2 minutes. Pour into the prepared pan.

3 Bake until a toothpick inserted in the center comes out clean, 35 to 40 minutes. Immediately poke holes all over the top of the cake using the handle of a wooden spoon. Pour on the chocolate syrup and carefully spread it with a butter knife. Allow to cool.

4 Meanwhile, make the frosting: Place the chocolate chips in a microwave-safe bowl and microwave for 45-second intervals, stirring between each, until just melted and smooth. Set aside to cool for a few minutes.

5 Place the heavy cream in a large mixing bowl. Beat with an electric mixer at medium speed until soft peaks form, 2 to 3 minutes. Add the confectioners' sugar and beat until stiff peaks form. With the mixer on low speed, slowly add the melted chocolate and blend until well combined. Cover and refrigerate the frosting until the cake has cooled completely, then frost the cake.

Dark Chocolate Mousse Cake will keep, covered in the refrigerator, for up to 1 week.

Bowl-Licking Buttermilk Cake
with Brown Sugar Fudge Icing

This cake is the type that brought folks running to family reunions and church socials generations ago, and you'd be hard-pressed to find any store-bought version that could hold a candle to it. With my supermoist buttermilk cake topped with a brown sugar fudge

icing, you can't go wrong. I strongly suggest baking this as a 9 x 13-inch sheet cake rather than a layer cake due to the thickness of the icing. *Serves 12*

Nonstick cooking spray, for coating
    the baking pan
1 cup (2 sticks) unsalted butter,
    at room temperature
2 cups granulated sugar
5 large eggs
2 1/2 cups all-purpose flour
1 teaspoon baking soda
1 teaspoon baking powder
1/4 teaspoon salt
1 teaspoon vanilla extract
1 cup buttermilk (see page 277)
Brown Sugar Fudge Icing
    (recipe follows)

1 Preheat the oven to 350°F. Lightly coat a 9 x 13-inch baking pan with cooking spray and set aside.

2 Cream the butter and sugar together in a large mixing bowl with an electric mixer at medium speed until very smooth, at least 4 minutes. Add the eggs and beat well to incorporate.

3 In a separate medium-size bowl, stir together the flour, baking soda, baking powder, and salt. Add the flour mixture to the butter mixture along with the vanilla and buttermilk and mix with an electric mixer at medium speed, scraping down the side of the bowl as needed, until thoroughly blended and smooth, about 3 minutes.

4 Pour the batter into the prepared pan. Bake until a toothpick inserted in the center comes out clean, 30 to 35 minutes. Allow to cool completely in the pan.

5 Frost the top of the cake with the Brown Sugar Fudge Icing.

Bowl-Licking Buttermilk Cake with Brown Sugar Fudge Icing will keep, under a cake dome at room temperature, for 3 to 5 days.

Brown Sugar Fudge Icing

Makes 2 cups

> 1/2 cup (1 stick) butter
> 1 cup light brown sugar
> 1/4 cup buttermilk (see page 277) or whole milk
> 1 teaspoon vanilla extract
> 2 to 3 cups confectioners' sugar
> 1 to 2 tablespoons milk (optional)

1 Melt the butter in a medium-size heavy-bottomed saucepan over medium heat. Stir in the brown sugar and buttermilk and bring to a boil, stirring constantly. Once it reaches a full boil, continue stirring and boil for 2 minutes.

2 Remove from the heat, stir in the vanilla, and set aside to cool for 10 minutes.

3 Pour the mixture into a large mixing bowl and add the confectioners' sugar, 1 cup at a time (you may not need all of it), beating with an electric mixer at medium speed after each addition. Continue beating until the icing is smooth and thick, about 2 minutes. If the icing gets too thick, add a tablespoon or two of milk to thin it just enough to be able to frost the cake. Use immediately.

Lemon Custard Poke Cake

This is an old-fashioned cake that packs a wallop of flavor and is still small enough for a simple family dessert. There is something about a homemade custard that just can't be beat. This one partially soaks into the cake while some remains on top as a rich, thick frosting once it's refrigerated. Yum!

Serves 9

For the cake

Vegetable shortening and flour,
    for coating the baking dish

1 cup self-rising flour
    (see page 276)

³⁄₄ cup granulated sugar

¹⁄₄ cup vegetable shortening

¹⁄₂ cup buttermilk (see page 277)

1 large egg

1 teaspoon vanilla extract

1 teaspoon butter flavoring
    (optional; can use an additional
    teaspoon vanilla instead)

¹⁄₄ teaspoon almond extract
    (optional)

For the custard

1 cup granulated sugar

¹⁄₃ cup all-purpose flour

3 large eggs

2 cups milk

Dash of salt

¹⁄₂ cup lemon juice

1 teaspoon vanilla extract

1 Preheat the oven to 350°F. Lightly grease and flour an 8 x 8-inch baking dish and set aside.

2 Make the cake: Place the flour, sugar, and shortening in a large mixing bowl and beat with an electric mixer at medium speed until well incorporated. Add the buttermilk, egg, vanilla, butter flavoring, and almond extract, if using, and beat again, scraping down the side of the bowl as needed, until smooth and creamy, 2 to 3 minutes.

3 Pour the batter into the prepared baking dish. Bake until a toothpick inserted in the center comes out clean, 30 to 35 minutes. Remove from the oven and poke holes all over the top of the cake using the handle of a wooden spoon.

4 Meanwhile, make the custard: Place the sugar, flour, eggs, milk, salt, lemon juice, and vanilla extract in a medium-size heavy-bottomed saucepan over medium heat. Stir constantly until the sugar is dissolved and the mixture is thick, about 10 minutes. (Do not give in to the temptation to step away—the mixture will scorch if it's not stirred constantly.) Once the mixture thickens to a soft pudding-like texture, remove from the heat and let it cool until the cake is done.

5 Pour the custard over the cake. Allow to cool completely, then cover and refrigerate until you're ready to serve. The custard will cool and form a thick frosting-like layer atop the cake.

Lemon Custard Poke Cake will keep, covered in the refrigerator, for up to 3 days.

Time Travel via Swing

I often take walks with my daughter. Usually we walk around the neighborhood and sometimes we head to a nearby park, which is by far her favorite place for us to go. As we near it, her eyes begin searching for kids, and if she sees any she tugs on my hand to speed me up as she shouts, "There are kids, Mama! Hurry!" My child could make friends with a hole in the wall. I don't know where she gets that from.

The other day we headed over there and there weren't any other kids, so I pushed Katy in the swing a few times, and that empty swing next to her started getting the best of me. I couldn't help myself, so I sat down in it.

Now let me fill you in here: Mama don't swing no more. I spent half of my childhood swinging. But as I've gotten older, motion has become a bit of a problem for me. I learned this the hard way when we went to Disney World when Katy Rose was just two. My husband and son wanted to ride roller coasters, which Katy was too small to ride, so it ended up being just me and Katy for a good bit of the trip. We walked by Dumbo's Flight, and every day when she begged and begged to ride it, I said that her daddy would take her. This went on for three days until one day, when my husband was nowhere to be found, I gave in and said, "Baby, I know you want to ride this, so let's just go."

We got on that thing and it went up, up, up (have I mentioned I don't care for heights?). While it was going up, it was spinning, spinning, spinning. Katy was lit up like the morning sun,

Katy's Lemon Juice Cake

My daughter came up with the idea (and name) for this cake, and it tastes just as sunshiny as she is! She always loves lemon pie but wanted the same flavor in a cake. We especially love to make it in early spring, when we need a little sunshine after a long winter. Katy often makes several at a time to give as gifts to friends and family members.

This cake bakes perfectly in a 9 x 9-inch baking dish. You can bake it in an 8 x 8-inch dish, but whenever I do, the center sinks down slightly. My family doesn't mind this one bit, but I'm letting you know just in case yours does. *Serves 9*

happy as could be and having the time of her life. It was wonderful to see.

But when we got off, I could barely walk. I was gripping that rail and trying to convince my brain that the world was not still spinning. For weeks after that, the room would spin whenever I closed my eyes, so I spent as much time as possible keeping my eyes open!

This is why I avoid swings. But I couldn't help myself that day at the park. I decided in that moment that to swing by my little girl would be worth a few weeks of spinning rooms, so I hopped on.

"Mama! You're swinging!" Her eyes were big as dollars. "I didn't know you knew how!"

I laughed. "Katy baby, I used to do this every single day when I was a little girl, all day long!" She just kept looking at me in delight each time we'd swing past each other.

"Mama, you're so good at this!" Bless her heart, that was a moment to remember for both of us. I didn't feel sick, so I went higher and higher still, shedding off years of adulthood and once again trying to touch the clouds with my toes.

I grew younger that day. Those precious moments when I shed the yoke of deadlines, emails, and demands took years off my life. In fact, it felt as if a full three decades' worth had been removed. My heart smiles now just thinking about it.

Childhood, no matter how far away it seems, is always within us, and sometimes all we need to travel back in time is a child and a trusty old park swing.

For the cake
Nonstick cooking spray, for coating the baking dish
3/4 cup (1 1/2 sticks) butter or margarine, at room temperature
1 cup granulated sugar
1 3/4 cups self-rising flour (see page 276)
2 large eggs
2 teaspoons lemon juice
1 teaspoon vanilla extract

For the lemon syrup
1/2 cup lemon juice
1/2 cup granulated sugar

For the glaze
1 1/2 cups confectioners' sugar
4 to 5 tablespoons milk
1 teaspoon butter flavoring or vanilla extract

1 Preheat the oven to 350°F. Lightly coat a 9 x 9-inch baking dish with cooking spray and set aside.

2 Make the cake: Cream together the butter and sugar in a large mixing bowl. Mix with an electric mixer at medium speed until light and fluffy, 1 to 2 minutes. Add the flour, eggs, lemon juice, and vanilla and mix until incorporated, scraping down the side of the bowl as needed, about 2 minutes. The batter will be thick like cookie dough.

3 Pat the dough into the prepared dish and bake until lightly golden around the edges, 25 to 30 minutes. Allow to cool.

4 Meanwhile, make the syrup: Combine the lemon juice and sugar in a small bowl and stir until the sugar is dissolved. (Alternatively, heat the mixture in the microwave for 30 seconds to help speed up the process.) Poke holes all over the top of the cake with the handle of a wooden spoon and pour the syrup evenly over the top.

5 Make the glaze: Place the confectioners' sugar, milk, and the butter flavoring in a small bowl and stir with a spoon until smooth. Pour over the top of the cake, spreading to cover the edges. Allow the glaze to harden. Once the glaze is hard, cover the cake with aluminum foil and allow to sit at room temperature for several hours while the cake completely absorbs the syrup.

Katy's Lemon Juice Cake will keep, covered at room temperature, for up to 3 days, or in the refrigerator for up to 5 days.

Coca-Cola Cake

If you're ever in a diner or café in the South and see Coca-Cola cake on the menu, you know you're in for some wonderful food! This fluffy and moist cake takes chocolate to a whole new level. Finished with a soft fudge icing, it's sure to be a fast family favorite, if it isn't already.

I try to keep some of those old-fashioned glass-bottled Coca-Colas in my pantry for recipes such as this. They retain their flavor a little longer than canned Coke, and just add a touch of nostalgia. *Serves 12*

For the cake
Nonstick cooking spray, for coating
   the baking pan
1 box (15 to 18 ounces) white
   cake mix
4 tablespoons unsweetened
   cocoa powder
1/2 cup (1 stick) butter or
   margarine, melted
1 cup Coca-Cola
1/2 cup buttermilk (see page 277)

2 large eggs

1 teaspoon vanilla extract

1½ cups mini marshmallows

For the frosting

½ cup (1 stick) butter

4 tablespoons unsweetened
  cocoa powder

⅓ cup Coca-Cola

4 cups confectioners' sugar, sifted

1 cup chopped pecans (optional)

1 Preheat the oven to 350°F. Lightly coat a 9 x 13-inch baking pan with cooking spray and set aside.

2 Make the cake: Place the cake mix, cocoa powder, melted butter, Coca-Cola, buttermilk, eggs, and vanilla in a large mixing bowl. Beat with an electric mixer at medium speed until well combined, scraping down the side of the bowl as needed, about 1 minute. Increase the mixer speed to medium-high and beat for 2 minutes. Fold in the marshmallows with a large spoon.

3 Pour the batter into the prepared pan. Bake until a toothpick inserted in the center comes out clean, 40 to 42 minutes.

4 Meanwhile, make the frosting: Place the butter in a medium-size saucepan over medium heat. When the butter starts to melt, stir in the cocoa powder and Coca-Cola. Let the mixture come to a boil, stirring constantly. Once the mixture comes to a boil, remove from the heat and stir in the confectioners' sugar with a large spoon until the frosting is thick and smooth. Fold in the pecans, if using.

5 Pour the frosting over the top of the cake while both are still warm, spreading the frosting with a rubber spatula so that it reaches the edges of the cake. Allow to cool for 20 minutes before serving.

Coca-Cola Cake will keep, covered at room temperature, for up to 3 days.

Mama Reed's Caramel Apple Cake

Mama Reed didn't really have a recipe for this cake, but I took one of her recipes and used it as a base to build on, so I decided to give her credit. It's sort of like a collaboration with the great-grandmother I know only through stories, and I like how that feels. After making a spiced baked apple cake I decided to top it with Caramel Fudge Icing, which has the crumbly, melt-in-your-mouth texture of fudge but tastes even better, because it's caramel!

Mama Reed's Caramel Apple Cake

If you were born after 1950, you are probably not familiar with boiled icing. This icing is very different from the kind cooks use today, and it's a rare thing indeed to find someone who can successfully frost a layer cake with it. It starts out spreadable but gets hard very quickly. My best advice is to stick with icing 9 x 13-inch sheet cakes with it. *Serves 12*

For the cake:
Nonstick cooking spray, for coating
    the baking pan
2 cups self-rising flour
2 large or 3 small apples, peeled
    and chopped
2 large eggs
1 1/2 cups granulated sugar
1/2 cup vegetable oil
2 teaspoons ground cinnamon
1 teaspoon ground allspice
1 teaspoon vanilla extract

For the icing:
1/4 cup (1/2 stick) butter or
    margarine
8 tablespoons heavy cream or
    whole milk
1 cup packed dark brown sugar
    (light is okay)
2 cups confectioners' sugar,
    plus extra if needed
1 teaspoon vanilla extract

1 Preheat the oven to 350°F. Lightly coat a 9 x 13-inch baking pan with cooking spray and set aside.

2 Make the cake: Combine the flour, apples, eggs, sugar, oil, 1/2 cup water, cinnamon, allspice, and 1 teaspoon of the vanilla in a large mixing bowl and stir with a wooden spoon until well blended and smooth. Spread into the prepared pan and bake until a toothpick inserted in the center comes out clean, 45 minutes. Allow to cool slightly while you prepare the icing.

3 Make the icing: Place the butter, heavy cream, and brown sugar in a medium-size saucepan over medium heat and cook, stirring constantly, until the butter is melted and the mixture is well blended, 2 to 3 minutes.

4 Turn the heat up to medium-high and stir constantly until it comes to a rolling boil. Once boiling, cook for 2 minutes and then remove from the heat. Working quickly, stir in the confectioners' sugar and remaining teaspoon of vanilla with a wire whisk or an electric mixer at medium speed until smooth. Add up to 1/2 cup more confectioners' sugar if needed to thicken. Ice the slightly cooled cake as soon as possible (the icing wants to harden, so don't let it do that until it's on the cake!).

Mama Reed's Caramel Apple Cake will keep, covered at room temperature, for up to 3 days.

Italian Cream Cake

This cake is in my top ten favorite desserts of all time, right up there with Red Velvet Cupcakes (page 103), Cappuccino Cake (page 113), and Old-Fashioned Banana Pudding (page 168). It's pillowy soft, moist, and just all-around perfect. Topped with a pecan-studded cream cheese frosting this luscious cake will insure you'll bring back an empty pan every time.

I make this as a sheet cake but you can make it as a layer cake if you like—see the Variation that follows. *Serves 12*

Nonstick cooking spray, for coating
    the baking pan
1/2 cup vegetable shortening
1/2 cup (1 stick) unsalted butter,
    at room temperature
2 cups granulated sugar
5 large eggs
2 cups all-purpose flour
1 teaspoon baking soda
1 cup buttermilk (see page 277)
2 teaspoons vanilla extract
1 cup sweetened shredded coconut
Cream Cheese Frosting
    (page 123), for finishing
1 cup chopped pecans, plus pecan
    halves for garnish (optional)

1 Preheat the oven to 350°F. Lightly coat a 9 x 13-inch baking pan with cooking spray and set aside.

2 Cream together the shortening, butter, and sugar in a large mixing bowl with an electric mixer at medium speed until light and fluffy, 1 to 2 minutes. Add the eggs and beat on medium speed, scraping down the side of the bowl as needed, until smooth, about 2 minutes.

3 In a separate small bowl, stir together the flour and baking soda. Add the flour mixture to the egg mixture along with the buttermilk, vanilla, and coconut and mix at medium speed until well blended and completely smooth, about 2 minutes more.

4 Pour the batter into the prepared pan. Bake until a wooden toothpick inserted in the center comes out clean, 40 to 45 minutes. Allow to cool on a wire rack.

5 Stir the chopped pecans into the cream cheese frosting to combine. Frost the top of the cake and garnish with the pecan halves, if desired.

Italian Cream Cake will keep, covered at room temperature, for up to 2 days, or in the refrigerator for up to 1 week.

How a Homemade Cake Says "I Love You"

When my mother was a little girl, her mother worked full-time as a secretary, so my mama's grandmother stayed home and took care of her each day. My grandmama didn't have the ease and mastery in the kitchen that her mother had, mostly from lack of experience. But one year, on my mama's birthday, Grandmama decided that she was going to make Mama's birthday cake herself. She made a white cake and iced it with homemade fluffy white icing. Not knowing how to decorate it beyond that, she got creative and cut several pieces of cotton string and then dipped them into different colors of food coloring before carefully laying them across the cake and picking them up to leave colorful stripes. When she was done, Mama had a cake decorated in myriad rainbow stripes; and to this day she still says that was the prettiest cake she'd ever seen.

VARIATION

ITALIAN CREAM LAYER CAKE: Divide the batter between two prepared 9-inch round cake pans. Bake for 30 to 35 minutes, then allow to cool on a wire rack. Turn one cake layer out onto a large plate and frost the top with one third of the frosting, then top with the second layer, frost the top and side with the remaining frosting, and decorate with the pecan halves.

Pecan Pie Cake

This cake has all the flavors we love in a pecan pie but in cake form: What's not to love about that? Whenever I serve this cake, I am asked for the recipe, and the cake is usually all gone by the time I leave. I've found that this holds up to travel a little better than pecan pie as well. *Serves 12*

Nonstick cooking spray, for coating
    the baking dish
1 box (15 to 18 ounces) yellow cake
    or butter cake mix
4 large eggs
1/2 cup (1 stick) butter or
    margarine, melted
1 1/2 cups light corn syrup
1/2 cup packed dark brown sugar
1 teaspoon vanilla extract
1 1/2 cups chopped pecans

1 Preheat the oven to 350°F. Lightly coat a 9 x 13-inch baking dish with cooking spray and set aside.

2 Place the cake mix, 1 egg, and the melted butter in a large mixing bowl. Beat with an electric mixer at medium speed until well blended, 2 minutes. Place 2/3 cup of the batter in a medium-size mixing bowl and set aside.

3 Spread the remaining batter in the prepared baking dish and bake until just lightly browned, 15 minutes.

4 While the crust is cooking, add the remaining 3 eggs, the corn syrup, brown sugar, vanilla, and pecans to the reserved batter and mix with an electric mixer at medium speed until well combined, 1 to 2 minutes.

5 Pour the filling on top of the crust and bake until set in the center, 50 to 60 minutes. Allow to cool completely before serving.

Pecan Pie Cake will keep, covered at room temperature, for up to 3 days, or in the refrigerator for up to 1 week.

Oatmeal Cake

Oatmeal is one of my favorite baking ingredients. It adds flavor, density, and texture unlike anything else. This is a dense, lightly sweet cake, perfect for snacks, breakfast, or with coffee. The topping adds even more flavor and moistness, but it is mostly absorbed into the cake shortly after it's added, so the cake will appear to be "naked" when served. For those folks who aren't fans of a super-sweet topping, this is a plus! *Serves 12*

For the cake
1 cup old-fashioned oats
Nonstick cooking spray, for coating
    the baking dish
1 cup granulated sugar
1 cup light brown sugar
1/2 cup (1 stick) unsalted butter,
    at room temperature

2 large eggs

1¹/₂ cups all-purpose flour

1 teaspoon baking soda

¹/₂ teaspoon ground cinnamon

For the topping

¹/₂ cup (1 stick) butter

¹/₂ cup granulated sugar

1 cup shredded coconut
    (sweetened or unsweetened)

¹/₄ cup evaporated milk

1 cup chopped pecans

1 Make the cake: Bring 1¹/₄ cups water to a boil in a saucepan over high heat. Place the oats in a medium-size heatproof bowl. Pour the boiling water over the oats and allow them to soak for 30 minutes.

2 Meanwhile, preheat the oven to 350°F. Lightly coat a 9 x 13-inch baking dish with cooking spray and set aside.

3 Place the oats and their soaking liquid in a large mixing bowl. Add the granulated sugar, brown sugar, butter, eggs, flour, baking soda, and cinnamon. Beat with an electric mixer at medium speed, scraping down the side of the bowl as needed, until well combined, about 2 minutes.

4 Pour the batter into the prepared dish and bake until a toothpick inserted in the center comes out clean, 30 to 35 minutes. Remove

the cake from the oven, move a rack to the center of the oven, and set to a low broil.

5 As soon as the cake comes out of the oven, make the topping: Melt the butter in a medium-size saucepan over medium-high heat. Add the sugar, coconut, evaporated milk, and pecans and stir until well mixed. Pour evenly over the cake.

6 Place the cake on the center rack and broil, until the topping is lightly browned, 5 to 6 minutes (watch carefully to make sure it doesn't burn). Allow to cool slightly before serving.

Oatmeal Cake will keep, covered at room temperature, for up to 3 days.

Black Pepper Cake

from WENDY BALL

"My father-in-law, Ray, and his siblings lost their parents and were sent to a foster home back in the Depression. Their foster parents, like all folks back then, had to make everything count when there were hungry mouths to feed. Ray told me he used to sneak out at night and raid the trash looking for chicken bones so he could suck the marrow out of them because he was so hungry. One thing his foster mother did make as a special treat for him, however, was Pepper Cake.

"He would ask me to make it for him on occasion only because my mother-in-law didn't want to. Not out of spite mind you, but because in my husband's family there were ten mouths to feed so there really wasn't enough to make desserts very often.

"I am always happy to make this dessert to remind him that a bit of sweetness still exists, even during sad times." *Serves 12*

Nonstick cooking spray, for coating
   the pan
2 cups granulated sugar
1 cup vegetable shortening
2 teaspoons baking soda
1 teaspoon baking powder
Pinch of salt
2 teaspoons ground cinnamon
1 teaspoon ground nutmeg
2 teaspoons ground cloves
1 teaspoon ground black pepper
3 cups all-purpose flour
2 cups buttermilk (see page 277)
Ice cream or whipped topping,
   for serving (optional)

1 Preheat the oven to 375°F. Lightly coat a 9 x 13-inch baking pan with cooking spray and set aside.

2 In a large mixing bowl, cream together the sugar and shortening with an electric mixer at medium speed until light and fluffy, about 1 minute.

3 In a medium-size mixing bowl, stir together the baking soda, baking powder, salt, cinnamon, nutmeg, cloves, black pepper, and flour with a spoon.

4 Add the baking soda mixture to the sugar mixture, alternating with the buttermilk. Mix well by hand until smooth.

5 Pour the batter into the prepared pan and bake until a toothpick inserted in the center comes out clean, 35 to 40 minutes. Allow to cool completely in the pan.

6 Serve topped with ice cream or whipped topping, if you like.

Black Pepper Cake will keep, covered at room temperature, for up to 3 days.

CHRISTY'S NOTE: This recipe piqued my curiosity and I'm so glad I tried it! This is an amazingly easy and delicious spice cake. The black pepper enhances the flavor of the spices without overpowering it. It is almost like having a band playing in your mouth. Now when is the last time you had a band play in your mouth? Maybe it is time you gave this a try.

Lotsa Crumb Cake

This cake is my heartsong! It's one of those cakes I always wanted to make myself but had to settle for purchasing for quite some time until I got determined to come up with a recipe for it. My version features a buttery cake bottom and a piled-high crumb topping that stays put and allows you to get all of that in your mouth without the mess. Even better, the recipe is easy and starts with a cake mix. But since we're switching up the usual ingredients that you would add to a mix in order to add more richness and a homemade flavor, we can keep that little secret to ourselves. *Serves 12*

For the cake
Nonstick cooking spray, for coating
    the baking dish
1 box (15 to 18 ounces) yellow,
    butter golden, or white cake mix
¾ cup whole milk
3 large eggs
2 teaspoons vanilla extract
½ cup (1 stick) butter, melted and
    cooled slightly

For the crumb topping
1 cup (2 sticks) butter, at room
    temperature
3 cups all-purpose flour
1 cup packed light brown sugar
1 tablespoon ground cinnamon
Confectioners' sugar, for dusting
    the cake (optional)

1 Preheat the oven to 350°F. Lightly coat a 9 x 13-inch baking dish with cooking spray and set aside.

2 Make the cake: Place the cake mix, milk, eggs, vanilla, and melted butter in a large mixing bowl. Beat with an electric mixer at medium speed until blended and smooth, scraping down the side of the bowl if needed, about 2 minutes. Pour the batter into the prepared baking dish.

Lotsa Crumb Cake, page 83

3 Make the crumb topping: Combine the butter, flour, brown sugar, and cinnamon in a medium-size bowl, and cut together using a long-tined fork or pastry cutter until well mixed and crumbly. Sprinkle the crumb mixture over the top of the cake batter.

4 Bake until a toothpick inserted in the center comes out clean, about 45 minutes. Allow to cool slightly and then sprinkle the top with confectioners' sugar, if desired.

Lotsa Crumb Cake will keep, covered at room temperature, for up to 3 days.

Tropical Pig Pickin' Cake

This is a deluxe version of mandarin orange cake (often called Pig Pickin' Cake), a family reunion classic. It's light, creamy, fruity, and delicious! It's even better if it sits in the refrigerator for three days to allow the flavors to blend together and the cake to moisten before serving. My mother used to manage this, but the longest I've been able to wait before diving in is one day! *Serves 12*

For the cake
Vegetable shortening and flour,
   for coating the pan(s)
1 box (15 to 18 ounces) yellow
   cake mix
4 large eggs
1/2 cup vegetable oil
1 can (8 ounces) crushed
   pineapple, drained
1 can (11 ounces) mandarin
   oranges, drained and diced
1 jar maraschino cherries, drained
   and chopped

For the frosting
1 box (3.4 ounces) vanilla instant
   pudding
1 can (8 ounces) crushed
   pineapple, with juice
1 container (13 ounces) frozen
   whipped topping (such as
   Cool Whip), thawed
1 cup sweetened shredded coconut
   (optional)

1 Preheat the oven to 350°F. Lightly grease and flour three 8-inch round cake pans or one 9 x 13-inch baking pan and set aside.

2 Make the cake: Place the cake mix, eggs, and oil in a large mixing bowl and beat with an electric mixer at medium speed, scraping down the side of the bowl as needed, until well blended, about 2 minutes. Add the

Choosing the Scenic Route

Most folks, when asked, will tell you that they want to be happy. Oftentimes, though, our actions give a different answer. It is as if we become miserable out of habit and don't even notice that the way we act, speak, and even live all help create an environment that's the opposite of the one in which we want to live.

There comes a time when you've got to say enough is enough. Stand up to yourself. Become your own inner drill sergeant. Hold yourself to a higher standard. If you want to be happy, you have to think happy:

Tell yourself you're happy, listen to music that makes you happy, constantly be on the lookout for even the tiniest moments of joy!

Don't just wish to be happy, then spend your days in puddles of despair. Look at all the people around you clinging to their misery: You've got to decide to hold on just as tightly to your happiness.

Decide today to live in hope. Declare that you are happy and build up from there. Life is a journey no matter which path you take. Isn't it time you chose the scenic route?

pineapple, oranges, and cherries and mix at low speed until incorporated, less than 1 minute.

3 Pour the batter into the prepared pans. Bake until a wooden toothpick inserted in the center comes out clean, 30 minutes. Allow to cool in the pans for 10 minutes, then turn the cakes out of the pans onto a rack to cool completely.

4 Make the frosting: Place the pudding mix and pineapple in a medium-size bowl and stir together with a spoon. Fold in the whipped topping and beat with an electric mixer at medium speed until creamy and smooth, 1 to 2 minutes. Frost the cake and sprinkle with the coconut, if using. For best results, refrigerate the cake for 2 or 3 days before serving.

Tropical Pig Pickin' Cake will keep, covered in the refrigerator, for up to 1 week.

Always Moist Pineapple Upside Down Cake

There are two secrets to making this cake "always moist." One is to use the pineapple juice from the can of pineapple in place of the water called for on the box of mix. The second secret is to cover the cake while it is still warm. As moisture forms on top of the covering, gently pat it down with your hands so that it falls back into the cake. Some might call this cheating, but once you take a bite, you won't care.

Don't skimp on the brown sugar in this recipe. Just make the best pineapple upside down cake you can, have a piece, enjoy it, and eat a salad tomorrow. *Serves 12*

½ cup (1 stick) butter
1 cup dark or light brown sugar
1 can (20 ounces) pineapple slices,
    juice reserved in a measuring cup
6 whole maraschino cherries

1 box (15 to 18 ounces) yellow cake mix, plus the ingredients called for on the package (except for water; see Note)

1 Preheat the oven to 350°F.

2 Place the butter in a 9 x 13-inch baking pan and place the pan in the preheating oven just until the butter is melted, about 5 minutes. Remove the pan from the oven, tilt the pan to distribute the butter evenly, and sprinkle the brown sugar all over the bottom of the pan (careful—it's hot!). Be generous with the brown sugar; a cup may seem like a lot, but it melts and becomes a luscious layer of goodness.

3 Place 6 pineapple slices on top of the brown sugar, evenly spaced. Place a cherry in the center of each pineapple slice.

4 Prepare the cake batter as directed on the package, substituting the reserved pineapple juice for the water. (You probably will not have enough juice; in that case, add water until the liquid measures the amount of water called for on the box.) Slowly pour the cake batter over the pineapple slices and cherries.

5 Bake until a toothpick inserted in the center comes out clean, about 45 minutes.

6 Allow to cool in the pan for 5 minutes. Turn it out onto a large cake board or tray, being careful not to let the hot cake touch your skin. Cool completely before serving.

Always Moist Pineapple Upside Down Cake will keep, covered at room temperature, for up to 2 days.

NOTE: I make this cake with a store-bought mix, but you can use my homemade yellow cake recipe (see page 65) for the batter if you prefer. (Omit the pineapple juice.)

Classic Cheesecake Made Easy

When I was in college at the University of North Alabama, I spent my first semester living in a dorm and having supper every night downstairs in the dorm cafeteria. Once a month they'd have a special "fancy" night where the food got a bit more upscale than the standard fare. That is where I saw my first cheesecake bar and was struck at the simple genius of it all. Now if I'm making cheesecake for a party, I'll set up a toppings bar (see page 89) and let my guests choose their favorites.

Most cheesecake recipes call for a springform pan, but most of the folks I know don't actually own any—myself included. Rather than fretting over it, I make my cheesecake in a 9 x 13-inch pan and serve it directly from the pan. No muss, no fuss, and you have a GIANT cheesecake. Life is good! *Serves 12*

Nonstick cooking spray, for coating
    the baking pan
1/2 cup (1 stick) butter, melted
2 cups graham cracker crumbs
1¼ cups granulated sugar
4 packages (8 ounces each) cream
    cheese, at room temperature
4 large eggs
2 tablespoons lemon juice
1 teaspoon vanilla extract

1 Preheat the oven to 350°F. Lightly coat a 9 x 13-inch baking pan with cooking spray.

2 Combine the melted butter, graham cracker crumbs, and ¼ cup of the sugar in a medium-size bowl. Stir until well combined and crumbly. Press into the bottom of the prepared pan and bake until very lightly browned, about 10 minutes. Remove from the oven and reduce the oven temperature to 300°F.

3 Combine the cream cheese and the remaining 1 cup sugar in a medium-size mixing bowl. Beat with an electric mixer at medium speed until light and fluffy. Add the eggs, lemon juice, and vanilla. Mix until well combined and creamy, 2 to 3 minutes.

4 Pour the batter over the crust and bake until set in the center, about 55 minutes.

5 Allow to cool in the pan, then refrigerate for several hours before serving.

Classic Cheesecake will keep, covered in the refrigerator, for up to 1 week.

Hummingbird Cake

This is a classic Southern cake loaded with all kinds of goodness like pineapple, pecans, and even mashed bananas, yielding a very moist and dense cake, perfectly crowned with a homemade frosting. Most people serve this around holidays, but you certainly won't get complaints for making an "average" day that much sweeter by putting this cake on the table! *Serves 12*

How to Set Up a Cheesecake Bar

At several of my son's gatherings he has requested I set up a cheesecake bar. I usually make up several of my large cheesecakes (see page 88) and then supply toppings so that everyone has a choice of flavors to add to their dessert. I have provided the following toppings in the past, but feel free to experiment with others to make this cheesecake your own.

- Canned fruit pie filling (such as blueberry, strawberry, cherry, and so on)
- Canned mandarin oranges, drained
- Caramel sauce (add chopped pecans if you want to turn it into a super-easy praline sauce)
- Chocolate syrup (such as Hershey's)
- Chocolate chips
- Whipped topping (such as Cool Whip)

Hummingbird Cake

Vegetable shortening and flour,
    for coating the baking pan(s)
3 cups all-purpose flour
2 cups granulated sugar
1 teaspoon salt
1 teaspoon baking soda
1 teaspoon ground cinnamon
3 large eggs
1¹/2 cups vegetable oil
1¹/2 teaspoons vanilla extract
1 can (8 ounces) crushed
    pineapple, drained
2 cups mashed ripe bananas
    (5 to 6 bananas)
Cream Cheese Frosting
    (page 123), for finishing
1 cup chopped pecans

1 Preheat the oven to 350°F. Lightly grease and flour two 9-inch round cake pans or a 9 x 13-inch baking pan and set aside.

2 Place the flour, sugar, salt, baking soda, and cinnamon in a large mixing bowl and stir together by hand. Add the eggs, oil, vanilla, pineapple, and bananas and stir again by hand, scraping down the side of the bowl as needed, until smooth and well blended.

3 Pour the batter into the prepared pan(s). Bake until a toothpick inserted in the center comes out clean, 25 to 30 minutes for two 9-inch pans, 60 to 70 minutes for a 9 x 13-inch pan. Allow to cool on a wire rack.

4 If making a layer cake, turn one cake layer out onto a large plate and frost the top with one third of the cream cheese frosting; top with the second layer and frost the top and side with the remaining frosting. For a sheet cake, leave the cake in the pan and frost the top. Sprinkle with the pecans.

Hummingbird Cake will keep, covered at room temperature for up to 2 days, or in the refrigerator for up to 1 week.

Butter Rum Cake

Before the computer age, women found their best recipes at work and at get-togethers. Mama always loved when Grandmama came home with a new recipe that someone had brought to work. If she took the time to get the recipe, it had to mean that it was really tasty. Some of our best recipes have come from the Reed family reunions—Butter Rum Cake is one of those. When Mama looked it up in her recipe file box, the words "Delicious—Sept. 30, 1972" were written in the top corner. If it has Grandmama's stamp of approval, it is definitely a cake worth making! *Makes one 10-inch tube cake*

For the cake
Vegetable shortening and flour, for
    coating the pan
1/2 cup chopped pecans
1 tablespoon rum flavoring
1 package (3¾ ounces) vanilla
    instant pudding mix
1 box (15 to 18 ounces) butter
    cake mix
1/2 cup vegetable oil
4 large eggs

For the glaze
1½ teaspoons rum flavoring
1 cup granulated sugar
1/2 cup (1 stick) margarine

1 Preheat the oven to 325°F. Lightly grease and flour a 10-inch tube pan. Sprinkle the nuts in the bottom of pan. Place the rum flavoring in a measuring cup and add water to equal 1 cup.

2 Make the cake: Place the vanilla pudding, butter cake mix, diluted rum flavoring, oil, and eggs in a large mixing bowl and beat with an electric mixer at medium speed, scraping down the side of the bowl as needed, until well blended, 2 to 3 minutes.

3 Pour the batter into the pan, covering the nuts. Bake until a toothpick inserted in the center comes out clean, 50 to 60 minutes. Allow to cool in the pan.

4 Meanwhile, make the glaze: Place the rum flavoring in a measuring cup and add water to equal 1/2 cup. Combine the sugar, margarine, and diluted rum flavoring in a medium-size saucepan over medium heat. Cook, stirring constantly, until it comes to a boil, then stop stirring and let boil for 2 to 3 minutes. Immediately pour over the cooled cake in the pan. Let the glaze soak into the cake for 10 to 15 minutes, then invert the cake onto a large plate and remove it from the pan.

Butter Rum Cake will keep, in an airtight container or under a cake dome at room temperature, for 3 to 4 days.

Lovelight Yellow Two-Egg Chiffon Cake

This is another of Mama Reed's recipes. After she was moved to a nursing home, my mama went to her house and borrowed all of her recipes to copy. They were rolled together and stuck down into a wide-mouth mason jar. It took my mama several days, but these recipes are still some of our most cherished, and we count ourselves lucky that she thought to do that.

This chiffon cake was also one of Mama Reed's favorites. Mama Reed usually served it with a custard sauce or fresh strawberries or peaches. It is light and wonderfully moist. If you have never tasted a chiffon cake, you are in for one mouthwatering adventure. *Makes one 10-inch tube cake*

Vegetable shortening and flour, for coating the pan

2 large eggs, separated

1½ cups granulated sugar

2¼ cups sifted cake flour

3 teaspoons baking powder

1 teaspoon salt

⅓ cup vegetable oil

1 cup milk

1½ teaspoons vanilla extract

Thinned Custard Glaze (page 129), for serving

Fresh fruit, for serving (optional)

1 Preheat the oven to 350°F. Lightly grease and flour a 10-inch tube pan and set aside.

2 Beat the egg whites in a large mixing bowl with an electric mixer at medium speed until frothy, about 2 minutes. Gradually beat in ½ cup of the sugar. Continue beating until stiff peaks form to create a meringue. Set aside.

3 Sift together the remaining 1 cup sugar with the flour, baking powder, and salt into a separate large mixing bowl. Add the oil, ½ cup of the milk, and the vanilla. Beat with an electric mixer at medium speed, scraping down the side of the bowl as needed, 1 minute. Add the remaining ½ cup milk and the egg yolks and beat for 1 minute. Gently fold in the meringue with a spatula until well incorporated.

4 Pour the batter into the prepared pan and bake until a toothpick inserted in the center comes out clean, 30 to 35 minutes. Serve with the custard sauce or fruit, or serve plain as a wonderfully light cake.

Lovelight Yellow Two-Egg Chiffon Cake will keep, under a cake dome at room temperature, for 3 to 5 days.

Wind Cake

Oh, what a treasure this recipe is to me! When I was looking through Grandmama's old cookbook, I found this handwritten recipe on a piece of crumbling, yellowed paper tucked inside. Grandmama's instructions were vague, as they were likely notes she jotted down after a friend explained

The Longing and the Finding

We are all guilty of longing for what others have—a house, a job, a seemingly perfect life, a talent, or even a disposition. When surrounded by people with different things and different situations, it is a natural human response to compare and consider what our lives would be like if only . . .

And then there is how we view ourselves when measured by the same stick we use to measure others. So often, when looking at someone else's presentation of their life (which is not necessarily reality), our own character comes up short.

But if we would only look at our wealth as it stands on its own. The unique blessings and gifts that have been carefully crafted and beautifully wrapped just for us. If we would only stand back and look at the wonderful people in our lives, at how dearly we are held, at the beautiful ministry we have been given charge of, how dear and precious we are to our friends and family.

Throughout my life, there have been times when I read passages, verses, and writings that I've taken to heart. From time to time I read something and I think, *I need to memorize this so I can have it with me whether I have this book or not.* I have no idea how many sonnets, verses, and poems are floating around in my head as a result, but once I've deemed something important enough to be memorized, I've never regretted it. One such thing was Shakespeare's twenty-ninth sonnet. It is the Elizabethan equivalent of a kick in the pants whenever you find yourself envious of another and not in full and rightful appreciation of your blessings:

the recipe to her. I was thrilled to get into the kitchen and flesh them out a bit.

Wind Cake no doubt got its name from the method of making the batter. First, you whip large amounts of air into egg yolks, then into egg whites. The final step is adding all of the other ingredients, which help stabilize the air in the egg white mixture before you fold it into the egg yolk mixture. In my twist on the recipe, though, I whip the egg whites in a stand mixer first and set them aside in a separate bowl, so we can use the original mixing bowl for the rest of the batter.

This is the ideal cake for serving with lightly sugared fresh strawberries or other seasonal fruit. *Serves 12*

*When, in disgrace with fortune and men's
 eyes
I all alone beweep my outcast state,
And trouble deaf heaven with my bootless
 cries, and look upon myself and curse
 my fate
Wishing me like to one more rich in hope,
Featured like him, like him with friends
 possessed,
Desiring this man's art and that man's scope,
With what I most enjoy contented least;
Yet in these thoughts myself almost despising,
Happily I think on thee, and then my state
(like to the lark at break of day arising from
 sullen earth)
sings hymns at heaven's gate;
For thy sweet love remembered such wealth
 brings
that then I scorn to change my state with
 kings.*

Do you get that? He is comparing himself to others, sinking further and further the more he does. Wishing he was popular like one, talented like the other, wise like the third. He compares and compares, always coming up short when he holds himself up to their measure in his mind.

And then, he remembers who loves him. And all of his wealth, all of the blessings in his life come rushing in and his soul breaks free from the comparison, from the envy, from the jealousy of others . . . because he realizes what he has. And that sweet love remembered helps him put his life into perspective to the extent that if he were offered a kingdom in exchange, he wouldn't even consider it.

Next time you find yourself longing for something, step back and consider all that you have, because the quickest way to put a stop to longing is to move yourself to the finding. Therein lies the sweetness.

4 large eggs, separated
Pinch of salt
1 teaspoon lemon juice or
 distilled white vinegar
2/3 cup cold water
1 1/2 cups granulated sugar
2 cups all-purpose flour
1 teaspoon vanilla extract
Fresh fruit, for serving

1 Preheat the oven to 300°F.

2 Place the egg whites and salt in a large mixing bowl and beat with an electric mixer at medium speed until soft peaks form, 2 to 3 minutes. Add the lemon juice and continue beating until stiff peaks form. Use a rubber spatula to scrape the mixture into another bowl and set aside.

3 Place the egg yolks and water in the mixing bowl you just used (no need to wash it). Beat with an electric mixer at high speed until the mixture reaches within 1 to 2 inches of the top of the bowl, 3 to 5 minutes.

4 With the mixer running, slowly add the sugar, followed by the flour and vanilla, scraping down the side of the bowl if needed, until the mixture is well blended. Reduce the speed to the lowest setting and add the beaten egg whites, mixing just until incorporated.

5 Pour the batter into an ungreased 12-cup Bundt or tube pan. Bake until golden brown and fully set in the center (no wiggle when you jiggle it), about 1 hour.

6 Allow to cool in the pan for 10 minutes, then turn the cake out onto a large plate (see Note). Serve with the fruit.

Wind Cake will keep, covered at room temperature, for up to 4 days.

NOTE: It's important to use an ungreased pan so the cake clings to the sides as it rises. If the baked cake sticks to the pan, run a butter knife around the edge to release it before turning it out of the pan.

Dark Chocolate Pound Cake

Once, when my mother was going on a quilt retreat, she mentioned needing to take something for the snack table (ladies generally baked a little treat to share). I told her not to worry, that I'd just make her a chocolate pound cake. Knowing I had been on a newfangled diet at the time, she assumed it was a diet recipe. She called from the retreat to tell me how much everyone was enjoying the cake and that no one could believe it was a diet recipe!

"MAMA!" I exclaimed in horror and surprise. "Do you have any idea what is in that cake?" I recited this recipe to her from memory and we both decided it would be best to just keep the details under wraps until the retreat was over.

If you've read my first cookbook, *Southern Plate*, you might recognize this recipe. I've included it here because it's one of my all-time favorites, and no book of sweet recipes would be complete without it! *Serves 12 to 16*

For the cake
Vegetable shortening and flour,
    for coating the pan
1¹/₂ cups (3 sticks) butter or
    margarine
3 cups granulated sugar
5 large eggs
3 cups all-purpose flour
¹/₂ cup unsweetened cocoa powder
¹/₂ teaspoon baking powder
1 cup milk
3 teaspoons vanilla extract

For the glaze
1¹/₂ cups granulated sugar
7 tablespoons milk
¹/₂ cup unsweetened cocoa powder
2 tablespoons vegetable
    shortening
2 tablespoons butter
1 teaspoon vanilla extract

1 Preheat the oven to 325°F. Lightly grease and flour a 10-cup Bundt pan and set aside.

2 Make the cake: Cream together the butter and sugar in a large mixing bowl with an electric mixer at medium speed until light and fluffy, 1 to 2 minutes. Add the eggs, one at a time, beating well after each addition.

3 Stir together the flour, cocoa, and baking powder in a separate medium-size bowl. Measure the milk and stir the vanilla into it. Add the milk mixture and flour mixture alternately to the butter mixture, mixing after each addition. Beat with an electric mixer at medium speed, scraping down the side of the bowl as needed, until well combined and smooth.

4 Pour the batter into the pan and bake until a toothpick inserted in the center comes out clean, 1 hour and 20 minutes. Allow to cool for 10 minutes, then remove the cake from the pan and place it on a large cake plate. Allow it to cool completely.

5 Make the glaze: Combine the sugar, milk, cocoa, shortening, and butter in a medium-size heavy-bottomed saucepan over medium heat. Bring to a rolling boil, stirring constantly. Once it reaches a boil, allow to boil without stirring, exactly 2 minutes.

6 Remove from the heat and add the vanilla. Stir until cooled just slightly. Spoon over the cooled cake.

Dark Chocolate Pound Cake will keep, covered at room temperature, for up to 5 days.

Pound Cakes in Jars

Pound Cakes in Jars

from SHAY BAUGH

"Being the quintessential Southern grandparents, there were certain things you could always count on at Papaw and Granny's house in Locust Fork, Alabama: There would always be food, and plenty of it. You were going to have to eat, whether you were hungry or not. There would be at least one update on Aunt Helen and her kids, the neighbors who weren't blood-related. We would all end up on the front porch in the rocking chairs or on the swing. And best of all, there were always pound cake leftovers to take home.

"Sometime in the mid-1970s my grandmother brought home the recipe for pound cake from her job at the flower shop. It was an instant staple at her house from then on. The recipe stayed the same until the late '90s. Granny heard that someone had been making bread in mason jars and decided that was a great way to preserve her pound cake for her grandson who was leaving for his first military tour of duty in Qatar. She tweaked the temperature, time, and quantities until she had perfected her craft. The final product was pound cake in a wide-mouth pint canning jar that would stay fresh for months at a time.

"When Wes packed his duffle bag, he secured the jars by sliding them into socks and stuffing them in his combat boots. They arrived safely and brought him comfort in the time that he was away from our family.

"Since those first days of the pound cake in jars, they have been mailed to Iraq and South Korea, have traveled with grandkids to college, have been given as gifts, and have been made on countless occasions to store in our pantries for visitors. And to this day, we can all still count on the delicious pound cake being ready anytime we travel to Papaw and Granny's house down that sunny dirt road deep in Locust Fork." *Makes 9 pint-size jars*

CHRISTY'S NOTE: I am so grateful to Shay for sharing this recipe because it is one of the most delicious pound cakes I've ever had. The batter is just like velvet, and it's so pretty to bake up and deliver in mason jars! I'll be making these as Christmas gifts from here on out. As far as storing the cake in mason jars, conditions and methods of storage vary, and it is up to you to determine whether or not a cake stored long-term is safe to consume. For best results, if you would like to store these long-term, I recommend placing the sealed jars in your freezer for up to 6 months or delivering them fresh within 2 to 3 days. Note that you'll need 9 pint-size wide-mouth mason jars for the recipe.

Nonstick cooking spray, for coating
   the jars
3 cups granulated sugar
1 cup vegetable shortening
6 large eggs
1 container (8 ounces) sour cream
3 cups all-purpose flour
1 teaspoon vanilla extract
1 teaspoon lemon or almond
   extract
¼ teaspoon salt
¼ teaspoon baking soda

1 Preheat the oven to 325°F. Spray the inside of 9 wide-mouth pint jars with cooking spray, wipe off the rims, and set aside.

2 Cream together the sugar and shortening in a large mixing bowl with an electric mixer at medium speed until fluffy, about 1 minute. Add the eggs, one at a time, beating well after each addition.

3 Add the sour cream, flour, vanilla, lemon extract, salt, and baking soda. Mix again with the electric mixer at medium speed, scraping down the side of the bowl as needed, until well incorporated, 2 to 3 minutes.

4 Fill the jars halfway with batter (no more). Place the jars on a rimmed baking sheet, making sure they aren't touching. Bake until a toothpick inserted in the center comes out clean, about 1 hour.

5 Remove from the oven and wipe off the rims. Place a lid and ring on each jar and screw it shut securely, but not with force. You'll need to use a dish towel to do this as the jars will be hot. After a few moments, you'll hear a pop as the lids seal. Allow to cool entirely before storing.

Pound Cakes will keep, stored and sealed in jars, for at least 1 year.

Wonder Cake

Wonder cake is one of those old recipes I found written in my grandmother's hand on her work stationery from Morton-Thiokol, Inc. No doubt it was exchanged across desks back during her days as a secretary. Mama said Grandmama used to make it a lot but that they hardly ever got to eat any because every time Grandmama made it, she took it straight to the office! This recipe yields a fruit-studded, lightly spiced version of a pound cake, perfect with a dusting of confectioners' sugar to finish it off.

One thing to note: Sometimes we can get away with just spraying our cake pans with cooking spray, but with this recipe it is important that you grease and flour your Bundt pan or the baked cake will stick. *Serves 12 to 16*

Vegetable shortening and flour, for coating the pan
4 large eggs, separated
2 1/2 cups self-rising flour (see page 276)
2 cups granulated sugar
1 1/2 cups vegetable oil
1 can (8 ounces) crushed pineapple with juice
2 teaspoons ground cinnamon
1 teaspoon ground nutmeg
1/2 teaspoon ground allspice
1 cup chopped pecans
Confectioners' sugar, for serving (optional)

1 Preheat the oven to 350°F. Lightly grease and flour a 12-cup Bundt or tube pan and set aside.

2 Beat the egg whites in a large mixing bowl with an electric mixer at medium-high speed until stiff peaks form, 2 to 3 minutes. Gently scrape the egg whites into another bowl and set aside.

3 In the same large mixing bowl (no need to wash it), combine the egg yolks, flour, sugar, oil, pineapple with juice, cinnamon, nutmeg, allspice, and pecans and mix well with an electric mixer at medium speed, scraping down the side of the bowl as needed, until well blended. Fold in the egg whites with a wooden spoon until incorporated.

4 Pour the batter into the prepared pan and bake until a wooden toothpick inserted in the center comes out clean, about 1 hour. Allow to cool for 10 minutes before turning the cake out onto a plate. Serve plain, or dust with confectioners' sugar if desired.

Wonder Cake will keep, covered at room temperature, for up to 2 days, or in the refrigerator for up to 5 days.

Buttermilk Lime Pound Cake

This cake tastes like the marriage of an all-butter pound cake with a Key lime pie—and oh what a beautiful marriage it is! It's the perfect finish to any spring or summer meal. *Serves 12 to 16*

For the cake
Vegetable shortening and flour,
    for coating the pan
1½ cups (3 sticks) butter,
    at room temperature
2 cups granulated sugar
6 large eggs
3 cups all-purpose flour
½ teaspoon baking powder
¼ teaspoon salt
1 cup buttermilk (see page 277)
¼ cup lime juice
1 teaspoon vanilla extract
Green food coloring (optional)

For the glaze
1 tablespoon lime juice
3 to 4 tablespoons milk
About 1½ cups confectioners'
    sugar

1 Preheat the oven to 325°F. Lightly grease and flour a 10-inch Bundt pan and set aside.

2 Make the cake: Place the butter and sugar in a large mixing bowl. Mix with an electric mixer at medium speed until light and fluffy, 1 to 2 minutes. Add the eggs and mix until well incorporated.

3 Stir together the flour, baking powder, and salt in a separate large mixing bowl. Add the flour mixture to the butter mixture along with the buttermilk, lime juice, and vanilla. Mix with an electric mixer at medium speed until fully incorporated and well blended, scraping down the side of the bowl as needed, 2 to 3 minutes. Add a few drops of green food coloring, if desired, and mix again.

4 Pour the batter into the prepared pan and bake until golden brown and a toothpick inserted in the center of the cake comes out clean, 1 hour and 15 minutes. Allow to cool in the pan for 10 minutes before turning out onto a cake plate.

5 Make the glaze: Place the lime juice, 3 tablespoons of the milk, and the confectioners' sugar in a small bowl and stir together until smooth, about 1 minute. If the glaze is too thin, add another tablespoon or so of confectioners' sugar. If the glaze is too thick, add more milk in ½ tablespoon increments until it reaches the desired consistency. Drizzle over the cooled cake. Enjoy!

Buttermilk Lime Pound Cake will keep, covered at room temperature, for up to 3 days.

Red Velvet Cupcakes
with Cream Cheese Frosting

This is one of only a few recipes in this book that have appeared in my previous cookbooks. I wanted to make this book an all-in-one source for my family's favorite sweet recipes, and so our classic red velvet cupcakes, courtesy of family friend Tookie, had to make the cut. This cake is rich and moist, the best red velvet I've ever had. *Makes 18 cupcakes*

For the cupcakes
2 1/2 cups all-purpose flour
1 teaspoon unsweetened cocoa
   powder
1 teaspoon baking soda
1 teaspoon salt
1 1/2 cups granulated sugar
1 cup buttermilk (see page 277)
1 1/2 cups vegetable oil
2 large eggs
1 teaspoon distilled white vinegar
1 teaspoon vanilla extract
1 ounce red food coloring

For the frosting
1 package (8 ounces) cream cheese,
   at room temperature
1/2 cup (1 stick) butter or
   margarine, at room temperature
1 box (16 ounces) confectioners'
   sugar
1 teaspoon vanilla extract

1 Preheat the oven to 350°F. Line two 12-cup muffin tins with 9 paper muffin cups each and set aside.

2 Make the cupcakes: Stir together the flour, cocoa powder, baking soda, and salt in a medium-size bowl with a large spoon.

3 In a separate large mixing bowl, mix together the sugar, buttermilk, oil, eggs, and vinegar with an electric mixer at medium speed until combined, about 1 minute. Add the flour mixture to the wet mixture and beat on medium speed, scraping down the side of the bowl as needed, until well blended.

4 Add the vanilla and food coloring to the batter and mix again on low speed until well blended and uniform in color.

5 Fill each muffin cup about three-quarters full with batter. Bake until the center of a cupcake springs back when pressed lightly, 20 to 25 minutes. Allow to cool completely.

6 Meanwhile, make the frosting: Beat the cream cheese and butter in a large mixing bowl with an electric mixer at medium speed until well blended, about 1 minute. Add the confectioners' sugar and vanilla and beat with the mixer at medium speed, scraping down the side of the bowl as needed, until smooth and creamy, 1 to 2 minutes. Frost the cooled cupcakes.

Red Velvet Cupcakes will keep, in an airtight container at room temperature, for 2 to 3 days, or in the refrigerator for up to 1 week. I love them refrigerated!

Miss Barbara's Key Lime Cupcakes
with Cream Cheese Frosting

Miss Barbara Ingram is a local legend in the small town of Rogersville, Alabama. She owns a shop that serves as the town florist, caterer, and wedding chapel all rolled into one. In fact, I almost got married there, but we opted not to go any farther west from where we lived so folks driving from out of state wouldn't have to make a longer trip.

The great thing about Barbara, aside from all of this, is that she lives next door to my mother. From time to time, Mama will open the door to find a bouquet of flowers or a cake box of goodies from Barbara herself. Everything Barbara creates is wonderful, but Mama and I have to admit feeling a little extra gleeful whenever these delicious cupcakes come our way! *Makes 24 cupcakes*

For the cupcakes
1 box (15 to 18 ounces) lemon
　　cake mix
1 box (3 ounces) lime gelatin
3/4 cup buttermilk (see page 277)
1/3 cup vegetable oil
3 large eggs
3 drops green food coloring

For the frosting
1 package (8 ounces) cream cheese,
　　at room temperature
1/2 cup (1 stick) unsalted butter,
　　at room temperature
1 box (16 ounces) confectioners'
　　sugar
1 teaspoon vanilla extract

1 Preheat the oven to 350°F. Line two 12-cup muffin tins with muffin papers and set aside.

2 Make the cupcakes: Place the cake mix, gelatin, buttermilk, oil, eggs, and food coloring in a large mixing bowl and beat with an electric mixer at medium speed until smooth, about 1 minute. Scrape down the side of the bowl and mix again until smooth, 2 minutes more.

3 Divide the batter evenly among the prepared muffin cups. Bake until the cupcakes are lightly browned and spring back when lightly pressed in the center, 20 to 25 minutes. Cool completely.

4 Meanwhile, make the frosting: Beat the cream cheese and butter in a large mixing bowl with an electric mixer at medium speed. Add the confectioners' sugar and vanilla and beat again until smooth and creamy, scraping down the side of the bowl as needed, 1 to 2 minutes. Generously frost the cooled cupcakes.

Key Lime Cupcakes will keep, in an airtight container at room temperature, for up to 2 days, or in the refrigerator for up to 1 week.

Coconut Cake
with No-Fail
Seven-Minute Frosting

This is a favorite of our family for Easter and Christmas. I found the recipe in an old box of papers that belonged to my grandmother. She had typed it out on letterhead from the company where she worked and later came back to circle it and write "real good." After trying it for myself, I had to agree: When it comes to moist cakes, this is the mother of them all! If a crumb drops from your fork, don't be surprised if you find your finger chasing it around your plate—it's just that good. Top it off with No-Fail Seven-Minute Frosting and a sprinkling of coconut and get ready for a coconut cake experience unlike any other.

One of the great things about this seven-minute frosting is that you don't need a double boiler to make it. And you can forget fretting over whether or not the weather is dry enough for a seven-minute frosting to "turn out." This one comes out perfect every time. If you're making a layer cake and you like generous amounts of frosting, you may want to double the recipe. *Serves 12*

Coconut Cake with No-Fail Seven-Minute Frosting

Vegetable shortening and flour,
    for preparing the pans
1 cup (2 sticks) unsalted butter,
    at room temperature
2 cups granulated sugar
5 large eggs
1 teaspoon vanilla extract
1 teaspoon coconut flavoring
2 1/2 cups all-purpose flour
1 teaspoon baking soda
1 teaspoon baking powder
1/4 teaspoon salt
1 cup buttermilk (see page 277)
No-Fail Seven-Minute Frosting
    (recipe follows)
2 cups grated sweetened shredded
    coconut, for garnish

1 Preheat the oven to 350°F. Lightly grease and flour two 9-inch round cake pans or one 9 x 13-inch baking pan and set aside.

2 Cream together the butter and sugar in a large bowl with an electric mixer at medium speed until very smooth, at least 4 minutes. Add the eggs, vanilla, and coconut flavoring and beat well to combine. In a separate medium-size bowl, stir together the flour, baking soda, baking powder, and salt.

3 Add the flour mixture and the buttermilk to the butter mixture and beat with an electric mixer at medium speed, scraping down the side of the bowl as needed, until thoroughly blended and smooth, 2 to 3 minutes.

4 Pour the batter into the prepared pan(s). Bake until a toothpick inserted in the center comes out clean, 25 to 30 minutes for 9-inch pans, 30 to 35 minutes for a 9 x 13-inch pan. Cool completely and frost with No-Fail Seven-Minute Frosting. Sprinkle with the coconut immediately after frosting.

Coconut Cake with No-Fail Seven-Minute Frosting will keep, covered at room temperature, for up to 2 days, or in the refrigerator for up to 1 week.

No-Fail Seven-Minute Frosting

Makes enough to frost one 9-inch layer cake, one 9 x 13-inch sheet cake, or about 12 cupcakes

1 cup granulated sugar
1/4 teaspoon salt
1/2 teaspoon cream of tartar
2 large egg whites
1 teaspoon vanilla extract

1 Place the sugar, salt, cream of tartar, egg whites, and 3 tablespoons of water in a medium-size, stainless-steel, heavy-bottomed saucepan over medium-low heat.

Simple, No-Skill-Needed Ways to Decorate a Cake

The first thing I want to encourage you to do is get past trying to make a cake look "store-bought." Which would you rather have, a cake purchased from a store or one that someone made just for you? It is ridiculous that we take a homemade cake, the best of the best, and try to cheapen it by making it look store-bought. Go for that homemade look! It doesn't have to be decorated to the nines, and so what if it ends up a little lopsided? Like my father-in-law says, "I don't care, it all eats the same!"

Here are some easy ways to make your cake look extra special but still like it came from your kitchen:

Imperfect icing. Icing doesn't have to be smooth. In fact, many "boutique" bakeries go out of their way to spread icing so that it has lots of cracks and ridges, giving it a truly homemade look.

Top it with fruit. Fresh fruit makes a wonderful topping on a cake and draws the eye in. It also helps temper the sweetness of the icing.

Use a comb. If you want the sides of your cake to look more finished, purchase a hair pick at any department store (usually located in the hairstyling aisle). Label it clearly with permanent marker (FOR FOOD ONLY) and gently run it around the sides of the cake, creating perfectly spaced lines. You may have to practice a time or two to get the pressure just right, but as long as your icing hasn't set yet, it is simple to smooth it back down until you get it just how you want it.

Chocolate shavings. Place a chocolate bar in the freezer until it is good and cold. Using a vegetable peeler or paring knife, carefully scrape at the chocolate bar to produce shavings. Slower movements will create curls of chocolate while quicker ones will yield smaller pieces. Make as many as you like and sprinkle them all over the top of your cake.

Pecan halves. Carrot cake is usually decorated with pecan halves, and many red velvet cakes are as well. They are a pretty and natural complement to anything with cream cheese icing.

Assorted candies. Peeps make great toppings for Easter cakes and M&M's might be pretty for a birthday party. You can't go wrong with gumdrops, miniature candy bars, or rainbow sprinkles!

Keep it simple. Of course, my favorite way to adorn a cake is simply with a fork. Most times, nothing more is needed.

2 Beat with a handheld electric mixer at medium-high speed until fluffy and stiff peaks form, about 7 minutes.

3 Remove from the heat and stir in the vanilla. Use immediately.

Mama Reed's Jam Cake

My great-grandmother, Mama Reed, raised ten children and kept house all her life. She canned fresh vegetables that she grew herself, cooked three wonderful meals a day, and still managed to keep a nice home (I wish I had half her energy!). My mother had the blessing of living next door to Mama Reed from the time she was six years old, which is the same age she was when Mama Reed taught her how to embroider and quilt. Mama spent most of her free time at Mama Reed's elbow cooking, sewing, and just being together.

One day Mama Reed called her and told her to come down so that she could show her how to cut up a whole chicken. Mama went, thinking they had a fryer from the grocery store, but was surprised to find that first they had to kill the chicken and prepare it. I'm pretty sure Mama hasn't killed a chicken

since, but to this very day she can cut up a whole chicken just like Mama Reed taught her.

This is one of Mama Reed's recipes that Mama looked forward to every Christmas. It is a wonderful cake with lots of flavor thanks to the jam and raisins throughout. It is actually better the second day and tastes similar to an old-fashioned spice cake. If you'd rather, you can make this cake in a 9 x 13-inch pan instead of the two round cake pans and bake it for 40 to 45 minutes. *Makes one 9-inch layer cake*

For the cake
Vegetable shortening and flour,
    for coating the pans
3 cups all-purpose flour
1/4 teaspoon salt
1 teaspoon ground allspice
1 teaspoon ground cinnamon
1 teaspoon ground nutmeg
1 teaspoon baking soda
1/2 cup (1 stick) unsalted butter,
    at room temperature
2 cups granulated sugar
4 large eggs
3/4 cup buttermilk (see page 277)
1 cup raisins
1 cup blackberry or grape jam

For the filling
3 cups granulated sugar
1 large egg
5 tablespoons butter
1/2 cup milk

How to Make a Perfect Layer Cake

One of the most common problems I hear when it comes to cakes is round layer cakes sticking to the pan. There are a few ways to avoid this. First of all, a good heavy cake pan is essential. You don't have to buy an expensive one but chances are, if you bought the cheapest pan, you don't have a very good one. Look for a stainless-steel pan or even a nonstick pan that is dishwasher-safe and uniformly thick. This will allow it to cook your layers evenly and also ensure that the pan doesn't warp or rust over time.

Second, grease your pan. The standard way of greasing a cake pan—with shortening and then a coating of flour—is still one of the best ways to ensure a good cake release. Some of my better pans, though, need only a light coating of nonstick cooking spray. If you aren't sure what will work best for your pan, shortening and flour won't steer you wrong. To prepare a pan without all of the mess, fold a paper towel and use it to swipe the inside of a shortening container. Use the paper towel to spread the shortening all around the inside of your cake pan. Sprinkle about ¼ cup of flour into the pan and pat the pan, tilting as needed, until the entire inside is fully coated. Hold the pan over the trash can and continue patting to get rid of any excess. Now you have a perfectly greased and floured cake pan ready to go.

1 Preheat the oven to 350°F. Lightly grease and flour two 9-inch round cake pans and set aside.

2 Make the cake: Combine 2½ cups of the flour with the salt, spices, and baking soda in a large mixing bowl and stir well until combined.

3 In a medium-size bowl, cream together the butter and sugar with an electric mixer at medium speed until fluffy, about 1 minute. Add the eggs, one at a time, beating well after each addition.

4 Dump the flour mixture into the butter mixture and add the buttermilk. Beat with an electric mixer at medium speed, scraping down the side of the bowl as needed, until fully combined, 2 to 3 minutes.

5 Toss the raisins in the remaining ½ cup flour and fold them into the batter using a rubber spatula. Carefully fold the jam into the batter until combined. Pour the batter into the prepared pans.

6 Bake until a toothpick inserted in the center comes out clean, 40 to 45 minutes. Cool in the pans for 10 minutes. Remove the cake layers from the pans and cool completely.

7 Meanwhile, make the filling: Fill the bottom pot of a double boiler with water and bring to a boil over medium-high heat. Place the sugar, egg, butter, and milk in the top of the double boiler and cook, stirring every now and then, until the butter melts, the sugar has dissolved, and the mixture has thickened slightly, about 20 minutes. Allow to cool for 5 minutes.

8 Place one cake layer on a cake plate, and spread half of the filling on top of it. Place the second layer on top and add the remaining filling, letting it run down the sides of the cake.

Mama Reed's Jam Cake will keep, under a cake dome at room temperature, for 3 to 5 days.

Mama Reed: mother of ten and known near and far for her wonderful cooking

Fresh Strawberry Cake

This is one of those cakes that folks bring to family reunions and everyone ends up passing the recipe around because it is so good. One bite of this will win over the staunchest objector to using a mix. *Serves 12*

For the cake
Vegetable shortening and flour,
   for coating the pans
1 cup chopped fresh strawberries
1 box (15 to 18 ounces) white
   cake mix
3/4 cup milk
1 box (3 ounces) strawberry gelatin
3/4 cup vegetable oil
3 large eggs

For the frosting
1 package (8 ounces) cream cheese,
   at room temperature
4 tablespoons (1/2 stick) butter, at
   room temperature
3 cups confectioners' sugar
1/2 cup crushed, drained
   strawberries (optional; see Note)

Fresh Strawberry Cake

1 Preheat the oven to 350°F. Lightly grease and flour two 8-inch round cake pans or one 9 x 13-inch baking pan and set aside.

2 Make the cake: Gently mash the strawberries by placing them in a large zip-top bag and rolling over it with a rolling pin or large can.

3 Place the cake mix, milk, gelatin, oil, and eggs in a large mixing bowl. Beat with an electric mixer at medium speed until smooth and creamy, about 2 minutes. Add the strawberries and their juice and mix again until well combined.

4 Pour the batter into the prepared pans. Bake until a toothpick inserted in the center comes out clean, 25 to 30 minutes. If using two 8-inch pans, allow to sit for 10 minutes before turning out of the pans onto a wire rack to cool completely. If baking in a 9 x 13-inch pan, simply allow to cool in the pan on a wire rack.

5 Make the frosting: Combine the cream cheese, butter, and confectioners' sugar in a large mixing bowl and mix with an electric mixer at medium speed until smooth and creamy, 1 to 2 minutes. Stir in the strawberries, if using, until combined. Frost the cooled cake.

Fresh Strawberry Cake will keep, covered in the refrigerator, for up to 1 week.

NOTE: Some people add strawberries to this frosting as well. I leave them out to make the cake a bit prettier and easier to ice, but feel free to add them for more strawberry flavor!

Cappuccino Cake

We used to have a restaurant in our town that served Cappuccino Cake as its signature dessert. I always went there on my birthday just to have a slice of this cake. They closed many years ago, and I spent a decade or two pining away until I finally decided to come up with my own recipe.

After a little experimentation, I had a result that tasted even better in my opinion, and to this day, I ask my mother to bake this for me each year when my birthday rolls around—because the only thing better than not having to bake your own birthday cake is having your mother bake it for you! I hope you get to make this soon. It is definitely a showstopper cake, perfect for any special occasion. It also bakes well in a 9 x 13-inch pan if you'd like to save some time. *Serves 12 to 16*

For the cake

Vegetable shortening and cocoa
    powder, for coating the pans

2 heaping tablespoons
    unsweetened cocoa powder

1 box (15 to 18 ounces) any flavor
    chocolate cake mix (I use
    Duncan Hines)

1 container (8 ounces) sour cream

1/2 cup milk

1/4 cup vegetable oil

3 large eggs

1 to 2 teaspoons vanilla extract

For the frosting

1/2 cup milk

3 teaspoons instant coffee granules

1 cup (2 sticks) butter,
    at room temperature

1 teaspoon vanilla extract

5 cups confectioners' sugar

Chocolate ice cream,
    for serving (optional)

Chocolate syrup (such as
    Hershey's), for serving (optional)

1 Preheat the oven to 350°F. Lightly grease two 8- or 9-inch round cake pans with shortening and dust with cocoa powder. Set aside.

2 Make the cake: Place the cocoa, cake mix, sour cream, milk, oil, eggs, and vanilla in a large mixing bowl. Beat with an electric mixer at medium speed, scraping down the side of the bowl as needed, until well blended, about 2 minutes.

3 Divide the batter evenly among the prepared pans. Bake until a toothpick inserted in the center comes out clean, 25 to 30 minutes.

4 Allow to cool in the pans for 10 minutes, then turn the cakes out onto a rack to cool completely.

5 Meanwhile, make the frosting: Pour the milk into a small bowl. Stir the instant coffee granules into the milk until dissolved.

6 Place the butter in a large mixing bowl and beat with an electric mixer at medium speed until fluffy, about 2 minutes. Add the vanilla, confectioners' sugar, and coffee mixture and mix at medium speed, scraping down the side of the bowl as needed, until smooth. Turn the mixer to medium-high speed and beat until the frosting is whipped, 5 to 7 minutes more.

7 Frost the cake. Chill, in a covered cake container in the refrigerator, for several hours or overnight. Serve cold with chocolate ice cream and a drizzle of chocolate syrup.

Cappuccino Cake will keep, covered in the refrigerator, for up to 1 week.

Angel Food Dessert Cake

My grandmother brought this recipe home from work and my mother immediately fell in love with it. This is so easy to make and looks really impressive when you take it to a dinner because it comes out looking so beautiful. Even better than that, though, is the delicious taste. The angel food cake keeps things light, while the icing adds a touch of sweetness, and the pie filling makes it look so elegant. People will think you worked on it all day! *Serves 12 to 16*

1 package (8 ounces) cream cheese, at room temperature

1 cup confectioners' sugar

1 container (8 ounces) frozen whipped topping (such as Cool Whip), thawed

1 angel food cake from the bakery (14 ounces)

2 cans (21 ounces each) fruit pie filling (such as blueberry or cherry), chilled (see Note)

1 Beat together the cream cheese, confectioners' sugar, and whipped topping in a large mixing bowl with an electric mixer at medium speed until smooth and creamy, 1 to 2 minutes.

Make Lemons Out of Lemonade— or a Trifle Out of a Failed Cake

What if your cake falls apart or perhaps doesn't end up looking like you hoped it would? This can be due to several factors but most often either the cake wasn't allowed to cool long enough before being turned out (10 minutes after removing from the oven is ideal) or the pan is to blame. Either way, a broken cake can often be pieced back together using icing as "glue," but my husband's grandmother would take that cake, break it up fully, and layer it in a trifle bowl with layers of light and fluffy icing, pudding, or both! Add some fresh fruit between those layers and you have a beautiful and delicious dessert. What started out as a mishap can have a beautiful ending. Now *that's* finding the sweetness in life!

Don't Get Caught Up in the Swirliness of Life

Have you ever met a person who has a calming effect on everyone around them? While the rest of the world stresses, rushes, and frets, they seem to take it step by step with a calm smile and still arrive at the same time as everyone else—but a lot less frazzled.

From what I've experienced, it actually takes less effort to be the calm than it does to be the frenzy. So why don't more people do it?

Simple. We forget. We get caught up in the swirliness of life and we forget that while that funnel cloud spins us around, the space outside of it is not spinning. We simply lose sight of the option to step out of the storm and instead use our energy to kick it up even more.

Be the calm today. Put your smile on, still your heart, and do not be shaken. Our attitude reaches deeper than we could ever know. When we decide to have a good day, our actions and attitude can create a good day for all around us as well.

Psalm 16:8. That's the stuff.

---

2 Slice the angel food cake horizontally into 2 layers. Frost the bottom layer of the cake with one third of the cream cheese mixture. Place the other layer on top and coat the sides and top of the assembled cake with the remaining cream cheese mixture.

3 Just before serving, spoon the pie filling over the top of the cake, letting it drip down the sides. Serve immediately.

Angel Food Dessert Cake will keep, covered in the refrigerator, for up to 3 days.

NOTE: If taking this to an event, wait until you get there to pour the pie filling over the cake.

Caramel Tiramisu

I am an avid supporter of tiramisu. If it is on the menu at a restaurant, I'm ordering it. If a grocery store sells it, I'm buying it. And if I'm making it, it is going to be good! I don't have a T-shirt yet but I can come up with a pair of pom-poms if need be, and I even wrote a little jingle for it: "Tiramisu! It's so good for you! Tiramisu! It's so good for you!"

A few years back I got to thinking about my old tiramisu recipe. It was pretty standard and a little bit fussy, so I didn't make it very often because I'm just not a fussy recipe–type gal on a day-to-day basis. But then I came up with the idea of making a caramel tiramisu—because I love caramel anything—so I decided to simplify my recipe and give this new idea a whirl at the same time.

I was pleasantly amazed. This tiramisu was the best I'd tasted and so very simple to throw together! This is a rich and decadent, but not overly sweet, dessert that is served cold, making it the perfect dish to take to a summer barbecue or party. If you love tiramisu, I beseech you to try this.

Now seriously, when was the last time you were beseeched? *Serves 9*

3/4 cup hot water

2 tablespoons instant coffee granules

1 package (8 ounces) cream cheese, at room temperature

1/3 cup granulated sugar (or Splenda)

1 teaspoon vanilla extract

3 cups frozen whipped topping (such as Cool Whip), thawed

12 ladyfingers, broken in half

1 cup caramel ice cream topping

2 tablespoons unsweetened cocoa powder, for garnish (optional)

1 Place the hot water in a small bowl, add the instant coffee, and stir until it's dissolved. Set aside.

2 Place the cream cheese, sugar, and vanilla in a large mixing bowl. Beat with an electric mixer at medium speed until smooth and blended, 1 to 2 minutes. Add the whipped topping and beat again, scraping down the side of the bowl as needed, until creamy.

3 Place half of the ladyfingers in the bottom of an 8 x 8-inch baking dish. Spoon half of the coffee mixture over them. Top with a drizzle of the caramel ice cream topping. Place half of the cream cheese mixture on top and spread to cover the edges. Repeat the process once more.

Peanut Butter Cup Trifle

4 Sprinkle the cocoa powder on top, if desired. Cover and refrigerate for several hours before serving. Serve cold.

Caramel Tiramisu will keep, covered in the refrigerator, for up to 5 days.

Peanut Butter Cup Trifle

Before writing my book *Southern Plate*, I used to substitute teach from time to time. It was a fun side job that allowed me to be in the classroom, use my teaching degree, and have a change of pace. Years and years ago, I ended up with a rather unruly second-grade class. I immediately implemented one of my favorite classroom games called "Caught ya being good!" where every time I caught a child being good, whether it was sitting up straight, having a smile on her face, paying attention, or being respectful, I'd write their name on the board. It was quite a toss-up for them to actually want their name written on the board! Of course, my goal was to have every single child's name on the board with a series of checks beside it at the end of the day, and it worked like a charm. What was their reward? Well, earlier that morning, I had

asked them if they knew what a trifle was and began describing this one in great detail.

"Do you like peanut butter cups?"

"Oh, yeah!" they replied.

"Do you like brownies?"

"YES!" they called out.

"Hmmm, have you ever had peanut butter pudding?" Their eyes got big and they shook their heads. "Well, how would you like a dessert that combines all of this into one big old dish?"

So I had that unruly class on their best behavior all day long in hopes of being rewarded with this treat. Of course, I visited the class the very next day after their teacher returned and happily delivered. The teacher admitted that it was definitely an approach she had never tried, but it worked! *Serves 9 to 12*

1 box (family-size) brownie mix, plus the ingredients called for on the package

1 box (5.1 ounces) vanilla instant pudding mix

3 cups cold whole milk

1/2 cup creamy peanut butter

2 cups frozen whipped topping (such as Cool Whip), thawed

20 miniature-size peanut butter cups, or to taste

Today Is a Good Day

Today is a good day to notice the sky. Savor your food. Smile more. Sing along to the radio. Eat a piece of chocolate. Hold doors for others. *Let yourself feel hope.* Realize that our problems are smaller than they seem, and our impact on others is greater than we'll ever know. Today is a good day to pause and just breathe and know that *everything is gonna be all right*. So lift up your face, square your shoulders, and get ready to show the world what you're made of.

Smile, hon, you got this.

1 Prepare the brownies as directed on the package. Allow to cool completely in the pan.

2 Combine the pudding mix and milk in a large mixing bowl and beat with an electric mixer at medium speed until fully blended and thick, about 2 minutes. Add the peanut butter and beat again until well incorporated. Using a large spoon, fold in half of the whipped topping and stir until combined.

3 Cut the cooled brownies into 1-inch squares and set aside. Coarsely chop the peanut butter cups with a knife.

4 Place one third of the brownies in a layer on the bottom of a large mixing or punch bowl. Add one third of the chopped peanut butter cups in a layer covering the brownies, and one-third of the pudding mixture on top of the peanut butter cups. Repeat twice more, saving some peanut butter cups for the topping. Top the last layer with the remaining whipped topping and garnish with the reserved peanut butter cups. Cover and refrigerate for several hours before serving.

Peanut Butter Cup Trifle will keep, covered in the refrigerator, for up to 1 week.

Frostings, Icings, and Glazes

Classic Buttercream Frosting

This is the classic birthday cake frosting that you find on bakery cakes. It has a creamy, buttery flavor and makes any cake delicious. You will be amazed at how easy it is to make. *Makes 3 cups*

1 cup (2 sticks) butter, at room temperature

6 cups confectioners' sugar

4 teaspoons butter flavoring or vanilla extract

4 to 8 tablespoons milk

Combine and cream together the butter and 1 cup of the confectioners' sugar in a large mixing bowl with an electric mixer at medium speed until light and fluffy, 1 to 2 minutes. Add the butter flavoring, 4 tablespoons of the milk, and the remaining sugar and beat again, scraping down the side of the bowl as needed, until smooth and creamy. If the frosting is too thick, add just a tablespoon of milk at a time, stirring well after each addition, until it reaches your desired consistency.

Classic Buttercream Frosting will keep, in an airtight container in the refrigerator, for up to 2 weeks, or in the freezer for up to 3 months.

Creamy Chocolate Buttercream

This recipe takes the classic buttercream frosting to a whole new level. The addition of cocoa is sure to please all of the chocolate lovers in your house. *Makes about 2 cups*

1/2 cup (1 stick) butter or
　margarine, at room temperature
3 cups confectioners' sugar
2/3 cups unsweetened
　cocoa powder
6 tablespoons milk
1 teaspoon vanilla extract

Place the butter, 1 cup of the confectioners' sugar, the cocoa powder, and 2 tablespoons of the milk in a large mixing bowl. Beat with an electric mixer at medium speed, scraping down the side of the bowl as needed, until mixed well and no longer lumpy, 2 to 3 minutes. Add the vanilla and the remaining milk and sugar and beat until smooth and creamy.

Creamy Chocolate Buttercream will keep, in an airtight container in the refrigerator, for up to 1 week.

Whipped Cappuccino Buttercream

This is the perfect frosting for my Cappuccino Cake, but it would be equally good on any chocolate cake. It requires a little more time to prepare than some frostings but is well worth the effort—the end result is very light and fluffy. *Makes 3 1/2 cups*

1/2 cup milk
3 tablespoons instant coffee
　granules
1 cup (2 sticks) butter,
　at room temperature
5 cups confectioners' sugar
1 teaspoon vanilla extract

Place the milk in a small cup and add the instant coffee. Stir until it's dissolved; set aside. Place the butter in a large mixing bowl and beat with an electric mixer at medium speed until fluffy, 1 to 2 minutes. Add the coffee mixture, confectioners' sugar, and vanilla and mix until smooth, scraping down the side of the bowl as needed. Continue beating until whipped, 5 to 7 minutes.

Whipped Cappuccino Buttercream will keep, in an airtight container in the refrigerator, for up to 1 week. Before using, place in a large mixing bowl and beat again with an electric mixer at medium-high speed until rewhipped, 5 to 7 minutes.

Cream Cheese Frosting

Cream cheese frosting is good on just about everything from coconut cake to birthday cake, red velvet to carrot cake. It's even delicious on brownies or even cookie bars. This recipe is pretty basic; but sometimes pretty basic is pretty spectacular.

If I'm making a large layer cake and want to decorate it for a special occasion, I always double my frosting recipe so I have extra for borders and such. It's amazing how much frosting that uses up! If you have leftover frosting, you can always freeze it, then let it thaw slightly, and then give it a quick beating in the mixer and you're ready to go. *Makes about 4 cups*

1 package (8 ounces) cream cheese, at room temperature
1/2 cup (1 stick) butter, at room temperature
4 to 6 cups confectioners' sugar
1 teaspoon vanilla extract
1 teaspoon butter flavoring
1 tablespoon lemon juice

Combine the cream cheese, butter, 4 cups of the confectioners' sugar, vanilla extract, butter flavoring, and lemon juice in a large mixing bowl and beat with an electric mixer at medium speed, scraping down the side of the bowl as needed, until smooth and creamy, 2 to 3 minutes. Add up to 2 more cups of confectioners' sugar to reach a spreadable consistency.

Cream Cheese Frosting will keep, in an airtight container in the refrigerator, for up to 1 week.

Peanut Butter Cream Cheese Frosting

This creamy peanut butter frosting is a PB lover's delight—perfect on brownies, on cookies (especially chocolate), or on a simple cake for that peanut butter lover's birthday. *Makes about 3 cups*

1¹/2 cups creamy peanut butter
1 package (8 ounces) cream cheese,
    at room temperature
4 cups confectioners' sugar
2 tablespoons milk, plus extra as
    needed

Combine the peanut butter, cream cheese, confectioners' sugar, and 2 tablespoons of the milk in a large mixing bowl. Beat with an electric mixer at medium speed until incorporated. Scrape down the side of the bowl, add an extra tablespoon or so of milk if needed, and beat until smooth and creamy, 2 to 3 minutes.

Peanut Butter Cream Cheese Frosting will keep, in an airtight container in the refrigerator, for up to 1 week.

Coconut Pecan Icing

This is that wonderfully thick icing our grandmothers used on their German chocolate cakes. In fact, this is my grandmother's recipe. If you ever go back and look at photos of the cakes in vintage magazines, you'll notice that most of the cakes aren't iced on the sides. Instead, a generous amount is spread between each layer and on top to finish it. That is an ideal strategy with this icing because it is a bear to get it to hold to the sides. Make it easy on yourself and use this method if you decide to go with a round layer cake. Or, make it even easier and instead just make a 9 x 13-inch cake like I do! *Makes 4¹/2 cups*

3/4 cup (1¹/2 sticks) butter
1 can (12 ounces) evaporated milk
1¹/2 cups granulated sugar
3 large eggs
1¹/2 teaspoons vanilla extract
7 ounces sweetened shredded
    coconut
1¹/2 cups chopped pecans

Combine the butter, evaporated milk, sugar, eggs, and vanilla with a wire whisk in a large saucepan over medium heat. Cook, stirring constantly, until thick and golden brown, about 10 minutes. Remove from the heat and stir in the coconut and pecans. Beat with a wooden spoon until cooled and of spreading consistency, about 10 minutes (it will thicken as you beat it and it cools). If you prefer, you can use an electric mixer to beat the icing with ease.

Coconut Pecan Icing will keep, in an airtight container in the refrigerator, for up to 1 week.

Chocolate Fudge Icing

T his is what my grandparents referred to as a "boiled" icing. If you've ever had an old-fashioned cake where the icing broke off in big fudge chunks when you cut into it, that was this icing. Although it can be finicky at times, I've added another minute of boiling to the original recipe to help ensure the results you want every time. This one recipe can be either chocolate or peanut butter, depending on what you add at the end. The peanut butter version follows. *Makes about 3 cups*

Fudge Icings

I t is important to note that fudge icings work best when poured over cakes or brownies baked in 9 x 13-inch pans as they are extremely difficult to use on layer cakes. The icing must be used immediately while still hot and runny, before it sets. Once it sets, it will be the consistency of fudge.

My fudge icing recipes call for cooking the initial mixture to "soft ball stage," which is between 235°F and 240°F. I don't bother using a thermometer to check it. Instead I drop a very small amount of the mixture into a small glass of water; if it forms a soft ball before reaching the bottom of the water, it is good to go. If not, I cook it a little longer and test it again the same way.

1½ cups granulated sugar
7 tablespoons milk
2 tablespoons vegetable shortening
2 tablespoons butter or margarine
¼ teaspoon salt
1 teaspoon vanilla extract
½ cup unsweetened cocoa powder

Combine the sugar, milk, shortening, butter, and salt in a medium-size heavy-bottomed saucepan over medium heat. Bring to a rolling boil, stirring constantly. Once it reaches a rolling boil, stop stirring and boil until it reaches soft ball stage (a teaspoonful of the mixture should form a soft, pliable ball when dropped into a glass of water), 2 minutes. Remove from the heat and quickly stir in the vanilla and cocoa powder. Beat with a wooden spoon until smooth, 2 minutes. Use immediately.

VARIATION

PEANUT BUTTER FUDGE ICING: Substitute 1/2 cup creamy peanut butter for the cocoa powder.

Caramel Fudge Icing

This icing is nearly identical to the one used on Mama Reed's Caramel Apple Cake (page 75), but it's so fantastic and versatile, it's worth including here, too. It will make you the Pied Piper to caramel lovers everywhere! *Makes 2¹/₂ cups*

1/4 cup (1/2 stick) butter or
    margarine
8 tablespoons heavy cream or
    whole milk
1 cup packed dark brown sugar
    (light is okay)
1 teaspoon vanilla extract
2 cups confectioners' sugar,
    plus extra as needed

Combine the butter, heavy cream, and brown sugar in a heavy-bottomed saucepan over medium heat. Bring to a rolling boil, stirring constantly. Once it reaches a rolling boil, stop stirring and boil until it reaches soft ball stage (a teaspoonful of the mixture should form a soft, pliable ball when dropped into a glass of water), 2 minutes. Remove from the heat and use a whisk to quickly stir in the vanilla and confectioners' sugar. Add up to 1/2 cup more confectioners' sugar, if needed, to thicken. Use immediately.

Browned Butter Icing

When I first tasted browned butter icing, I was not prepared for the impact of flavor. Having never had browned butter anything (I have since remedied that) I didn't realize what intense caramel toffee-like icing this would be. A simple step, just browning the butter a little bit before adding, transforms your everyday buttercream into the cool and fascinating aunt of this traditional cake topper. This is excellent on chocolate cake but works just as well to bring your average yellow or white cake up a few notches. *Makes about 3 cups*

1 cup (2 sticks) unsalted butter, at
    room temperature
6 cups confectioners' sugar
1 teaspoon vanilla extract

1 Place 1 stick of the butter in a medium-size heavy-bottomed saucepan over medium heat. Cook, stirring constantly, until the butter turns light brown, about 10 minutes. Remove the pan from the heat and cool slightly, then transfer to a small bowl. Refrigerate for about 30 minutes.

2 Combine the refrigerated browned butter and remaining butter in a large bowl and beat with an electric mixer at medium speed until smooth, about 2 minutes. Add the confectioners' sugar and vanilla and beat, scraping down the side of the bowl as needed, until smooth and creamy, about 2 minutes.

Browned Butter Icing will keep, in an airtight container in the refrigerator, for up to 1 week.

Classic Confectioners' Sugar Glaze

This is that pretty white glaze that you see on top of many pound cakes, Bundt cakes, and cookie bars. It's a classic, all-purpose glaze that adds just an extra touch of sweetness. *Makes about 1 1/2 cups*

1 cup confectioners' sugar,
    plus extra as needed
1 to 3 tablespoons milk
1 teaspoon vanilla extract
2 tablespoons butter, at room
    temperature

Glaze Basics

I t is very common for folks to make their glazes too thin, which causes the glaze to sink down into the cake rather than form the pearly white drizzle that we are accustomed to seeing atop many Bundt cakes and sweet loaf breads. I made mine too thin for years until I saw someone else do it in person and the lightbulb went on as I realized that I was missing out on some beautiful cakes by not adding more confectioners' sugar! The consistency you want here is that of white school glue. If your glaze is too thin, add more confectioners' sugar, a tablespoon at a time, stirring well to remove the lumps after each addition. If it's too thick, add milk, just a teaspoon at a time, stirring well after each addition.

Place the confectioners' sugar, 1 tablespoon of the milk, and the vanilla in a small bowl. Add the butter and cut it into the other ingredients with a fork. Add an additional tablespoon of milk if needed. Use a spoon to stir until the glaze is creamy, with no lumps, and has the consistency of white school glue, adding a bit of milk if necessary. Should the glaze become too thin, add a little bit more confectioners' sugar. Use immediately.

Buttermilk Glaze

A simple buttermilk glaze, this is good poured over any Bundt cake, quick bread, or individual slices of pound cake. The slight tartness supplied by the buttermilk makes it so tasty.

This glaze soaks into a cake and leaves a thin layer on top. It is important to pour it on while the cake is still in the pan, and let the cake sit for a few minutes before turning it out—if you pour it over a cake on a plate, you are going to have a mess and a half! It is delicious spooned over individual slices of cake, though! *Makes about 2 cups*

½ cup (1 stick) butter or margarine

1½ cups granulated sugar

½ teaspoon baking soda

2 teaspoons vanilla extract

½ cup buttermilk (must be store-bought)

Combine all of the ingredients in a medium-size saucepan over medium heat. Bring to a boil, stirring constantly. Continue to boil gently until thick, about 2 minutes. Remove from the heat and use immediately. Allow the glaze to soak into the cake some before serving.

Thinned Custard Glaze

Τhis is a sauce that we use to pour over thick slices of pound cake, but it can also be drizzled over broken cookies (such as vanilla wafers) or angel food cake. A rich custard sauce like this one holds a place of honor on any dessert table, especially around the holidays. *Makes about 3 cups*

1/2 cup granulated sugar
1/3 cup all-purpose flour
1/8 teaspoon salt
2 1/2 cups milk
3 large egg yolks
1 teaspoon vanilla extract

1 Combine the sugar, flour, and salt in a medium-size heavy-bottomed saucepan over medium heat. Whisk in the milk and cook, stirring constantly, until just hot, 1 to 2 minutes.

2 Place the egg yolks in a small bowl and beat with a wire whisk until smooth. Add about 1/2 cup of the hot milk mixture to the beaten eggs and stir vigorously to temper the eggs.

3 Pour the milk and egg mixture back into the saucepan over medium heat and cook, stirring constantly, until the custard begins to thicken, 10 to 15 minutes. Remove from the heat and stir in the vanilla.

4 Pour the custard through a strainer to remove any lumps (if you like) and into a small pitcher or gravy boat and let cool. Cover with plastic wrap and press down lightly so it touches the surface. Refrigerate until ready to serve.

Thinned Custard Glaze will keep, covered in the refrigerator, for 3 days.

One-Minute Peanut Butter Glaze

This is an all-around delicious concoction that has multiple uses. We use it as a syrup over ice cream, on top of pancakes, and even on Bundt cakes. It is also excellent over biscuits, French toast, waffles, and toast. With a house full of peanut butter lovers, we can't go wrong! *Makes about ¾ cup*

1/2 cup honey (see Note)
1/4 cup creamy peanut butter

Combine the honey and peanut butter in a microwave-safe bowl or measuring cup. Microwave for 30 seconds. Stir and microwave for 30 seconds more. Stir until creamy and well combined.

One-Minute Peanut Butter Glaze will keep, covered in the refrigerator, for 3 to 5 days.

NOTE: This very versatile recipe has a simple formula: 2 parts syrup to 1 part peanut butter. Honey is the syrup used here, but you can also use maple syrup, corn syrup, or even pancake syrup in its place.

Lime Glaze

Here's a sunny lime glaze for a summertime treat or to bring a little cheer to wintery days. I especially like this glaze on a warm yellow cake (see page 65). *Makes about 2 cups*

1½ cups confectioners' sugar,
    plus extra as needed
1 tablespoon butter, melted
1 to 2 tablespoons milk
2 tablespoons lime juice
1 teaspoon butter flavoring or
    vanilla extract

Place the confectioners' sugar in a medium-size bowl. Stir in the butter, 1 tablespoon of the milk, the lime juice, and butter flavoring until the mixture is smooth and creamy with no lumps. If the glaze is too thin, add more confectioners' sugar, a tablespoon at a time, stirring well to remove the lumps after each addition. If the glaze is too thick, add just a teaspoon of milk at a time, stirring well after each, until the glaze reaches your desired consistency. Use immediately.

VARIATION

....

LEMON GLAZE: Substitute lemon juice for the lime juice.

Lemon Custard Sauce

Lemon custard is wonderful served over slices of warm yellow cake (see page 65). It's also good over any type of pound cake. We like to serve it the old-fashioned way by crumbling yellow cake in a bowl while it's still warm and spooning the custard over it for a special treat. *Makes about 3 cups*

1 cup granulated sugar
1/3 cup all-purpose flour
3 large eggs
2 cups milk
A dash of salt
1 teaspoon vanilla extract
1/2 cup lemon juice

Place the sugar, flour, eggs, milk, and salt in a medium-size heavy-bottomed saucepan over medium heat and cook, stirring constantly, until the mixture has thickened and looks like a soft pudding, 10 to 15 minutes. Immediately remove from the heat and whisk in the vanilla and lemon juice. Allow to cool slightly, then pour into a small bowl. Serve warm or, to serve cold, cover with plastic wrap, pressing down lightly so it touches the surface to keep a film from forming, and refrigerate for several hours.

Lemon Custard Sauce will keep, covered in the refrigerator, for up to 3 days.

4

Homemade Pies Made Easy

THERE IS NO better baked vehicle to show off colorful, beautiful fruit than a simple, old-fashioned pie, and there is nothing better than a slice of no-bake freezer pie on a hot summer's day. This chapter showcases some heritage recipes along with a few new ones sure to become favorites for generations.

Peach Buttermilk Pie

If you like buttermilk and peaches, this one won't disappoint. This is an old-fashioned buttermilk custard pie with juicy bites of peaches throughout and a hint of cinnamon in every bite.

It's as good hot as it is cold, as good for dessert as it is for breakfast. Oooh, did I say that? Pie for breakfast? Oh, I meant . . . mid-morning snack with your coffee, as long as you got up at four AM and skipped breakfast just to have this "snack" at seven. It has buttermilk (calcium!), eggs (protein!), and peaches (fruit!). Toss in the starches in the crust and all ya gotta do is throw a green bean on the side and you've practically eaten the food pyramid! *Serves 8*

1 can (29 ounces) yellow cling peaches in heavy syrup, drained
One 9-inch deep-dish pie crust
2 heaping tablespoons all-purpose flour
1 cup granulated sugar
3 large eggs
1/3 cup buttermilk (see page 277)
1/2 cup (1 stick) butter, melted
1 teaspoon vanilla extract
1/2 teaspoon ground cinnamon

1 Preheat the oven to 350°F. Place the peaches in the bottom of the pie crust and set aside.

2 Combine the flour, sugar, eggs, buttermilk, melted butter, vanilla, and cinnamon in a medium-size mixing bowl and mix with a whisk until well combined. Pour over the peaches.

3 Place the pie on a rimmed baking sheet and bake until lightly golden and the middle doesn't jiggle when moved, about 40 minutes. Allow to cool on a wire rack until ready to serve. Serve warm or cold.

Peach Buttermilk Pie will keep, covered in the refrigerator, for up to 5 days.

Strawberry Cream Pie

This recipe is a favorite of my strawberry-loving husband. It's a wonderful combination of fresh strawberries and lightly whipped cheesecake, blended into a creamy, fruity, delicious summer concoction and served up in a graham cracker crust! *Serves 8*

Strawberry Cream Pie

1 package (8 ounces) cream cheese,
    at room temperature
1 teaspoon vanilla extract
1/2 cup granulated sugar (see Note)
1 cup chopped fresh strawberries
1 container (8 ounces) frozen
    whipped topping (such as Cool
    Whip), thawed (see Note)
One 9-inch graham cracker
    pie crust
About 1 cup strawberry preserves,
    for garnish (optional)

1 Place the cream cheese, vanilla, and sugar in a large mixing bowl and beat with an electric mixer at medium speed until light and fluffy, 1 to 2 minutes. Add the strawberries and beat again until well combined. Dump in the whipped topping and beat again, scraping down the side of the bowl as needed, until smooth and creamy. There will be lumps from the strawberries and that is fine.

2 Spoon the filling into the pie crust. Cover and refrigerate for several hours before serving.

3 Spoon the strawberry preserves into a microwave-safe bowl and microwave until just warm, about 45 seconds. Stir vigorously until it is of syrup consistency and spoon a little over each slice to serve.

Strawberry Cream Pie will keep, covered in the refrigerator, for up to 3 days, or in the freezer for up to 1 month.

NOTE: Feel free to substitute Splenda for the sugar and use light whipped topping.

Apple Doozie Dessert Pizza

This is a recipe I whipped up because I LOVE the apple dessert pizzas that are served at all of the pizza chains. I got to thinking that it would have to be a quick and easy recipe in order to be made on such a large scale. After taking a few minutes to wrap my head around it and dream up the ingredients, I went shopping and made this little baby. Bingo. Bull's-eye. Jackpot. We just passed "GO" *and* collected two hundred dollars!

My only suggestion is that you *not* make this in the evening after the kids have gone to bed, because then it will be just you and your husband and this big old apple pizza . . . and if you eat a slice, it will keep calling you back for more, and I am not responsible if the two of you eat nearly the whole thing. *Serves 8 to 10*

One store-bought 12-inch pizza
   crust
1 can (20 ounces) apple pie filling
1/2 cup quick-cooking oats
1/2 cup dark brown sugar
1/2 cup all-purpose flour
1 tablespoon ground cinnamon
1/4 cup (1/2 stick) butter,
   at room temperature
1 cup confectioners' sugar,
   plus extra as needed
2 tablespoons milk,
   plus extra as needed
1 teaspoon vanilla extract

1 Preheat the oven to 350°F. Place the pizza crust on an ungreased baking sheet and set aside.

2 Open the pie filling and use a paring knife to dice it up a bit while it is inside the can. Spread the filling over the pizza crust, leaving about a 1-inch border around the edge.

3 Place the oats, brown sugar, flour, and cinnamon in a small bowl and stir to combine. Using a long-tined fork, cut the butter into the mixture until crumbly to make a streusel.

4 Sprinkle the streusel over the top of the pie filling. Bake until lightly golden brown, about 25 minutes.

5 Meanwhile, make the glaze: Place the 1 cup confectioners' sugar, 2 tablespoons milk, and vanilla in a small bowl and stir until smooth. If the mixture is too thick, add an additional tablespoon of milk. If it's too thin, add confectioners' sugar, 1 tablespoon at a time, until it reaches the desired consistency. Drizzle the glaze over the apple pizza with a spoon.

Apple Doozie Dessert Pizza will keep, covered at room temperature, for up to 2 days.

NOTE: You can substitute fresh apples for the apple pie filling, if you'd like. Peel and chop 3 medium-size apples. Heat 2 tablespoons butter in a medium-size pan over medium heat and sauté the apples until tender, about 5 minutes. Add a few tablespoons of sugar if you like, but keep them a bit tart, because the topping adds a lot of sweetness.

Faux Apple Pie

I 'd heard about the famous "mock apple pie" for years but, never having made it for myself, I was more than skeptical. At a book signing in Knoxville, Tennessee, a precious older lady pulled me aside and told me that she'd lost her recipe for mock apple pie and asked if I had a recipe I'd share with her. As soon as I got home, it was time to get into the kitchen! I found the classic recipe but it seemed to be lacking a bit so I added more crackers (to make a fuller pie) and amped up the flavor with the addition of vanilla, a little butter, more lemon juice, and the spices I would normally use in an apple pie. I also changed up the assembly of the pie, letting the crackers soak in the syrup for a little bit before adding the filling to the pie crust to keep it from becoming soggy. After all that, I held my breath while it baked.

The result has managed to fool every single person who has tasted it. Even after making it, I can't help but feel disbelief every time I have a bite. Go ahead and give up on convincing people the small bits inside this pie aren't apples. This is just one of those kitchen miracles that I encourage you to see for yourself! *Serves 8*

1 package (14.1 ounces) pie crust dough (2 roll-out crusts)

2 cups plus 1 tablespoon granulated sugar

1 tablespoon all-purpose flour

2 teaspoons cream of tartar

1 teaspoon ground cinnamon

1/2 teaspoon ground allspice

4 tablespoons lemon juice

5 tablespoons butter

1 teaspoon vanilla extract

60 Ritz crackers (about 2 sleeves)

Make It a Pie!

Just about anything can be turned into a pie—all you have to do is bake it in a pie plate! One of the best ways to convert a recipe into a pie is to take your favorite 8 x 8-inch brownie recipe, pour it into an unbaked shell, and bake. Serve topped with whipped cream and a drizzling of chocolate syrup for a decadent dessert.

Congealed salads (see page 221) make excellent summer pies when spooned into a fully cooked crust and refrigerated until firm, and even cookie dough can be patted out to form a pie crust with a little experimenting. Get in the kitchen and play around! You're more creative than you realize. ☺

1. Preheat the oven to 425°F. Roll out one crust in the bottom of a 9-inch pie plate and set aside.

2. Place 1 1/2 cups of water, the 2 cups of sugar, the flour, cream of tartar, cinnamon, and allspice in a medium-size saucepan over medium-high heat and cook, stirring until it comes to a boil.

3 Once it reaches a boil, reduce the heat and simmer for 5 minutes. Remove from the heat. Add the lemon juice, 3 tablespoons of the butter, and the vanilla. Set the syrup aside to cool slightly.

4 Coarsely break the crackers and place them in a medium-size heatproof bowl. Pour the syrup over the crackers and stir until well coated. Allow to soak for 5 minutes.

5 Pour the cracker mixture into the pie crust. Top with the remaining crust and crimp the edges with a fork to seal. Cut a few vents in the top of the pie with a paring knife and place on a rimmed baking sheet.

6 Melt the remaining 2 tablespoons butter in a small pan over low heat or in a microwave-safe bowl in the microwave at 30-second intervals. Brush the butter over the top of the crust and sprinkle with the remaining 1 tablespoon sugar.

7 Bake until golden, 30 to 35 minutes. Allow to cool before serving.

Faux Apple Pie will keep, covered at room temperature, for up to 3 days, or in the refrigerator for up to 1 week.

Fruit Cocktail Pie

While I was going through my grandmother's old cookbook to gather recipes for this book, I was reminded of my friend Jyl's discovery in her grandmother's cookbook: this Fruit Cocktail Pie. She found it on aged paper, written in her grandmother's handwriting with instructions that were a little bit on the cryptic side, as so many of my grandmother's have been! Trial and error allowed Jyl to create the pie she remembered from childhood—and she gave me the honor of sharing this recipe with you. *Serves 8*

1 can (15 ounces) fruit cocktail
  with juice
1 cup brown sugar
1 cup self-rising flour
  (see page 276)
1 large egg
One 9-inch deep-dish pie crust

1 Preheat the oven to 375°F.

2 Stir together the fruit cocktail, brown sugar, flour, and egg in a medium-size mixing bowl until well mixed. Pour the mixture into the pie crust.

3 Bake until the top is browned and the pie is set, 30 to 45 minutes. Allow to cool before serving.

Fruit Cocktail Pie will keep, covered in the refrigerator, for up to 5 days.

Golden Apple Pie

I t is said that we all have a twin somewhere in the world. Having had the pleasure of meeting mine, I can say this is true, for me at least! Angela Mitchell lives in the next town over from me and when she and I met it was like looking in a mirror. As fate would have it, we have more in common than just our appearance. We share a love of cooking, family, and passing on recipes. This is her Golden Apple Pie recipe that she's been using for nearly thirty years. It is her son-in-law's favorite and easy as pie to make. The end result is a golden pie with delicious pieces of apple on the top and a custardy pecan pie–like filling in the center. *Serves 6*

1½ cups granulated sugar
3 tablespoons all-purpose flour
2 large eggs, beaten
½ cup (1 stick) butter, melted and
   cooled slightly
½ teaspoon ground nutmeg
1 teaspoon ground cinnamon
1 teaspoon vanilla extract
3 cups chopped or diced apples
   (about 3 medium-size apples)
One 9-inch deep-dish pie crust
Good-quality vanilla ice cream,
   for serving (optional)

1 Preheat the oven to 425°F.

2 Stir together the sugar and flour in a medium-size mixing bowl. Add the eggs, butter, nutmeg, cinnamon, and vanilla and stir until well combined.

3 Stir the chopped apples into the batter and pour the mixture into the pie crust.

4 Bake for 15 minutes, then reduce the oven temperature to 350°F and bake until golden and set in the center, 30 to 35 minutes. Serve hot on its own or with a scoop of vanilla ice cream.

Golden Apple Pie will keep, covered in the refrigerator, for up to 3 days.

Best Ever Orange Meringue Pie

One of my all-time favorite recipes is the classic lemon meringue pie that I grew up eating. A few years back, though, I happened upon an orange pie for sale in a grocery store bakery. My curiosity was piqued as I schemed and prepared the recipe in my head. But how would you get the orange flavor concentrated enough without having the pie be runny? Orange juice concentrate! This recipe is a simple modification of my lemon meringue pie, with orange juice concentrate lending the perfect orange-ness to an incredibly delicious pie! *Serves 6 to 8*

1 can (14 ounces) sweetened
　　condensed milk
1/2 cup thawed frozen orange juice
　　concentrate
2 large egg yolks
One 9-inch graham cracker crust or
　　Cookie Crumb Crust (page 275)
3 large egg whites
1/4 cup granulated sugar

1 Preheat the oven to 325°F.

2 Place the sweetened condensed milk, orange juice concentrate, and egg yolks in a medium-size mixing bowl and mix with an electric mixer at medium speed until well blended, 1 to 2 minutes. Pour the mixture into the pie crust.

3 Place the egg whites in a separate medium-size mixing bowl (make sure it's very clean). Use clean beaters and beat with an electric mixer at medium-high speed until foamy, 3 to 5 minutes. Add the sugar and continue beating at high speed until soft peaks form, 3 to 5 minutes more. Spread the meringue on top of the pie, making sure to spread it to the edge of the crust to seal.

4 Bake until the meringue is golden, about 15 minutes. Allow to cool completely on a wire rack, then cover and refrigerate until cold before serving.

Best Ever Orange Meringue Pie will keep, covered in the refrigerator, for up to 3 days.

VARIATION

LEMON MERINGUE PIE: To make an amazing lemon meringue pie, just substitute bottled or fresh lemon juice for the orange juice concentrate.

Best Ever Orange Meringue Pie

Japanese Fruit Pie

I have no idea why this is called a Japanese Fruit Pie, but I found the same recipe in the cookbooks of two different grandmothers. The pages were stained, a telltale sign of a well-loved recipe, so I had to bake one up to try. Oh my goodness! I took one bite and instantly recognized this rich buttery pie from my childhood. It was like running into an old friend again. Of course, I had to add it to my cookbook, too!

Serves 6

> 1/2 cup raisins
> 1 cup boiling water
> 1/2 cup (1 stick) butter,
>   at room temperature
> 1 cup granulated sugar
> 2 large eggs, beaten
> 1 teaspoon vanilla extract
> 1/2 cup pecans, chopped
> 1/2 cup sweetened shredded
>   coconut
> One 9-inch pie crust (or Mix-in-Pan
>   Pie Crust, page 275), unbaked

1 Preheat the oven to 350°F. Place the raisins in a small heatproof bowl and cover with the boiling water. Set aside and soak for 5 minutes. Drain the liquid.

2 Cream together the butter and sugar in a large mixing bowl with an electric mixer at medium speed until light and fluffy, 1 to 2 minutes. Add the eggs and beat again, scraping down the side of the bowl as needed. Add the vanilla, pecans, coconut, and soaked raisins and stir until well combined.

3 Pour the batter into the pie crust and bake until set in the center, 35 to 40 minutes. Allow to cool before serving.

Japanese Fruit Pie will keep, covered at room temperature, for up to 2 days, or in the refrigerator for up to 4 days.

Homemade Chocolate Pie

from ERICA DEERMER

"We always called my grandmother 'Maw' and this is her chocolate pie recipe. Her given name was Lillie Mae Edwards and she was a sweet Christian lady whom I adored. Even though she was a diabetic, she still loved her sweets.

"This is the recipe that taught me how to temper my eggs. I learned the hard way! My first few pies had scrambled eggs in them. Now it seems I have perfected this pie. I have requests for it often and it is a family favorite. I think part of that is due to all of the love and memories it calls to mind each time we make it." *Serves 6*

One refrigerated 9-inch pie crust
　(or Mix-in-Pan Pie Crust,
　page 275), unbaked
1 cup granulated sugar
2 tablespoons unsweetened
　cocoa powder
2 tablespoons flour (all-purpose
　or self-rising)
1¼ cups milk
3 large eggs, separated, whites
　reserved, yolks beaten
1 tablespoon butter
1 teaspoon vanilla extract

1 Bake the pie crust according to the package directions and allow to cool completely.

2 Preheat the oven to 325°F.

3 Combine ¾ cup of the sugar, the cocoa, and the flour in a medium-size saucepan and stir with a wire whisk. Gradually stir in the milk and cook, stirring constantly, over medium-low heat until the mixture starts to thicken, 8 to 10 minutes.

4 Working quickly, place the egg yolks in a small bowl and add about ⅓ cup of the hot mixture to temper them. Beat well with a fork to combine, then add the egg mixture to the saucepan. Continue to cook, stirring continuously, over low heat, until the mixture thickens (it will look like a soft-set pudding), 8 to 10 minutes. Remove from the stove, add the butter and vanilla, and mix with a whisk until the butter is completely melted and the mixture is well blended. Pour into the pie crust and set aside.

5 Place the egg whites in a large mixing bowl and beat with an electric mixer at medium-high speed until foamy, 1 to 2 minutes. Add the remaining ¼ cup sugar and continue beating on high speed until soft peaks form. Spread the meringue on top of the pie and to the edge of the crust to seal well.

6 Bake the pie until the meringue is golden, about 10 minutes. Allow to cool for 1 hour, then cover and store in the refrigerator overnight. (The pie can be eaten warm if you prefer—it's still wonderful.)

Homemade Chocolate Pie will keep, covered in the refrigerator, for up to 3 days.

Hey You, Time to Sparkle

A couple of years back, I was in an accident and ended up breaking both of my legs. It was a bit of a trial, as you can imagine, but I can honestly say that I am grateful for the experience and am a better person because of it. I often get asked about the accident and how I am doing since then. I still have a little ache, but that's just pain. I'm used to it, so I don't really think about it anymore. It's just become part of my life, and like anything in life, you have to weigh the cons against the pros and give the pros extra credence.

It's all in your focus. What you focus on tells a lot about who you've decided to be. And we all decide who we are going to be. Whether we are going to be an encourager or a discourager, a grateful person or a complaining person. Whether we are going to use our life victoriously or sit back and whine about not being given the ideal circumstance or opportunity for us to shine. You can shine with broken legs, or no legs, or perfectly working legs.

You can shine when you're unemployed or overworked, eating filet mignon or living on ramen noodles. You can shine when the odds are stacked against you—and it will actually be a brighter gleam because of it.

The thing is, if you're going to shine, you've got to shine right now. If you say you can't shine, right now, where you are, then you're making excuses. And if you can't shine in a dark spot, if you want to shine only when it's midday and sunny and the winds are perfectly aligned for you like they are in your dreams—then you don't want to shine.

And that's a shame. Because you have a spark within you that could really make a difference in this world. But the biggest fire that spark could light—the biggest change it can make—is in your own life.

Me? I'm doing great. Whenever I have pain or issues, they just remind me that it's time to crank up the wattage. Do yourself a favor today. Dust off the sparkle.

Coca-Cola Pie

Anyone who has ever had Coca-Cola Cake (page 74) knows how amazingly well Coca-Cola and chocolate go together. This chocolate refrigerator pie has a little something different thanks to the addition of Coke. Chocolate ganache takes it over the top, as chocolate ganache always does! *Serves 8*

1¹/2 cups Coca-Cola
¹/4 heaping cup unsweetened
    cocoa powder
¹/3 cup brown sugar
¹/4 cup cornstarch
¹/4 cup (¹/2 stick) butter
1 teaspoon vanilla extract
One 9-inch graham cracker crust
1¹/2 cups semisweet chocolate
    chips
¹/2 cup half-and-half or heavy
    cream
Whipped cream (see page 277), for
    serving (optional)
Maraschino cherries, for garnish
    (optional)

1 Combine the Coca-Cola, cocoa powder, brown sugar, cornstarch, and butter in a medium-size saucepan over medium heat. Stir constantly with a whisk until thickened (it will look like a soft-set pudding), 5 to 10 minutes.

2 Remove from the heat and stir in the vanilla. Pour the mixture into the graham cracker crust. Cover and place in the refrigerator until thoroughly chilled.

3 For the ganache, place the chocolate chips and half-and-half in a large microwave-safe measuring cup. Place the cup in the microwave and heat at 45-second intervals, stirring after each, until the chips are melted. Stir together until thoroughly blended and creamy. Allow to cool for 5 to 10 minutes before spreading on top of the pie. Refrigerate the pie, uncovered, until the ganache is set, about 1 hour.

4 To serve, top each slice with a dollop of whipped cream and a cherry, if desired.

Coca-Cola Pie will keep, covered in the refrigerator, for up to 4 days.

Orange Chess Pie

This tastes similar to a classic chess pie with just enough orange to brighten it up a bit. I usually use store-bought juice for this recipe but if you have a fresh orange on hand, feel free to use that and a bit of the zest for more flavor. *Serves 8*

½ cup (1 stick) butter,
    at room temperature
1 cup granulated sugar
3 large eggs
3 tablespoons cornmeal
1 cup orange juice
1 tablespoon lemon juice
One 9-inch pie crust, unbaked

1 Preheat the oven to 350°F.

2 Cream together the butter and sugar in a medium-size mixing bowl with an electric mixer at medium speed until fluffy, 1 to 2 minutes. Add the eggs and mix, scraping down the side of the bowl as needed, until well blended. Add the cornmeal, orange juice, and lemon juice and mix again until smooth.

3 Pour the mixture into the pie crust and bake until set in the center and lightly golden, about 30 minutes.

Orange Chess Pie will keep, covered in the refrigerator, for up to 1 week.

Pineapple Chess Pie

This recipe from my husband's grandmother Granny Jordan is one of the prettiest chess pies I've ever seen. It comes out of the oven golden yellow, just like sunshine! The juicy bits of pineapple are a perfect complement to the classic chess pie.

This pie will just barely fit into a deep-dish crust, so make sure you drain the pineapple well and level off your ingredients when measuring. *Serves 8*

1½ cups granulated sugar
3 tablespoons cornmeal
2 tablespoons all-purpose flour
¼ teaspoon salt
4 large eggs, lightly beaten
¼ cup (½ stick) butter,
    melted and cooled
1 teaspoon vanilla extract
1 can (15 ounces) crushed
    pineapple, drained
One 9-inch deep-dish pie crust,
    unbaked

Granny Jordan was the epitome of a Southern lady with a kind heart. She showed gracious hospitality to everyone she met.

1 Preheat the oven to 350°F.

2 Stir together the sugar, cornmeal, flour, and salt in a large mixing bowl. Add the eggs, butter, and vanilla and stir until smooth and blended. Add the crushed pineapple and stir again until evenly distributed.

3 Pour the mixture into the pie crust. Bake until set, 1 hour (cover with aluminum foil after 30 minutes if needed to prevent the crust from overbrowning). Allow to cool completely before serving. Serve at room temperature or chill before serving.

Pineapple Chess Pie will keep, covered in the refrigerator, for up to 1 week.

Chocolate Chess Pie

If you make no other pie from this book, make this one. This incredible pie was another one of Grandmama's handwritten treasures. The paper was worn and stained, which is always a good sign. This intense chocolate pie forms a wondrous thin chocolate crust on top with a fudgy filling. My friend Jyl likes to peel the top off and eat that first! I love that it uses cocoa powder. You'll notice that most of my chocolate recipes use that because it's budget-friendly and my ancestors usually had that on hand, as I do. I also prefer the no-fuss method of stirring cocoa powder into a recipe rather than melting baking chocolate. *Serves 8*

1 1/2 cups granulated sugar
1/4 cup (1/2 stick) butter, melted
3 1/2 tablespoons unsweetened
    cocoa powder
2 large eggs
1 teaspoon vanilla extract
1/2 cup evaporated milk
One 9-inch pie crust, unbaked
Confectioners' sugar, for garnish
    (optional)

Chocolate Chess Pie

1 Preheat the oven to 350°F.

2 Combine the sugar, butter, cocoa powder, eggs, vanilla, and evaporated milk in a large mixing bowl and beat with an electric mixer at medium speed until well combined, 1 to 2 minutes.

3 Pour the mixture into the pie crust and bake until set in the center, 35 to 40 minutes. Allow to cool completely. Dust with confectioners' sugar before serving, if desired. It is excellent served warm from the oven or chilled.

Chocolate Chess Pie will keep, covered in the refrigerator, for up to 1 week.

Old-Fashioned Coconut Pie

from SHELIA TEASLEY

"This recipe was handed down to me from my late grandmother. She loved to cook and I have memories of helping her bake in the kitchen. She passed away in August 1998. I think about her every time I step into my kitchen to bake up something. I can see her now with her apron on as if it were yesterday. I miss her so much! I am keeping her memory alive, though, by handing her recipes down to my daughter and granddaughter.

"This is an old-fashioned coconut pie. Not the usual custard pie with meringue but a baked coconut pie that my aunt always called French Coconut Pie. It is one delicious pie that just seems to get even better as it cools."
Serves 6

3 large eggs
1 cup granulated sugar
1/2 cup buttermilk (see page 277)
1 teaspoon vanilla extract
1/4 cup (1/2 stick) butter, melted
　　and cooled slightly
1 1/2 cups sweetened flaked
　　coconut
One refrigerated 9-inch pie crust
　　(or Mix-in-Pan Pie Crust,
　　page 275), unbaked

1 Preheat the oven to 350°F.

2 Stir together the eggs, sugar, buttermilk, and vanilla in a large mixing bowl until well mixed. Add the melted butter and coconut and stir again until well combined.

3 Pour the mixture into the pie crust and bake for 10 minutes, then reduce the oven

The Magic of Grandparents

"You're only spending one night, Katy."

"But PLEASE, Mama, can't I just spend ten nights?"

"Oh, Katy," I said, in an exaggerated voice. "We'd just miss you SO MUCH if you were gone more than one!"

This was a recent conversation we had on the way to take Katy to spend the night at my mama's house. My kids don't get to spend nearly as much time as I'd like with my parents because they live a pretty good bit away from us, and I understood her excitement completely. There really is something magical about grandparents.

We used to beg to spend the night with my grandparents. Grandmama, Granddaddy, and my great-grandmother Lela all lived in one house when we were kids, and getting to spend a Saturday night at their house was like hitting the jackpot for us for many reasons, but the two main ones were:

1. We were the center of their universe the entire time we were there and being the center of the universe of these three people was about as good as it gets.

2. Saturday night was *Hee Haw* night on television! On those special Saturday nights, we'd eat supper at their large table and then head on into the den as Grandmama made us glasses of milk (sweet milk for us, buttermilk for them) to crumble our cornbread into and eat with a spoon. I'd curl up next to Granddaddy on the couch, his arm draping around me.

We'd watch Buck Owens and Minnie Pearl, giggling and singing "You Were Gone." The little jokes told in the cornfield had us laughing hysterically, and then they'd get down to the picking and grinning, one of Granddaddy's favorite parts of the show. "I'ma pickin'—and I'ma grinnin'!" I'd give anything to be able to have one more Saturday night at Grandmama and Granddaddy's house in good old Huntsville, Alabama.

But life has changed and I've grown up. *Hee Haw* doesn't show on any of my channels anymore and Granddaddy isn't here to wrap his arm around me. I bet Granddaddy would be tickled at how a few stories and recipes from the days of milk and cornbread have ended up in books sold around the world.

Still, when I am missing my childhood days, it strengthens my heart to see my own children living out theirs and making memories with their grandparents.

With that bit of nostalgia, I'm sharing a classic Southern recipe for Buttermilk Pie. I'll save ya a slice, Granddaddy.

temperature to 325°F and bake until the filling is set in the center, about 50 minutes.

Old-Fashioned Coconut Pie will keep, covered in the refrigerator, for up to 1 week.

Buttermilk Pie

Buttermilk pie is a classic Southern recipe that is kissing cousins with Chess Pie. Simple yet delicious, with our beloved buttermilk as the headlining ingredient, this pie was a mainstay in traditional Southern kitchens. *Serves 8*

1½ cups granulated sugar

½ cup (1 stick) butter or
   margarine, at room temperature

3 tablespoons all-purpose flour

3 large eggs, lightly beaten

1 cup buttermilk (see page 277)

1 tablespoon lemon juice

1 tablespoon vanilla extract

One 9-inch pie crust (or Mix-in-Pan
   Pie Crust, page 275), unbaked

Ground cinnamon, for garnish
   (optional)

Confectioners' sugar, for garnish
   (optional)

Fresh berries, for serving
   (optional)

Me with my sister, Patti, and my granddaddy Jay Pockrus.

1 Preheat the oven to 350°F.

2 Cream together the sugar and butter in a large mixing bowl with an electric mixer at medium speed until light and fluffy, 3 to 4 minutes. Add the flour, eggs, buttermilk, lemon juice, and vanilla and mix again, scraping down the side of the bowl as needed, until well combined, about 1 minute. Pour the batter into the pie crust. Sprinkle the cinnamon over the top, if desired.

3 Bake until golden on the top and set in the center, 40 minutes. Allow to cool slightly. Serve warm with confectioners' sugar sprinkled over the top and berries on the side, if desired.

Buttermilk Pie will keep, covered in the refrigerator, for up to 1 week.

Basic Fried Pies

This recipe is from my great-grandmother Lela. Everything she made was delicious, but she was known for her fried pies. The dried fruit makes all the difference in these because it has a much more concentrated flavor than fresh fruit. I like to dry my own fruit when it is in season and most affordable. Katy and I keep our dehydrator going nonstop in the summertime and have made all sorts of fun snacks by dehydrating every fruit and berry we can find. You don't have to dehydrate your own fruit, though: Simply purchase a package of dried fruit in your grocery store next to the raisins. *Serves 8 to 10*

6 to 7 ounces dried peaches,
   apples, apricots, or other fruits
1 cup granulated sugar
1/4 cup (1/2 stick) butter or
   margarine
1 tablespoon lemon juice
   (optional, but recommended)
1/2 teaspoon ground cinnamon
   (optional, but recommended)
2 cups all-purpose flour, plus extra
   for rolling out the dough
1 teaspoon salt
1/2 cup vegetable shortening

1/2 cup milk, plus extra as needed
Vegetable oil, for frying

1 Place the dried fruit, sugar, and 2 cups water in a medium-size saucepan over medium-high heat. Bring to a boil, stirring often, then reduce the heat to a simmer and cook until the fruit is tender, about 20 minutes. Remove from the heat.

2 Add the butter and the lemon juice and cinnamon, if using, and mash together with a potato masher or fork. Set aside to cool.

3 Meanwhile, prepare the dough: Stir together the flour and salt in a medium-size bowl. Add the shortening and cut together with a long-tined fork. Add the milk and stir until the dough sticks together. Divide into 8 to 10 portions (depending on the desired thickness of the dough).

4 On a floured surface and with a rolling pin, roll out each portion into a 5- or 6-inch circle. Place 2 tablespoons of the filling on one half of each circle. Wet the edges and fold the dough over the filling, crimping the edges with a fork. Repeat with the remaining circles of dough.

5 Pour vegetable oil to a depth of 1 inch into a large skillet and place over medium-high heat to preheat for about 5 minutes. Sprinkle a little flour into the oil to check the heat: If the flour sizzles, the oil is ready. Reduce the heat to medium and add the pies, a few at a time, being careful not to let them touch. Cook until browned on both sides, 2 to 3 minutes per side. Remove the pies and place them on a paper towel–lined plate.

Basic Fried Pies are at their absolute best the day they are made, but they will keep, covered at room temperature, for up to 3 days.

Water Pie

from KAY WEST

My grandmother had eight children and served ten people three meals every day. This was a recipe that she developed in order to have a dessert during leaner times, with ingredients most folks always have in their kitchen. I have used this many times when I do not have a dessert for unexpected guests. In order to get the measurements right, I had to have my grandmother do her 'pinch of this and pinch of that' and then measure what she had used."

Serves 6

One 9-inch deep-dish pie crust
4 tablespoons all-purpose flour

1 cup granulated sugar
2 teaspoons vanilla extract
5 tablespoons butter,
   cut into 5 pats

1 Preheat the oven to 400°F. Set the pie crust on a baking sheet.

2 Pour 1½ cups water into the pie crust. Stir together the flour and sugar in a small bowl until combined. Using a spoon, evenly sprinkle the flour mixture over the water in the pie crust. Add the vanilla; do not stir. Distribute the pats of butter evenly on top.

3 Bake for 30 minutes, then reduce the oven temperature to 375°F and bake until set, about 30 minutes more. Let sit until the pie cools and the filling gels.

Water Pie will keep, covered in the refrigerator, for up to 3 days.

CHRISTY'S NOTE: I had never heard of a pie like this one. I was pleasantly surprised when it set up beautifully and tasted really buttery and creamy. I can surely understand how someone came up with this pie when times were hard and supplies were scarce. It is amazing how smart people were back in the day.

Wake Up and Say Thank You

At the beginning and end of each day, there is so very much for which we can be grateful. Wake up and look for it. Set your alarm ten minutes early if you have to just to give yourself time to lie there and think about it. It's a crying shame that so many folks spend their time counting their sorrows instead of counting their blessings. What you nurture is what you grow. I sure don't want to be caught nurturing negativity!

So sit back and count your blessings today. If this isn't something you normally do each day, then I challenge you to try it for a week. One whole week of taking just a few minutes every day to think about how very good life is right now. Do you have a house? Food on the table? Healthy kids?

If you have ever found yourself sitting around hoping to someday have more, I'm challenging you to contemplate the abundance you already have. When you wake up to find you've been given an entire day, the world and all its possibilities, complete with sunshine, love, and hope, the best first response would be, "Thank you."

Cracker Pie

This is a simple pie with simple ingredients and it's easily altered to suit whatever you have on hand. I like to use a can of drained fruit cocktail but it would also be good with a can of drained pineapple. I use saltine crackers but I've heard of other folks using Ritz-type crackers. Mama always adds a little coconut to hers, and you could also add dried fruit instead of canned without having to alter the recipe. When I got ready to make this recently, I found I had everything I needed on hand, which is why old-fashioned pies like this have been favorites of home cooks for as long as stoves have been in kitchens. *Serves 6*

One 9-inch deep-dish pie crust

3 large egg whites

1 cup granulated sugar

1/2 teaspoon baking powder

1/2 cup chopped pecans or walnuts (optional)

1 can (15 ounces) fruit cocktail of your choice, drained

16 saltine crackers, crushed

1 teaspoon vanilla extract

Whipped cream (see page 277) or frozen whipped topping (such as Cool Whip), thawed, for serving

Maraschino cherries, for garnish

1 Preheat the oven to 325°F.

2 Prick the bottom of the pie crust several times with a fork and bake for 10 minutes.

3 Place the egg whites in a large mixing bowl and beat with an electric mixer at medium-high speed until stiff peaks form, 3 to 5 minutes. Add the sugar and baking powder and beat again until the sugar is incorporated, about 1 minute more.

4 Using a large spoon, gently fold the nuts, if using, fruit, cracker crumbs, and vanilla into the egg whites and stir until well combined.

5 Pour the batter into the prebaked pie crust. Bake until lightly browned on top, 20 to 25 minutes. Allow to cool completely.

Serve each piece with a dollop of whipped cream and a cherry on top.

Cracker Pie will keep, covered in the refrigerator, for up to 4 days.

Vinegar Dumplings

from **GWEN PERRY**

66 In 2002 my grandmother, Annie Seaton (Maw), was diagnosed with congestive heart failure and given six months to live. After her diagnosis, one evening she and I were sitting and talking about some of her recipes that I wanted to have in order to carry on her wonderful cooking. While we talked, my uncle came in to visit and said, 'You need to get her recipe for vinegar pie.' My first thought (and I voiced it) was, 'That doesn't even sound good!' But I asked her if she remembered how to make it and what was in it. As she told me, I realized it really wasn't pie but dumplings: Back in the day, if it was sweet, they called it pie.

"Once we got her home from the hospital, I made a batch of the dumplings for her from a recipe I found. I put a small bite on the spoon, blew on it real good so as not to burn her mouth, and gave her a taste. She smiled really big and said, 'Yep, that's just about right!' We talked for another minute or so and then she said, 'Well, aren't you going to give me another bite?' I couldn't help but giggle. Of course I fed her every bite I had in that little bowl.

"That day she had lots of company coming by to visit and check on her. With every group that came in, she'd say, 'Gwen made vinegar pie and you have just got to have some of it!' I bet I made vinegar pie four or five times that day in order to share with everyone.

"I had so much fun watching her enjoy her visitors and share a dessert full of fond memories for her and her children while they were growing up; it allowed me to have just a glimpse into their world so many years ago. Of course, I got the added bonus of keeping this heirloom recipe to share for many more years to come!

"And believe it or not, they are really, really good!" *Serves 4 or 5*

1/2 cup apple cider vinegar
1 cup granulated sugar
1/2 cup (1 stick) plus 2 tablespoons
    butter or margarine
1 cup all-purpose flour
2 teaspoons baking powder
1/2 teaspoon salt
6 tablespoons milk

1 Stir together the vinegar, sugar, the 1/2 cup of butter, and 1 cup water in a medium-size stockpot over medium-high heat. Bring to a boil, then reduce the heat to a simmer.

2 Stir together the flour, baking powder, and salt in a medium-size mixing bowl. Add the remaining 2 tablespoons butter and cut with a long-tined fork or pastry cutter until crumbly. Stir in the milk until the mixture forms a dough.

3 Carefully drop the dough by spoonfuls into the hot liquid. Simmer until the dumplings are somewhat firm and the syrup is thick, 10 to 15 minutes. Serve the dumplings and syrup immediately.

CHRISTY'S NOTE: I wish I had had this recipe when my grandmother Lucille was still living. She often talked of a vinegar pie that her mother made when they ran out of fruit to bake cobblers. She said her mother always fixed a little something sweet for supper and this was what she made at the end of the season when she had used up all that she had canned or dried. Grandmama described it as similar to lemon with its tartness. I would describe it as buttery and tart but more of a dumpling or cobbler than a pie, even though that is what all of my ancestors called it, too.

Cherry Pecan Pies

If you're looking for a cool, sweet pie with just a bit of tang, you've found it! From Granny Jordan's recipe collection, this pie comes together in a flash and is reminiscent of the classic cherry cheese pie that is so popular around the holidays. The main difference is that this pie is a bit subtler in flavor and all of the flavors are blended together rather than separated into layers. I like to top mine with a generous helping of whipped topping (just heaped in the center so the pretty pink color of the pie can still be seen) and a big red cherry. This recipe yields two pies, and honestly, I've yet to find someone who objected to taking one off my hands. *Makes 2 pies; serves 16*

1 cup chopped pecans
1 can (14 ounces) sweetened
   condensed milk
1 container (8 ounces) frozen
   whipped topping (such as
   Cool Whip), thawed (or 1 cup
   whipped cream, see page 277)
¼ cup lemon juice
1 teaspoon vanilla extract
1 can (21 ounces) cherry pie filling
Two 8-inch graham cracker
   pie crusts

1 Preheat the oven to 350°F.

2 Place the pecans on a rimmed baking sheet and toast them in the oven until they just barely darken, 5 to 10 minutes. Remove immediately and set aside to cool.

3 Pour the sweetened condensed milk and whipped topping into a large mixing bowl and beat with an electric mixer at medium speed until smooth and creamy, about 1 minute. Add the lemon juice and vanilla and mix again until incorporated. Fold in the toasted pecans and the cherry pie filling until well blended.

4 Divide the filling evenly between the two pie crusts. Cover and chill in the refrigerator or freezer for several hours before serving. If frozen, allow the pies to thaw for 5 minutes before cutting and serving.

Cherry Pecan Pies will keep, covered in the refrigerator, for up to 1 week, or in the freezer for up to 3 months.

Pecan Pie Cheesecake

Pecan pie is one of those desserts usually served at special occasions such as holidays, big family meals, and family reunions. This recipe has a lovely cheesecake surprise at the bottom! I find the cheesecake not only adds a whole other flavor that complements the traditional pecan layer, but it also cuts the sweetness we are accustomed to with traditional pecan pie. And since I'm such a honey lover, my recipe uses honey where most tend to use light corn syrup. This switch-up really gives the pie a wonderful flavor. While it is baking, the cream cheese layer floats through the pecan pie layer to the top, and the pecan pie layer sinks to the bottom. They do this little magical dance and it ends up as the best pecan pie I've ever had. *Serves 6 to 8*

1 package (8 ounces) cream cheese, at room temperature
1¼ cups granulated sugar
4 large eggs
2 teaspoons vanilla extract
One 9-inch deep-dish pie crust (or double the recipe for Mix-in-Pan Pie Crust, page 275)

½ cup honey
¼ cup (½ stick) butter, melted
1 cup pecan halves or pieces

1 Place the cream cheese, ¼ cup of the sugar, 1 egg, and 1 teaspoon of the vanilla in a large mixing bowl and beat with an electric mixer at medium speed until smooth and creamy, 1 to 2 minutes. Scrape the mixture into the pie crust.

2 Place the remaining 1 cup sugar, the honey, the butter, the remaining 3 eggs, and the remaining 1 teaspoon vanilla in the same bowl (no need to clean). Beat with an electric mixer at low speed until very well blended and smooth, about 2 minutes. Stir in the pecans and pour over the cheesecake mixture.

3 Place the pie on a rimmed baking sheet in a cold oven and heat the oven to 325°F. Bake until set in the center, about 1 hour. Allow to cool completely before cutting. This pie is best if refrigerated for several hours before serving.

Pecan Pie Cheesecake will keep, covered in the refrigerator, for up to 1 week.

Pecan Pie Cheesecake

Black Walnut Pie

My mother's friend Pam Ritter brought this recipe to my mama's New Year's Day lunch. It was an instant hit, and after trying it, I can see why. The pie has a wonderful flavor and doesn't seem quite as sweet as a pecan pie.

To most people, black walnuts taste rich and delicious, but to others they have a very bitter and harsh taste. Before making this pie for other people, you might want to ask. I know that Granddaddy would have loved it, since he loved anything with black walnuts in it. Granddaddy, this recipe is for you. *Serves 8*

2 large eggs
1/2 cup granulated sugar
1/4 teaspoon salt
1/4 cup (1/2 stick) butter, melted
3/4 cup light corn syrup
3/4 cup chopped black walnuts
One 9-inch pie crust, unbaked

1 Preheat the oven to 375°F.

2 Place the eggs, sugar, salt, butter, and corn syrup in a large mixing bowl and beat with an electric mixer at medium speed until well mixed, 1 to 2 minutes. Stir in the nuts with a spoon.

3 Pour the mixture into the pie crust. Bake until the filling is set and the crust is golden brown, 40 to 50 minutes. Allow to cool slightly before serving.

Black Walnut Pie will keep, covered at room temperature, for up to 3 days.

Oatmeal Raisin Cookie Pie

I first had this pie at the Loveless Cafe in Nashville, and let me tell you, I fell for it hard. I contacted the Sun-Maid raisin company and got permission to share the recipe. If you, like me, love a delicious warm oatmeal raisin cookie, you'll think this one is a treasure! *Serves 6 to 8*

3 large eggs
1 cup light corn syrup
1/2 cup packed brown sugar
3 tablespoons butter or margarine, melted
3/4 cup quick-cooking oats
1 tablespoon all-purpose flour
1 teaspoon ground cinnamon

¹/4 teaspoon salt

³/4 cup raisins (preferably Sun-
  Maid natural)

One 9-inch graham cracker pie
  crust (or Cookie Crumb Crust,
  page 275, or Mix-in-Pan Pie
  Crust, page 275)

1 Preheat the oven to 325°F.

2 Beat together the eggs, corn syrup, brown sugar, and butter with a whisk or spoon in a medium-size mixing bowl.

3 Add the oats, flour, cinnamon, salt, and raisins and stir again until well mixed. Pour the batter into the pie crust and place the pie on a rimmed baking sheet.

4 Bake until the top is golden brown and the filling is just set in the center, 45 to 50 minutes. Allow to cool completely.

Oatmeal Raisin Cookie Pie will keep, covered at room temperature, for up to 3 days.

My Nephew's Peanut Butter Pie

from JUDY WATTS

"I never had anyone to hand me down recipes, but my nephew Nicky just loved peanut butter cups as a baby, so I set out to find a recipe that I'd make just for him. I found this recipe a long time ago and it was an immediate favorite. I've been making it for him ever since. Even though he is grown and married and lives far away now, he still requests this pie whenever he comes home." *Serves 8*

1 cup creamy peanut butter

1 package (8 ounces) cream cheese,
  at room temperature

1¹/2 cups confectioners' sugar

¹/2 teaspoon vanilla extract

3 cups frozen whipped topping
  (such as Cool Whip), thawed

One 9-inch chocolate graham
  cracker crust (preferably
  store-bought)

1 Beat the peanut butter, cream cheese, confectioners' sugar, and vanilla in a large mixing bowl with an electric mixer at medium speed until smooth, 1 to 2 minutes. Fold in 2 cups of the whipped topping until well incorporated.

2 Pour the mixture into the pie crust. Smooth the remaining 1 cup of the whipped topping over the top of the pie.

3 Cover and freeze until firm, at least 3 hours. Let sit at room temperature for 20 minutes before serving.

My Nephew's Peanut Butter Pie will keep, covered in the freezer, for up to 2 weeks.

CHRISTY'S NOTE: This pie is amazing. If you have a peanut butter lover in your house, this is for them. It is creamy and peanut buttery without being so very rich. The chocolate crust turns it into a pie that reminds me of Reese's Peanut Butter Cups.

Frozen Oreo Pie

Oreos are my son's favorite store-bought cookie, but most desserts involving Oreos layer ultra sweet ingredients on top of an already sweet cookie. This frozen pie has the texture of ice cream but is light and creamy. I make it with less sugar by using sugar-free pudding mix, but you can use the full-sugar version if you like. *Serves 8*

1½ cups milk
1 box (1 ounce) sugar-free white
    chocolate instant pudding mix
10 Oreos or other creme-filled
    chocolate sandwich cookies,
    plus extra for garnish (optional)
1 container (8 ounces) extra-
    creamy frozen whipped topping
    or regular whipped topping
    (such as Cool Whip), thawed,
    plus extra for serving (optional)
One 9-inch chocolate Cookie
    Crumb Crust (page 275)

1 Pour the milk in a large mixing bowl and sprinkle the pudding mix over it. Beat with an electric mixer at medium speed until well combined, about 1 minute.

Frozen Oreo Pie

2 Place 10 Oreos in a plastic bag and crush them by rolling over the bag with a rolling pin. Add the crushed Oreos to the pudding mixture along with the whipped topping. Beat again, scraping down the side of the bowl as needed, until well incorporated, about 2 minutes.

3 Spoon the mixture into the pie crust. Cover and refrigerate or freeze for several hours before serving. Top with extra whipped topping and crushed or whole Oreos, if you like.

Frozen Oreo Pie will keep, covered in the refrigerator, for up to 1 week, or in the freezer for up to 2 months.

Frozen Turtle Pie

Frozen Turtle Pie sounds decadent (and it is), but the beauty of it is that you can actually make it significantly lower in sugar with just a few substitutions. Now keep in mind, this is not going to be a low-calorie dessert, but you can certainly lessen the calories! The caramel and pecans on the bottom of each slice are two of my favorite parts, balanced perfectly with the thick and fluffy chocolate layer on top. *Serves 8*

1 box (3.4 ounces) chocolate
   instant pudding (see Note)
1½ cups milk
1 container (8 ounces) frozen
   whipped topping (such as
   Cool Whip), thawed (see Note)
1 cup caramel ice cream topping
One 9-inch chocolate cookie
   crumb crust
1 cup chopped pecans
Canned whipped cream,
   for garnish
Smucker's Chocolate Magic Shell,
   for garnish
Pecan halves, for garnish
   (optional)

1 Place the instant pudding and milk in a large mixing bowl and beat well with an electric mixer at medium speed, scraping down the side of the bowl as needed, until the pudding is dissolved, about 2 minutes. Add the whipped topping and mix again until well blended, about 1 minute.

2 Spread the caramel ice cream topping in the bottom of the pie crust and sprinkle with the chopped pecans. Spoon the pudding mixture over the nuts. Cover and place in the freezer until firm, about 2 hours.

3 Before serving, squirt the canned whipped topping around the edge of the pie (I usually make little rosettes). Drizzle a

Make a List and Check It Often

My mother has always been a list-maker. This came in very handy for her nosy children; if a gift-giving occasion was coming up, all we had to do was find the right notebook to see exactly what we were getting. I admit to doing this every chance I got!

As I've grown older, I have taken to list-making as well. I always keep a notebook within reach for things like grocery trips, chores I need to do, deadlines, projects, and so on. But within each notebook I always end up with another kind of list:

things I'm grateful for. I never plan these lists ahead of time, but rather, end up writing them in response to those days where I feel a little down, overwhelmed, or just not at my best. Opening up my book, I start numbering the page and listing, one by one, some of the wonderful things in my life that I am grateful for. This simple act resets my focus and leaves me with a wonderful gift to myself, because the momentary reflection on my life helps me realize how sweet it really is.

zigzag pattern of chocolate shell over the top and place in the freezer, uncovered, to set, 5 minutes.

4 Press the pecan halves into the border for decoration, if desired. Allow to sit out to soften slightly before cutting, 5 to 10 minutes. Enjoy!

Frozen Turtle Pie will keep, covered in the freezer, for up to 3 months.

NOTE: To decrease the amount of sugar in this recipe, use sugar-free chocolate instant pudding and light whipped topping.

5

Cobblers, Puddings, and Sweet Rolls

THERE IS A certain comfort that can be found only in the old pudding and cobbler recipes. These were usually made while fruit was in season, but now we are blessed with fruit in the grocery store year-round. Cobblers and puddings are always welcome additions to any meal. I've included the well-worn and beloved recipes from my grandmothers along with a few new favorites in this chapter.

Mimi's Peach Cobbler

One of my mother's neighbors, Camille, gave us this recipe for a peach cobbler that is made using whole wheat bread. Camille's grandmother picked up the recipe a few years ago. It makes preparing a cobbler so much easier, since you don't have to make a crust. It's an easy, delicious recipe, and you'd never guess it was made with sandwich bread. *Serves 6 to 8*

Nonstick cooking spray,
   for coating the pan
1 can (20 ounces) sliced peaches
   in juice, half the juice reserved
7 slices whole wheat sandwich
   bread
1 cup granulated sugar
1 large egg, beaten
2 tablespoons all-purpose flour
1/2 cup (1 stick) butter, melted
1 tablespoon vanilla extract
1 teaspoon ground cinnamon,
   plus extra for garnish

1 Preheat the oven to 350°F. Coat a 9 x 13-inch pan with cooking spray.

2 Pour the peaches and the reserved juice into the prepared pan. Trim the crusts from the bread slices and cut each slice into 3 strips. Arrange the bread strips on top of the peaches in the pan.

3 Mix the sugar, egg, flour, butter, vanilla, and the 1 teaspoon cinnamon in a medium-size bowl and spread on top of the bread slices. Sprinkle with extra cinnamon and bake until lightly browned, about 45 minutes. Serve warm.

Mimi's Peach Cobbler will keep, covered in the refrigerator, for up to 3 days.

Strawberry Cobbler (Mama's Favorite)

I first tasted strawberry cobbler at a cafeteria. I love strawberries any way you fix them, so this was a recipe that I set out to duplicate the minute I got my hands on some strawberries. You can make this recipe with fresh strawberries washed and cut up with a little sugar on them, or you can use frozen sliced sweetened strawberries. If you use fresh ones, let them sit for a little bit after you add the sugar to make some juice. If you use frozen ones, let them thaw.

This is a really forgiving recipe. If you have a little extra fruit, add it. If you are a little bit short, use what you have and don't give it a second thought. I often sprinkle about a tablespoon of sugar over the batter and strawberries before I put it in the oven—that was my grandmother's finishing touch.

This strawberry cobbler is delicious by itself, with ice cream, or with whipped topping. Some folks like to pour on a little "sweet milk," which is country talk for whole milk. Just serve it any way that suits your fancy. *Serves 5 or 6*

1/2 cup (1 stick) butter or
   margarine
2 cups fresh strawberries, washed,
   hulled, and sliced
1 1/2 cups granulated sugar, plus
   1 tablespoon extra if desired
1 cup self-rising flour
   (see page 276)
1/2 teaspoon ground cinnamon
   (optional)
1 cup milk
Ice cream, whole milk, or thawed
   frozen whipped topping (such
   as Cool Whip), for serving
   (optional)

1 Preheat the oven to 400°F. Place the butter in a 2- to 2 1/2-quart ovenproof casserole dish and put it in the preheating oven just until the butter melts.

2 Place the strawberries in a medium-size bowl. Add 1/2 cup of the sugar and stir to coat.

3 Stir together the flour, the 1 cup of sugar, and the cinnamon, if using, in a large mixing bowl. Add the milk and stir until smooth. Pour the batter over the melted butter in the casserole dish. Pour the strawberries into the center of the batter. Do not stir. Sprinkle the remaining sugar over the top, if you wish.

4 Bake until a toothpick inserted in the center comes out clean (the batter will bake up in a cake-like texture), 30 to 40 minutes. Serve on its own or with ice cream, if you like.

Strawberry Cobbler will keep, covered in the refrigerator, for up to 3 days.

Old-Fashioned Banana Pudding

I can't even begin to count all of the wonderful memories I have of my family sitting around a big avocado-green bowl of Mama's homemade banana pudding. There is truly nothing like this dish, and no shortcut holds a candle to the real thing. *Serves 6 to 8*

Old-Fashioned Banana Pudding

The Secret to Being a Morning Person

The secret to being a "morning person" has nothing to do with what time you wake up. It doesn't matter if your morning starts at 4 a.m. or at noon. I've learned that the way I treat the morning will determine what I get back from it. If I growl and grumble, it's gonna bite. Instead, I *decide* to be grateful I woke up. I *decide* to count my blessings instead of complaints. I *decide* to be patient instead of frazzled. I *decide* to smile instead of frown. I *decide* to notice every little joy and count them as such instead of taking them for granted: running water, a bed, a roof, a job, a family, blue sky out my window, tires on my car that take me where I want to go . . .

These are some of the things that helped me to become a morning person, and these are also some of the things that helped me to become a happy person—neat how that works.

A string of small decisions, made moment after moment, day after day. But it all begins—each day—with one: I decide to be grateful.

1 box (11 ounces) vanilla wafers
5 bananas
1/2 cup granulated sugar
   (or Splenda)
1/3 cup all-purpose flour
3 large egg yolks
2 cups milk
A dash of salt
1/2 teaspoon vanilla extract
Meringue (page 276), for topping
   (optional)

1 Place a layer of vanilla wafers in the bottom of a medium-size ovenproof mixing bowl. Slice the bananas and place a layer of them on top of the wafers. Repeat with two more alternating layers of wafers and bananas.

2 Combine the sugar, flour, egg yolks, milk, and salt in a medium-size saucepan or double boiler over medium-low heat and stir well with a whisk to combine. Cook, stirring constantly to prevent scorching, until thick (it will look like a soft-set pudding), about 15 minutes. Add the vanilla and stir.

3 Immediately pour the pudding over the wafers and bananas. Let sit to allow the wafers to absorb the pudding, about 5 minutes.

4 If using the meringue, spread it on top of the pudding, being sure to spread to the edges to seal well. Bake until the top is golden, 10 minutes.

Old-Fashioned Banana Pudding will keep, covered in the refrigerator, for up to 2 days.

Vanilla Wafer Pineapple Pudding

Banana pudding (see page 168) is about the best thing on the planet, but if you're someone who doesn't like bananas, no worries! There is more than one way to make pudding!

Crushed pineapple is an excellent substitution for banana and the light sunshiny flavor is perfectly complemented by the homemade custard. Banana pudding aficionados don't skip a beat when you place this before them, either. My kids can attest to that—and they usually don't like pineapple! *Serves 6 to 8*

3 large eggs, separated
2 cups milk
3/4 cup granulated sugar
    (or Splenda)
1/3 cup all-purpose flour
Dash of salt
1 teaspoon vanilla extract
1 box (11 ounces) vanilla wafers
1 can (20 ounces) crushed
    pineapple with juice

1 Place the egg yolks, milk, 1/2 cup of the sugar, the flour, and salt in a medium-size saucepan over medium heat and cook, stirring constantly, until the custard thickens (it will look like a soft-set pudding), 15 to 20 minutes. Remove from the heat and stir in the vanilla.

2 Preheat the oven to 350°F.

3 Place half the wafers in the bottom of an 8 x 8-inch baking dish. Spread half the crushed pineapple on top. Cover with half the custard. Repeat with the remaining wafers, pineapple, and custard.

4 Place the egg whites in a clean medium-size mixing bowl and beat with the clean beaters of an electric mixer at medium-high speed until soft peaks form, 1 to 2 minutes. Add the remaining 1/4 cup sugar and beat

Make Some Wrinkles Today

Hopefully you've known a kind older person in your lifetime. One whose face is filled with wrinkles from years of smiles, whose cheeks have a rosy glow from making the effort to be cheerful, and whose eyes have a twinkle of wisdom and memories. The only thing capable of rivaling such beauty is a smile from a newborn babe.

Forget wanting to look like movie stars and "perfect" folks. I want wrinkles—LOTS of them. I want laugh lines around my mouth and crinkles at my eyes. I want worn hands from preparing meals for generations and I want joints so used they begin to wear and ache in my older years. And don't you dare deny me white hair as a testament to the glory I am shown in being able to watch my kids and grandkids grow up!

God, keep me so busy and focused on the living at hand and the love, smiles, laughter, and joy that come with it that I could not possibly end up with a drawn and pinched face, stretched and taut from trying to hide the evidence of a life well lived. I want to leave this world with every blessed wrinkle I can possibly earn. When I grow old, stand back, 'cause I'll show them what beautiful really is. Look out, world. Granny's got cookies! Make some wrinkles today!

---

again until stiff peaks form. Spread over the top of the custard to the edges of the dish.

5 Bake until the top is lightly browned, about 15 minutes. Serve warm.

Vanilla Wafer Pineapple Pudding is best served the day it's made. Leftovers will keep, covered in the refrigerator, for 1 day.

Lemon Syllabub

You know how you always want a little more whipped cream because it is so good? Well, this dessert is basically glorified whipped cream! If you love lemon meringue pie like I do, you'll especially love this because it ends up tasting like lemon meringue pie–flavored whipped cream.

Most recipes for syllabub are pretty complicated, but I have a firm belief that food and life are really simple, we just insist on complicating them. One of the things I like to do is simplify—so here is my recipe. *Serves 6*

1¹/₂ cups heavy cream
¹/₄ cup granulated sugar
2 tablespoons apple juice
Zest and juice of 1 lemon
¹/₂ teaspoon vanilla extract

Place the heavy cream, sugar, apple juice, lemon zest and juice, and vanilla in a large mixing bowl and beat with an electric mixer at medium speed, scraping down the side of the bowl and stirring from the bottom once, until thick and slightly stiff, 2 to 3 minutes. Cover and chill until ready to serve.

Lemon Syllabub is best served the day it's made.

Sweet Potato Crème Brûlée

Until I had my first bite of crème brûlée, I didn't really understand the difference between a dessert being "rich" and being "sweet." Crème brûlée is a favorite of mine because it is light on the sweet and decadently heavy on the rich. Most recipes call for making it with a whole vanilla bean. A whole vanilla bean has never once stepped foot inside of my kitchen, so my recipe uses ingredients I have on hand, including bottled vanilla extract. *Serves 6*

Nonstick cooking spray
2 large sweet potatoes, scrubbed
1 cup granulated sugar (or Splenda)
¹/₄ cup (¹/₂ stick) butter or
    margarine, melted
¹/₂ teaspoon ground cinnamon
2 large eggs, plus 4 large egg yolks
2 cups heavy (whipping) cream
1 teaspoon vanilla extract
¹/₃ cup brown sugar

1 Preheat the oven to 425°F. Line a baking sheet with aluminum foil and coat it with cooking spray.

Sweet Potato Crème Brûlée

2 Pierce each sweet potato a few times with a fork, place them on the prepared baking sheet, and bake until soft when pierced with a paring knife, about 1 hour. Allow to cool completely.

3 Meanwhile, turn the oven down to 325°F. Coat an 8 x 8-inch baking dish with cooking spray.

4 Peel the sweet potatoes and place them in a large mixing bowl. Add ½ cup of the sugar, the butter, the cinnamon, and the 2 eggs and beat with an electric mixer at medium speed until smooth and creamy, 1 to 2 minutes. Spread the sweet potato mixture into the bottom of the prepared baking dish and set aside.

5 Place the cream, the remaining ½ cup sugar, the 4 egg yolks, and the vanilla in a medium-size heavy-bottomed saucepan and stir well. Place over medium-low heat and cook, whisking constantly, until just warm, about 5 minutes (it will be very runny). Using a measuring cup, gently scoop up the custard mixture and pour it evenly over the sweet potatoes.

6 Place the baking dish in the center of a larger baking dish. Pour water into the larger baking dish to reach a depth of 1 inch up the sides of the smaller one.

7 Bake until a knife inserted in the center of the custard comes out clean, about 1 hour. Carefully remove the smaller baking dish and place it on a heavy dish towel or wire rack to cool. Once cool, cover it with aluminum foil and refrigerate for 2 to 3 hours, or overnight.

8 Shortly before you're ready to serve, remove the custard from the fridge and let it sit at room temperature for 30 minutes. Preheat the oven to a high broil.

9 Sprinkle the brown sugar over the top of the custard and place it on a rimmed baking sheet. Broil, about 5 inches from the heat, until the sugar is mostly melted and forms a thin coat across the top of the dish, 5 to 7 minutes. Allow to cool until the sugar hardens, about 5 minutes.

Sweet Potato Crème Brûlée will keep, covered in the refrigerator, for 1 to 2 days.

Old-Fashioned Butter Rolls Saved from Extinction

We were having supper over at Grandmama's house and as soon as we walked in the door I honed in on an indescribably delicious smell.

"Grandmama, what is that?"

"Oh, I just made us some butter rolls for dessert." She said it with a wave of her hand, dismissing it as nothing special.

I was confused. Rolls for dessert? I thought she had taken rolls and slathered them with butter and was heating them up in the oven. It smelled so different, though—vanilla and sweetness and butter. I hardly ate any supper waiting on them. As soon as she pulled the pan out of the oven I was beside her, helping her serve—you know, in case she forgot to get me one first! I stuck my fork into it and was hooked.

"Grandmama, you have GOT to get me this recipe!"

"Well now t'ain't really no recipe, I just make 'em like Mama did. You take you a little bit of biscuit dough and put you a little bit of butter on it and then just sprinkle a little bit of sugar and make you up a sauce and then you bake it."

For five years, I had no idea how to make a butter roll. Every time I asked Grandmama, she'd just make them again for me, but they were always in the oven by the time I showed up at her house. I would say, "Grandmama, you have got to give me that recipe," and off she'd go again into her "t'ain't really no recipe . . ." Just when I had lost hope of getting a recipe for them, Mama found several recipes for butter rolls in a few church cookbooks. We tried them out, and chose the winner (see opposite page)—just like Grandmama's. After making it according to the recipe, I can now understand Grandmama's instructions fully: It really is that simple.

Still wondering just what a butter roll is? Think more in line with cinnamon rolls, only without so much cinnamon and baked in a rich homemade custard sauce.

I have a favor to ask as well, since this is a nearly forgotten recipe of days gone by: Help me bring it back again so it won't be lost to future generations. If you enjoy it, please pass the recipe on. 😊

Old-Fashioned Butter Rolls

One of the things I enjoy doing most on *Southern Plate* is posting those nearly lost recipes of days gone by in hopes of bringing them back from the brink of extinction. This is especially important to me in preserving our food heritage, because our most cherished recipes were never written down, instead being passed verbally from cook to cook with instructions like "you take a little bit of this and a little bit of that."

Well of course, that hardly works nowadays when cooks are thousands of miles apart or perhaps precious Granny has passed on and taken the recipe with her. I don't know if my great-grandmother ever followed a single written recipe in her life. She didn't get to go too far in school, and I know that writing a recipe would have been a difficult task for her. Instead, it was a bit of this and a bit

of that, humming along as she took whatever she had in the pantry and whipped up a little supper.

Some of our most beloved dishes begin with flour. Biscuits, milk gravy, chicken and dumplings, and this recipe: butter rolls. I wish I could say I'd grown up eating butter rolls, but the truth is I had them for the first time about ten years ago—it was worth the wait. *Makes 9 rolls*

Nonstick cooking spray, for coating the baking dish

2 cups self-rising flour (see page 276), plus extra for rolling out the dough

1/2 cup vegetable shortening

2 1/2 cups milk

1/2 cup (1 stick) butter or margarine, at room temperature

1/4 cup plus 2/3 cup granulated sugar

1 teaspoon ground cinnamon

1 teaspoon vanilla extract

1 Preheat the oven to 350°F. Lightly coat an 8 x 8-inch baking dish with cooking spray and set aside.

2 Place the flour in a medium-size bowl and add the shortening, cutting it into the flour with a fork. Add 1/2 cup of the milk and stir until it forms a dough.

177

Laughter

My family loves to laugh. That might seem like an odd statement because I'm sure most folks would say the same thing. In my family, though, we place a very high value on laughter and seek it as often as possible.

For ancestors who had very difficult lives as sharecroppers, laughter was something they learned to cling to. It kept them going, reminded them of joy in the middle of hardship, and ensured the family always had something to look forward to, even if it was wondering what the next punch line would be.

Some of my earliest memories include Mama playing little pranks on us, or my brother and me hiding and jumping out when Mama walked around the corner. Of course, in my family this wasn't a cause for surprise, it was just how our everyday lives worked and how

they still do today. If you bend over, you get goosed. If you say you have a headache, someone will say, "If I had a head like that and it didn't ache, I'd think something was wrong!" and headaches turn into giggles and grins.

A few years back while traveling with my husband and kids, I accidentally dialed Mama's number while putting my cell phone in my coat pocket. Mama could tell what had happened by the rustling sound of my jacket, but rather than hang up, she set aside what she was doing and spent the next thirty minutes shouting out, "Help me! I'm stuck in a jacket!" at random intervals and then giggling as she listened to me ask my husband, "Did you hear that? I keep hearing someone call for help . . ."

When I remember each of my grandparents, I always see them in a fit of joy, laughing. Picturing my mother when I was a girl, I see

---

3 Place the dough on a floured surface and use your hands to shape it into a ball. Roll the ball into a 7 x 10-inch rectangle with a rolling pin. Spread the butter over the dough and sprinkle ¼ cup of the sugar and the cinnamon over the top.

4 Starting with a long edge, roll the dough up like a jelly roll and press the ends together

lightly to seal. Cut into nine 1-inch-thick slices. Place the slices in the prepared dish.

5 Combine the remaining 2 cups milk, the remaining ⅔ cup sugar, the cinnamon, and vanilla in a medium-size saucepan over medium heat and stir constantly until the mixture begins to bubble lightly, 1 to 2 minutes. Pour the sauce over the rolls in the pan.

her face lit up in laughter, just as it so often is now. My dad's laugh still bellows through the house, in much the same way as my husband's. Looking for the next funny moment is a natural habit I've developed over the years—and the next generation of our family is very much the same.

Now that I'm grown, Mama and I have become accomplices in scheming up gags to play on the rest of our family. We've served the family grand birthday cakes that turned out to be meat loaf iced with mashed potatoes, and on several occasions we've packed school lunches with items of only one color, just to see if my kids and nephews would notice and hopefully spark a little unexpected grin in the middle of their day. When my kids visit Grandmama's house, they never know if they're going to be given the special "dribble" glass, which causes a tiny trickle of liquid to spill down the chin of whoever uses it.

I could spend days telling you some of the things we've done to get a laugh out of one another. We all look forward to these moments, wondering what someone is going to do next to elicit that wonderful belly-ache caused by laughing. Sometimes we even spend entire afternoons just sitting around retelling funny moments in the lives of our ancestors that have been passed down and retold as part of our family history. I know for a fact that a sense of humor can be quite the inheritance!

A few weeks ago, my teenage son and I found ourselves sitting on a couch together, our feet up on a large footstool, sharing tales of some of the pranks I've pulled on my husband over the years. With each one we'd laugh and talk over how we could possibly top them if we worked together. As the conversation was winding to a close, Brady looked at me proudly and said, "Mom, you're crazy."

I grinned back at the compliment and said, "Aren't you glad?"

"Yup!" he replied. And we found ourselves laughing together, yet again.

---

6 Bake until the rolls are lightly browned on top, 30 to 40 minutes. Allow to sit for a few minutes as the rolls soak up more sauce. Serve with a spoonful of extra sauce from the pan on top.

Old-Fashioned Butter Rolls are best served hot from the oven but will keep, covered in the refrigerator, for 1 to 2 days. (They reheat nicely in the microwave.)

Shortcut Butter Rolls

As much as I love from-scratch butter rolls, I have to admit that I like this shortcut version even better! They are dumpling-like in texture on the bottom and flaky on the top. Since they come together so quickly, now there is no excuse not to try this old-fashioned favorite. *Makes 10 to 12 rolls*

Nonstick cooking spray, for coating the pan

All-purpose flour, for rolling out the dough

1 can (8 ounces) crescent roll dough

1/4 cup (1/2 stick) butter or margarine, at room temperature

1/3 cup plus 2 tablespoons granulated sugar

1/2 teaspoon ground cinnamon

1 cup whole milk

1 teaspoon vanilla extract

1 Preheat the oven to 350°F. Lightly coat an 8-inch round cake pan with cooking spray.

2 Roll out the dough on a floured surface using a rolling pin. Press the seams together.

3 Spread the butter over the dough, leaving a 1/2-inch border on all sides. Sprinkle with the 2 tablespoons of sugar and the cinnamon. Starting with a long edge, roll the dough like a jelly roll and squeeze lightly with your hands to seal. Cut into 10 to 12 slices and place them in the prepared pan.

4 Place the milk and vanilla in a microwave-safe measuring cup and heat in the microwave until very warm. Stir in the 1/3 cup sugar until dissolved. Pour the mixture over the rolls.

5 Bake until golden brown on top, 30 to 35 minutes. Let sit to cool slightly, 5 to 10 minutes. Serve warm with additional sauce from the pan spooned over the rolls. Enjoy!

Shortcut Butter Rolls are best served hot from the oven but will keep, covered in the refrigerator, for 1 to 2 days. (They reheat nicely in the microwave.)

Momma's Chocolate Butter Rolls

from CAMILLE RITTER WILLIAMS

"This is one of my grand-mother Annette Howard's recipes. It was her moth-er's recipe, and she made it often for her family during the 1940s and '50s. She didn't use a written recipe, she just started pouring this and that until she ended up with the right consistency. My grand-mother (Momma) always did the same thing, until a few years ago when we asked for the recipe and she realized she couldn't give it to us. She carefully measured it out for us so that we could re-create one of our favorite des-serts in our own homes.

"Momma is the oldest of four girls. Growing up, her mother was sick a lot, so she began cooking at an early age. She always helped take care of her younger sisters and was pre-paring full meals by the time she was twelve years old. She has always had a servant's heart. To this day, when she prepares a big meal, she often fixes plates to send to neighbors or oth-ers in the community just to show she cares. She is a wonderful example to all the younger generations who are blessed to spend time with her." *Serves 8 to 10*

Nonstick cooking spray, for coating the baking dish

1½ cups self-rising flour (page 276), plus extra for rolling the dough

½ cup vegetable shortening

2½ cups plus ⅓ cup milk

2 heaping tablespoons unsweetened cocoa powder

1 cup plus 2 heaping tablespoons granulated sugar

½ cup (1 stick) butter, cut into small pats

1 teaspoon vanilla extract

1 Preheat the oven to 350°F. Lightly coat a 9 x 13-inch baking dish with cooking spray.

2 Place the flour in a medium-size mixing bowl. Add the shortening and cut together with a long-tined fork. Add ⅓ cup of the milk and stir until a dough forms.

3 On a floured surface, roll the dough out with a rolling pin into a large rectangle about ¼-inch thick.

4 Stir together the cocoa powder and the 2 heaping tablespoons of sugar in a small bowl. Sprinkle the mixture over the dough and top evenly with the slices of butter.

5 Starting with the long edge, roll the dough into a tight log and cut it crosswise into ¾-inch-thick slices. Place the slices in the prepared baking dish (it's okay if they touch). Set aside.

6 Place the 2½ cups of milk, the remaining 1 cup sugar, and the vanilla in a medium-size saucepan. Stir over medium heat until the sugar is dissolved and the mixture is hot, about 5 minutes. Pour the mixture over the rolls in the baking dish.

7 Bake until the tops of the rolls are golden brown, 30 to 40 minutes. Serve warm.

Momma's Chocolate Butter Rolls will keep, covered in the refrigerator, for up to 3 days. Leftovers can be served cold or reheated in the microwave until warm.

Sweet Potato Dumplings

This is a recipe that Mama shared with me immediately after she got home from an event where the sides and desserts were potluck. To her, they were the best new old-fashioned dessert she had tasted in a long time.

Mama shares: "If you love sweet potatoes as much as I do, you may not want to try this recipe—I almost make myself sick every time I make them because they are so delicious that I can barely stop eating them!"

Mama got this recipe from an older lady at the event, who graciously emailed it to her. Thank you, Ms. Earlean, for the recipe. Our family thanks you, and now the *Southern Plate* family will thank you, too! *Makes 16 dumplings*

½ cup (1 stick) butter
1 large can (16.3 ounces) jumbo flaky layered biscuits (such as Grands! Flaky Layers Original Biscuits)
8 slices frozen sweet potato rounds, thawed (see Note)
Dash of ground cinnamon, nutmeg, or ginger (whichever you like best)
2 cups granulated sugar
2 tablespoons light corn syrup

1 Preheat the oven to 350°F. Place the butter in a 9 x 13-inch baking dish and put the dish in the oven while it preheats. Remove from the oven once the butter is just melted.

2 Divide each biscuit in half by pulling the layers apart. Pat each layer flat with your hands and place on a plate until all of the layers are divided.

heat and allow to simmer until the sugar is completely dissolved, 2 to 3 minutes. Pour the hot syrup around the dumplings.

6 Bake until golden brown, 25 to 35 minutes. Allow to cool slightly before serving (the sauce will thicken as it cools).

Sweet Potato Dumplings will keep, covered in the refrigerator, for up to 3 days. Leftovers can be served cold or reheated in the microwave until warm.

NOTE: If you are not able to find frozen sweet potato rounds, you can substitute canned sweet potatoes and cut them into 1/2-inch-thick slices. Note that sweet potatoes are often labeled "yams" in many grocery stores. If you check the ingredients on "yams," you'll see "sweet potatoes." Sometimes you just go with the crazy.

3 Slice the sweet potato rounds in half (to form semicircles) and sprinkle each with a dash of cinnamon.

4 Place a sweet potato slice on a biscuit half. Fold the biscuit over and seal by gently pressing the edges together with the tines of a fork or your fingers, as you would a fried pie or turnover. Place the biscuits in a single layer in the baking dish with the melted butter.

5 Stir together 2 1/2 cups of water, the sugar, and the corn syrup in a medium-size saucepan over medium-high heat and bring to a boil, stirring occasionally. Reduce the

6

Quick Breads, Muffins, and Breakfast (or Anytime) Treats

THERE IS SOMETHING so sweetly nostalgic about fresh baked breakfast breads, snack cakes, and muffins. I can't recall many times in my life when there wasn't a loaf of banana bread on a platter with a knife resting beside it should anyone want a quick little bite. In a time of mixes and store-bought baked goods, a basket of homemade muffins or a fresh loaf of sweet bread holds a charm that captures the heart and brings us back to simpler times.

Shortcut Amish Friendship Bread

The original recipe for this bread is legendary. It was wildly popular when I was a child and Mama kept the starter carefully nursed in her fridge, dutifully baking loaves of bread each week and passing on the extra starter to a friend so that she, too, could make the delicious, moist, cinnamon-flavored concoction known as Amish friendship bread. I never met a single person who didn't fall in love at first bite.

But goodness, that bread is high maintenance! My version doesn't require a starter or any forethought beyond, "Hey, I think I'll go make some Shortcut Amish Friendship Bread!" but it still has that wonderfully moist flavor that is perfect for an after-school snack or coffee-time treat. It's so simple, you can just make a loaf for a friend rather than saddling them with a starter that they'll have to remember each day. Low-maintenance deliciousness is just another reason to love this version. *Makes two 5 x 9-inch loaves*

Nonstick cooking spray,
   for coating the pans
3 cups self-rising flour
   (see page 276)

2 cups granulated sugar
1 box (5.1 ounces) vanilla instant
   pudding mix
1 tablespoon ground cinnamon
1½ cups buttermilk
   (see page 277) or whole milk
½ cup vegetable oil
½ cup (1 stick) butter, melted and
   cooled slightly
2 large eggs, lightly beaten
1 teaspoon vanilla extract

1 Preheat the oven to 325°F. Lightly coat two 5 x 9-inch loaf pans with cooking spray and set aside.

2 Place the flour, sugar, pudding mix, and cinnamon in a large mixing bowl. Stir together with a wooden spoon until well blended. Add the buttermilk, vegetable oil, butter, eggs, and vanilla, and beat with an electric mixer at medium speed, scraping down the side of the bowl as needed, until smooth and fully blended, about 2 minutes.

3 Divide the batter among the prepared pans. Bake until a toothpick inserted in the center comes out clean, about 1 hour. Allow to cool for 10 minutes in the pan, then turn out onto a wire rack to cool completely.

Shortcut Amish Friendship Bread will keep, in an airtight container or bread bag at room temperature, for up to 4 days.

Mom's Banana Bread

from MARY ALICE DOBBERT

This recipe is from my mom, Mary Anne Christiano. Mom always made this around Easter time when I was a young girl. Mom and Dad had four children and we all really enjoyed Mom's baking, especially her banana bread. Mom is still a wonderful cook. I remember that I would sit in the kitchen and watch my mom cook and bake during my childhood. I think this is where I get my love for baking. I still love to sit and chat and watch her cook.

"Even though I know this recipe by heart, I always take out her recipe card because I love to look at Mom's handwriting. It's just so beautiful to have these old memories from your past on a little recipe card." *Makes one 5 x 10-inch loaf or two 4 x 8-inch loaves*

CHRISTY'S NOTE: Every baker must have a recipe for banana bread in her lineup. This one is a sure keeper. It is delicious served warm slathered with butter and also freezes well. I love to keep some on hand for when company drops over for coffee.

Nonstick cooking spray, for coating the pan
3/4 cup (1 1/2 sticks) butter, at room temperature
1/2 cup brown sugar
1/2 cup granulated sugar
4 bananas, mashed
3 large eggs
1/3 cup milk
1 teaspoon vanilla extract
2 1/2 cups all-purpose flour
1/2 teaspoon salt
1 teaspoon baking powder
1/2 cup chopped walnuts (optional)

1 Preheat the oven to 350°F. Lightly coat a 10 x 5-inch loaf pan (or two 8 x 4-inch loaf pans) with cooking spray and set aside.

2 Cream together the butter and sugars in a large mixing bowl with an electric mixer at medium speed until combined, 1 to 2 minutes. Add the bananas, eggs, milk, and vanilla and blend until smooth. Add the flour, salt, and baking powder to the banana mixture and mix until just incorporated. Stir in the walnuts, if using.

3 Pour the batter into the prepared pan. Bake until the edges are dark brown and there is a nice crack down the center of the bread, or until a toothpick inserted in the center comes out clean, 50 to 60 minutes.

4 Allow to cool on a wire rack for 15 minutes, then remove the loaf from the pan. Return the banana bread to the wire rack and cool completely before slicing.

Mom's Banana Bread will keep, in an airtight container or bread bag at room temperature, for up to 4 days, or wrapped in aluminum foil in the freezer for 3 months.

Amazing Pineapple Bread

This loaf is decadently moist with sweet juicy bits of pineapple and a crispy crust that makes your mouth sing! This is a very dense and heavy bread with a tender crumb. If you are going to give it as a gift, I suggest making four smaller loaves, since they will travel a bit easier. *Makes one 5 x 9-inch loaf or four 3 x 5-inch loaves*

Nonstick cooking spray,
    for coating the pan
1 can (20 ounces) pineapple
    tidbits, drained
1/2 cup vegetable oil
1/4 cup milk
2 large eggs
1 teaspoon vanilla extract
2 cups granulated sugar
2 cups self-rising flour
    (see page 276)
2 teaspoons ground cinnamon

1 Preheat the oven to 350°F. Lightly coat a 5 x 9-inch loaf pan with cooking spray and set aside.

2 Place the pineapple, vegetable oil, milk, eggs, vanilla, and sugar in a large mixing bowl and stir with a large spoon until well blended. Add the flour and cinnamon and stir again until well combined.

3 Spoon the batter into the prepared pan. Bake until a toothpick inserted in the center comes out clean, 1 hour. Allow to cool in the pan for 5 minutes, then turn out onto a wire rack. For best results, allow to cool before cutting.

Amazing Pineapple Bread will keep, in an airtight container or bread bag at room temperature, for up to 3 days.

Oatmeal Banana Bread

This makes the most gorgeous loaf of banana bread you've ever seen, with a lightly golden top that mounds up beautifully with a lovely split right down the center. It looks like it deserves an honored place in a bakery store window. The addition of oats helps make an already moist bread even more so, and their faintly nutty flavor works well with the bananas. For added flavor, I soak my oats overnight before making this bread. Just place them in a mason jar, add water to cover, and place the lid on it. Leave them out on the counter until you're ready to make the bread the next day. This develops a richer flavor in the oats and adds just a hint of yeastiness. I often leave oats out like this for a full twenty-four hours to allow them to start to ferment and then place them in my fridge. Breakfast is ready in a flash since soaked (and fermented) oats don't require as much cooking time as raw oats. When I have them waiting in my fridge and want to make this bread, I just strain out a cup of oats and add them to my recipe! *Makes one 5 x 9-inch loaf*

Nonstick cooking spray,
   for coating the pan
1 cup light brown sugar
3 medium-size ripe bananas
   (the ones with brown spots
   on them are sweetest)
1/2 cup (1 stick) unsalted butter,
   at room temperature
2 large eggs
1/2 cup buttermilk (see page 277)
1 teaspoon vanilla extract
2 1/4 cups self-rising flour
   (see page 276)
1 cup soaked oats (old-fashioned
   or quick-cooking oats), drained
   (see headnote)

Baking in Quantity

*T*he only thing I enjoy more than baking for my family is baking for a small regiment. Here are some things to keep in mind:

Choose the recipe wisely. If you are going to be baking for fifty or even five hundred, layer cakes aren't the way to go. They don't travel well and they require a great deal of fuss when cooking on that scale. Instead, think bar cookies, cupcakes, congealed salads, and desserts that can be prepared in single servings. These will be easier to transport, won't require a dedicated person to serve them, and in many cases won't even require silverware.

Some of my favorite baked goods to take for large crowds are:

Muffins: These can be made days in advance and stored, carefully wrapped, in the freezer until needed.

Bar Cookies: No fussing with scooping out dough onto endless pans!

Sheet Cakes: Stick with ones that don't require refrigeration so you can set them out ahead of time.

If you are going to be serving these types of desserts on a buffet, it's easy to simply place them on a tray, but you can also make them more of a grab-and-go treat by wrapping each serving individually in plastic wrap. Sheet cake slices can be placed on small disposable plates.

When serving a crowd, keep serving sizes slightly smaller than usual, as most people prefer smaller portions of dessert; they can always come back for another bite. This will also help your dish serve more people.

---

1 Preheat the oven to 350°F. Lightly coat a 5 x 9-inch loaf pan with cooking spray and set aside.

2 Place the brown sugar and bananas in a large mixing bowl and beat with an electric mixer at medium speed until the bananas are liquefied, about 1 minute. Add the butter, eggs, buttermilk, and vanilla and mix again until well blended. Add the flour and oats and mix, scraping down the side of the bowl as needed, until smooth and well blended, about 2 minutes.

3 Pour the batter into the prepared pan. Bake until a toothpick inserted in the center comes out clean, 60 to 65 minutes. Allow to cool in the pan for 10 minutes, then turn out onto a wire rack or towel to cool completely.

Oatmeal Banana Bread will keep, in an airtight container or bread bag at room temperature, for up to 5 days.

Strawberry Pecan Bread

I love fruit in just about any shape and form. I actually don't know of any fruit offhand that I don't love, but I do know that strawberries definitely make my top-ten list. This bread is a great way to use strawberries that might be getting a wee bit past their prime, but it is definitely worthy of freshly picked berries as well. It is great just sliced and served, but if you really want to gussy it up a bit, butter each slice and toast it in the oven for a few minutes. Don't forget to call dibs on the first slice! *Makes one 5 x 9-inch loaf*

Vegetable shortening and flour,
   for preparing the pan
1 cup fresh strawberries, hulled,
   washed, and sliced
1 cup plus 2 tablespoons
   granulated sugar
1½ cups self-rising flour
   (see page 276)

½ cup vegetable oil
2 large eggs, beaten
2 teaspoons ground cinnamon
1 cup chopped pecans

1 Preheat the oven to 350°F. Lightly grease and flour a 5 x 9-inch loaf pan and set aside.

2 Place the strawberries in a small bowl and pour the 2 tablespoons of sugar over them. Stir and set aside.

3 Place the flour, the remaining 1 cup of sugar, the vegetable oil, eggs, and cinnamon in a large mixing bowl and mix with a spoon until well combined. Add the pecans and strawberries and mix again until well combined.

4 Pour the batter into the prepared pan. Bake until a toothpick inserted in the center comes out clean, 45 to 50 minutes. Allow to cool in the pan for 10 minutes before removing from the pan to cool completely.

Strawberry Pecan Bread will keep, covered at room temperature, for up to 3 days.

Miss Molcie's Hawaiian Banana Nut Bread

from AMANDA DOBBS

"Molcie Dobbs is a phenomenal woman. As a twenty-two-year-old (mind you, the age I am now), my grandmother moved out of her family home and took a man's job driving a forklift at the Tennessee Coal, Iron, and Railroad Company. She had put in an application every afternoon until she got the job, about which she knew nothing.

"There, she met my grandfather, fell in love, and started our wonderful family. Her Hawaiian Banana Nut Bread is just like her: On the outside it looks like your average old-fashioned favorite, but once you slice it open and experience it, you notice that there is something distinctly different and special about it. Grandmama has been making this bread for about as long as I can remember. She uses this recipe to show her talent and appreciation for numerous people around the community, including the garbage man who would pause his work just to take her garbage can back up to her house for her.

Sunken Centers

If your quick breads and cakes are consistently sunken in the center, try leaving them in the oven just a bit longer. The center of a loaf is the last part to finish baking, so taking it out before the center is fully done will cause it to sink. This can vary by oven but at my house, when a loaf looks done, I usually let it cook another 3 to 4 minutes just to give the center time to set. You can test it by pressing lightly on the center with your finger. If it springs back, the center is done. Or use the trusty toothpick test: The bread or cake is done when a toothpick inserted in the center comes out clean.

"She is known for her bread among our family and acquaintances; however, I know her for much more than that. Grandmama has taught me more about hard work, true love, and the importance of independence than I could have ever asked for. Every time I see banana nut bread, I think of Grandmama and how her special twist makes a very ordinary recipe extraordinary—just like Grandmama makes my very ordinary life that much more extraordinary, simply by being in it." *Makes two 5 x 9-inch loaves*

Turn Quick Breads into Muffins

I often turn quick bread recipes into muffins in order to have more shareable servings! Simply prepare your favorite quick bread recipe as the directions state, but instead of pouring the batter into a loaf pan, pour it in greased or paper-lined muffin cups. Cooking time will be reduced by about half, but you'll still need to check on them after 20 minutes to see if they are done. The recipe for one 5 x 9-inch loaf of quick bread usually yields about 12 muffins. Don't forget, muffins become cupcakes when you ice them! Try some of my favorite frostings in chapter 3. Banana Bread Muffins with Cream Cheese Frosting? Yes, please!

CHRISTY'S NOTE: I love pineapple, coconut, and bananas. Add some pecans and you take the combo over the top. I'm sure this recipe could easily win a blue ribbon. When my mother made some and gave it to a neighbor, she called immediately and wanted the recipe. You will definitely not be disappointed with this delicious bread.

Vegetable shortening and flour,
   for preparing the pans
3 cups all-purpose flour
2 cups granulated sugar
1 teaspoon baking soda
1 teaspoon salt
1 heaping teaspoon ground
   cinnamon
1 cup chopped pecans
1 cup sweetened shredded coconut
3 large eggs, beaten
2 cups mashed bananas
   (5 to 6 bananas)
1½ cups vegetable or canola oil
2 teaspoons vanilla extract
1 to 2 teaspoons coconut extract,
   to taste
1 can (8 ounces) crushed
   pineapple, drained

1 Preheat the oven to 350°F. Lightly grease and flour two 5 x 9-inch loaf pans and set aside.

2 Whisk together the flour, sugar, baking soda, salt, cinnamon, pecans, and the coconut in a large bowl. In a separate large bowl, whisk together the eggs, bananas, oil, vanilla, coconut extract, and crushed pineapple.

3 Add the wet mixture to the dry mixture and stir with a rubber spatula until just moistened.

4 Pour the batter evenly into the prepared pans. Bake until a toothpick inserted in the center comes out clean, 1 hour and 15 minutes. Cool the pans on a wire rack for 10 minutes. Remove the breads from the pans and allow to cool completely.

Hawaiian Banana Nut Bread will keep, in an airtight container or bread bag at room temperature, for up to 4 days, or in an airtight container in the freezer for up to 3 months.

Amazing Apple Bread

My family has always loved quick breads. They make a delicious snack, simple dessert, or great quick bite for breakfast as you head out the door. This bread greets your family with a heavenly aroma. It bakes up moist and tender, studded with juicy bits of apple, with a decadent soft-crisp crust on top. It's great on its own or spread with a smear of butter or apple butter.

Feel free to use any kind of apple you want, even apples that are going a little soft. In the interest of being neighborly, I like to double this so I have one loaf to keep and one to give away as a nice surprise to someone who would enjoy a little pick-me-up. *Makes one 5 x 9-inch loaf*

Nonstick cooking spray,
    for coating the pan
3 to 4 medium-size apples, peeled
    and diced (about 2 cups)
1/4 cup milk
2 large eggs, lightly beaten
1/2 cup vegetable oil
1 teaspoon vanilla extract
2 cups granulated sugar
2 cups self-rising flour
    (see page 276)
2 teaspoons ground cinnamon
1/2 teaspoon ground allspice

1 Preheat the oven to 350°F. Lightly coat a 5 x 9-inch loaf pan with cooking spray and set aside.

2 Place the apples in a large mixing bowl. Add the milk, eggs, oil, vanilla, and sugar and stir with a large spoon until well blended.

Add the flour, cinnamon, and allspice and stir again until well combined.

3 Spoon the batter into the prepared pan. Bake until a toothpick inserted in the center comes out clean, about 1 hour. Allow to cool in the pan for 5 minutes, then turn out onto a wire rack. For best results, allow to cool completely before cutting.

Amazing Apple Bread will keep, in an airtight container or bread bag at room temperature, for up to 3 days.

Super Easy King Cake

King cake is a classic Mardi Gras favorite that is fun to make at home. This ring-shaped treat is a cross between a bread and a cream cheese-filled cinnamon roll, without too much sweetness to it. Instead of reserving this for Mardi Gras season, I make it whenever the mood strikes and just switch up the sprinkles. *Serves 8 to 10*

Nonstick cooking spray, for coating the baking sheet

1 loaf (1 pound) frozen bread dough, thawed
All-purpose flour, for rolling out the dough
1 package (8 ounces) cream cheese, at room temperature
2 1/2 cups confectioners' sugar
1 teaspoon lemon extract
3 tablespoons milk, plus extra as needed
1 teaspoon butter flavoring or vanilla extract
Colored sprinkles, for garnish (optional, see Note)

1 Lightly coat a baking sheet with cooking spray and set aside.

2 Place the bread dough on a floured surface and roll it out to a 10 x 18-inch rectangle with a rolling pin. To make this easier, partially roll out the dough, allow it to rest for 5 minutes, then roll it out the rest of the way.

3 Combine the cream cheese, 1 cup of the confectioners' sugar, and the lemon extract in a medium-size mixing bowl and beat with an electric mixer at medium speed until creamy and well blended, 1 to 2 minutes.

4 Spread the cream cheese mixture over the dough, leaving a 1-inch border around the edges. Starting with a long edge, roll the dough up into a log about 17 inches long and 1/2 inch thick. Brush the open edge with water and press it into the log, then gently squeeze the log together with your hands to seal it.

5 Form the log into a ring, pressing the short ends into each other and brushing with water, if needed, to seal together. Place the dough on the prepared baking sheet and spray the top of the dough lightly with cooking spray. Cover with plastic wrap and set in a warm, draft-free place to rise for 45 minutes to 1 hour. (I have found that the top of my dryer is a great place to let the dough rise, especially if I have a load of laundry drying.)

6 Preheat the oven to 350°F.

7 Remove the plastic wrap and bake the ring until golden brown, 30 to 35 minutes. Allow to cool.

8 Stir together the remaining 1½ cups confectioners' sugar, the milk, and the butter flavoring in a small bowl until smooth. Drizzle over the top of the cake with a spoon. Immediately sprinkle with colored sprinkles, if desired. Allow to sit until the glaze hardens.

Super Easy King Cake will keep, covered at room temperature, for up to 3 days.

NOTE: Traditional king cake sprinkles are purple, yellow, and green. I rarely come across purple sprinkles, so I use whatever colors my kids want and we enjoy our cake just the same!

Bake Shop Blueberry Muffins

This recipe yields beautiful, light, and fluffy muffins with a wonderful crunchy topping. Feel free to substitute other berries for the blueberries. These are excellent for the office or teacher treats because they taste as good as they look! *Makes 15 muffins*

Nonstick cooking spray, for coating
   the muffin tins (optional)
2 cups self-rising flour
   (see page 276)
1 cup granulated sugar
¾ cup buttermilk (see page 277)
½ cup vegetable oil
1 large egg, lightly beaten
1 cup blueberries
½ cup all-purpose flour
¼ cup light brown sugar
¼ cup old-fashioned or quick-
   cooking oats
¼ cup (½ stick) cold butter
1 teaspoon ground cinnamon

1 Preheat the oven to 350°F. Lightly coat 15 muffin cups (you'll have to use 2 tins) with cooking spray or line them with muffin papers and set aside.

Bake Shop Blueberry Muffins

2 Place the self-rising flour, granulated sugar, buttermilk, vegetable oil, and egg in a large mixing bowl and stir together with a wooden spoon until well blended. Fold in the blueberries. Divide the batter evenly among the muffin cups.

3 Place the all-purpose flour, brown sugar, oats, butter, and cinnamon in a medium-size bowl. Cut together with a long-tined fork or pastry cutter until well mixed and crumbly. Sprinkle a little of the topping over each muffin.

4 Bake until lightly browned, 25 to 30 minutes. Allow to cool slightly, then remove from the muffin tins.

Bake Shop Blueberry Muffins will keep, in an airtight container at room temperature, for up to 3 days.

Apple Oat Muffins

Another keeper from my sister-in-law, Tina. What could be better on a cold winter morning than a muffin made with apples and oats? I especially like them when prepared with buttermilk as I find it gives them just a little more of a rich tang. These muffins make a delicious hearty breakfast and are perfect with a cold glass of milk. *Makes 12 muffins*

For the muffins
Nonstick cooking spray, for coating
   the muffin tin (optional)
1¼ cups self-rising flour
   (see page 276)
¾ cup quick-cooking oats
½ cup packed light brown sugar
1 teaspoon ground cinnamon
1 large egg
½ cup whole milk or buttermilk
   (see page 277)
¼ cup vegetable oil
2 tablespoons lemon juice
1 cup finely chopped, peeled apple
½ cup chopped nuts (optional)

For the glaze (optional)
2 tablespoons butter, melted
1 tablespoon lemon juice
½ cup confectioners' sugar

1 Preheat the oven to 400°F. Lightly coat a 12-cup muffin tin with cooking spray or line the cups with muffin papers and set aside.

2 For the muffins: Stir together the flour, oats, brown sugar, and cinnamon in a large bowl with a spoon. Set aside.

When You Need a Song, Start Singing

Often, I wake up to the sound of birds chirping in the dark. I love that they sound just as happy in darkness as they do in the sunshine. When we realize that joy and happiness come from a spring inside us that's not dependent on outward circumstance, droughts and darkness from this world of ours can't dry it up.

So those birds just start singing when they want to—and eventually the sun will rise to the song. I think I'll join them.

3 Beat the egg, milk, vegetable oil, and lemon juice in a medium-size bowl with a wooden spoon. Stir in the apples and nuts, if using. Dump the apple mixture into the flour mixture and stir until just moistened and no dry spots remain.

4 Spoon the batter into the muffin cups and bake until golden and a toothpick inserted in the center comes out clean, 20 minutes. Remove to a wire rack to cool.

5 If you wish to make the glaze: Stir together the butter, lemon juice, and confectioners' sugar in a small bowl with a spoon until smooth. Once the muffins are cool, drizzle a bit of the glaze on top of each muffin and spread with the back of a spoon.

Apple Oat Muffins will keep, in an airtight container at room temperature, for up to 3 days.

Dried Apricot Muffins

With golden nuggets of deliciousness in every bite, these muffins are great to have on the weekends when you just want to sit and relax before starting the day or for brunch with an omelet or fruit salad. I have made them the day before and reheated them in the microwave and they are just like fresh from the oven. Don't be surprised if the dough doesn't look like normal muffin batter—it is much thicker but turns out wonderful results. These muffins would be equally good with dried peaches. If you are a muffin lover like me, please give them a try. You won't be disappointed. *Makes 12 muffins*

Nonstick baking spray, for coating the muffin tin (optional)
1 cup boiling water
1 cup chopped dried apricots
1 cup granulated sugar
1/2 cup (1 stick) butter or margarine
1 cup sour cream
2 cups all-purpose flour
1 teaspoon baking soda
1/2 teaspoon salt

1 Preheat the oven to 400°F. Lightly coat a 12-cup muffin tin with cooking spray or line the cups with muffin papers and set aside.

2 Place the boiling water in a small heatproof bowl and add the dried apricots. Allow them to soak for 5 minutes.

3 Cream together the sugar and butter in a large mixing bowl with an electric mixer at medium speed until fluffy, 1 to 2 minutes. Add the sour cream and mix well.

4 Stir together the flour, baking soda, and salt in a small bowl. Add the flour mixture to the butter mixture and beat again with an electric mixer at medium speed, scraping down the side of the bowl as needed, until fully combined, about 1 minute.

5 Drain the apricots, pat them dry with a paper towel, and stir them into the batter with a wooden spoon.

6 Divide the batter evenly among the muffin cups. Bake until a toothpick inserted in the center comes out clean, 15 to 20 minutes. Remove to a wire rack to cool.

Dried Apricot Muffins will keep, in an airtight container at room temperature, for up to 5 days.

Hot Cocoa Muffins

These intense chocolate muffins are speckled with marshmallows and look just like a muffin version of hot cocoa. The taste is enough to win over any chocolate lover with the first bite. *Makes 12 muffins*

Nonstick cooking spray, for coating
   the muffin tin (optional)
1½ cups self-rising flour
   (see page 276)
½ cup dark brown sugar
½ cup unsweetened cocoa powder
½ cup (1 stick) butter, melted
   and cooled
1 cup milk
2 large eggs, lightly beaten
1 cup mini marshmallows

1 Preheat the oven to 350°F. Lightly coat a 12-cup muffin tin with cooking spray or line the cups with muffin papers and set aside.

2 Stir together the flour, brown sugar, and cocoa powder in a medium-size mixing bowl. Add the butter, milk, and eggs and stir until just blended, being careful not to overstir (the batter will be lumpy and that is okay). Fold in the marshmallows.

3 Divide the batter evenly among the muffin cups, stirring as you do, since the marshmallows tend to float to the top. Bake until a toothpick inserted in the center comes out clean, 20 to 25 minutes. Serve warm.

Hot Cocoa Muffins are best served the day they are made.

Double Chocolate Chip Muffins

I f you've been flipping through this book, have looked at my website, or have read any of my other books, you've probably picked up on the fact that my daughter is a chocolate lover. The darker the better. In fact, when she wasn't even old enough to walk yet she would crawl over to me, pull herself up to standing by grabbing hold of my leg, look up at me, and say, "I need chocwat." That was her first full sentence! So of course you know why I developed these deep chocolate muffins. Katy gives them her resounding stamp of approval! *Makes about 12 muffins*

Nonstick cooking spray,
   for coating the muffin tin
2 cups self-rising flour
   (see page 276)
1 cup granulated sugar
¾ cup unsweetened cocoa powder
½ cup (1 stick) butter, melted
   and cooled
1 large egg
1 cup milk
1 teaspoon vanilla extract
1½ cups chocolate chips
   (I use semisweet)

1 Preheat the oven to 400°F. Lightly coat a 12-cup muffin tin with cooking spray or line the cups with muffin papers and set aside.

2 Combine the flour, sugar, and cocoa powder in a large bowl and stir together with a spoon until well blended. In a separate small bowl, beat together the butter, egg, milk, and vanilla with an electric mixer at medium speed until well mixed, about 1 minute.

3 Pour the butter mixture into the flour mixture and stir with a wooden spoon to mix well. Stir in the chocolate chips.

4 Divide the batter evenly among the muffin cups. Bake until a toothpick inserted in the center comes out clean, 20 minutes. Remove to a wire rack to cool.

Double Chocolate Chip Muffins are best served the day they are made.

Anytime, Any Kind Oatmeal Muffins

This is one of the most versatile muffin recipes I make, with countless flavor variations. I mix up a batch of batter and keep it in the refrigerator for up to 1 month, then make however many muffins I need, be it one or five dozen. Even better is that it calls for ingredients you most likely already have on hand and is a pretty healthy muffin overall. No matter what you add, the muffin is moist, tender, and delicious. And the freshly baked muffins freeze well, too! *Makes about 60 muffins*

To make the batter
6 cups old-fashioned oats
2 cups very hot tap water
5 cups all-purpose flour
5 teaspoons baking soda
2 teaspoons ground cinnamon
2 teaspoons salt
2 cups granulated sugar
4 large eggs
4 cups buttermilk (see page 277)
1 cup vegetable shortening, melted
   (or melted butter)

To bake the muffins
Nonstick cooking spray, for coating
   the muffin tins
Optional mix-ins: fresh
   blueberries; chocolate chips;
   sliced almonds; chopped
   walnuts; chopped pecans;
   diced apples; dried cranberries,
   cherries, or other dried fruit;
   chopped banana

1 Place 2 cups of the oats and the hot water in a medium-size bowl. Stir and set aside.

2 Place the remaining 4 cups of the oats, the flour, baking soda, cinnamon, salt, and sugar in a large bowl and stir to combine. Form a well in the center and crack the eggs into it; beat them lightly with a spoon. Add the buttermilk and stir the batter with a large spoon until well combined.

3 Pour the melted shortening into the hot oats mixture and stir to incorporate. Pour the hot oats mixture into the batter and stir again until well combined. Cover and refrigerate at least overnight or up to one month.

4 When you're ready to bake the muffins, preheat the oven to 400°F. Lightly coat the cups of a muffin tin with cooking spray—coat as many cups as muffins you plan to make.

5 Remove the batter from the refrigerator and stir gently, then measure the amount you need into a large bowl (¼ cup batter will make 1 muffin; 1 cup of batter will make 4). Add any mix-ins, if desired: about 2 tablespoons mix-ins for ¼ cup batter, or ½ cup mix-ins for every 1 cup. Stir until just incorporated, and transfer the batter to the prepared muffin cups.

6 Bake until lightly browned and a toothpick inserted in the center comes out clean, about 20 minutes. Remove to a wire rack to cool.

What Choice Are We Going to Make Today?

Ever look at folks who seem to always be smiling and think, "Well, they must have an easier life than I do"? That's just not the case. I don't know a single human being who has made it to adulthood without their share of hard times, so don't discount happy or optimistic people as folks who just have it easy. Each of us has a choice to make when we wake up every morning. If you see someone smiling and making the best of their life, you know what choice they made! What is yours gonna be today? P.S. The "morning" part was given to us free of charge. It's up to us to put the "good" in it!

Anytime, Any Kind Oatmeal Muffin batter will keep, in an airtight container in the refrigerator, for up to 1 month. Baked muffins will keep, in a zip-top bag in the freezer, for up to 3 months.

Delectably Moist Bran Muffins

This is my incredibly versatile bran muffin recipe. These muffins can be made plain, or with your favorite mix-ins. They can be made only slightly sweet for a dinner bread or muffin-sweet for breakfast.

This is just a good basic bran muffin recipe, so feel free to make them exactly as I do or take them in your own direction! *Makes 12 muffins*

Nonstick cooking spray,
    for coating the muffin tin
1 1/2 cups wheat bran (see Notes)
1 cup buttermilk (see page 277)
1 large egg
1/2 cup vegetable oil or 1/2 cup
    (1 stick) butter, melted
    and cooled
3/4 cup brown sugar (dark or light)
    (see Notes)

1 teaspoon vanilla extract
1 cup self-rising flour
    (see page 276)
1/2 cup dried cranberries, dried
    blueberries, or other dried fruit
1 cup chopped almonds, pecans,
    walnuts, or other nuts (optional)

1 Preheat the oven to 375°F. Lightly coat a 12-cup muffin tin with cooking spray or line the cups with muffin papers and set aside.

2 Stir together the wheat bran and buttermilk in a large mixing bowl with a spoon. Add the egg, vegetable oil, brown sugar, and vanilla. Stir well to combine.

3 Add the flour, cranberries, and nuts, if using, and stir well until completely moist.

4 Divide the batter among the muffin cups. Bake until golden and a toothpick inserted in the center comes out clean, about 20 minutes.

Delectably Moist Bran Muffins will keep, in an airtight container at room temperature, for up to 5 days, or in the freezer for up to 3 months.

NOTES: Wheat bran is usually available in the health foods section at grocery stores.

If you prefer sweeter muffins, use 1 cup brown sugar.

Baked Peach Oatmeal Pudding

If you love peach crisp and old-fashioned baked rice pudding, this is a blend of those flavors. Technically it is a breakfast, but it is so very good and just lightly sweet enough that it could also be a dessert at the end of a soothing meal. It has a custardy texture and taste, with warm peaches and a hint of brown sugar to keep you coming back for just one more bite. *Serves 6 to 8*

Nonstick cooking spray,
   for coating the baking dish
2 cups old-fashioned oats
2 teaspoons baking powder
1/4 teaspoon baking soda
1 teaspoon ground cinnamon
1/2 teaspoon salt
1/2 cup brown sugar (dark or light)
1 1/2 cups milk
1/2 cup (1 stick) butter or
   margarine, melted
1 teaspoon vanilla extract
2 large eggs
1 can (29 ounces) sliced peaches,
   drained
Heavy (whipping) cream or ice
   cream, for serving (optional)

1 Preheat the oven to 350°F. Lightly coat an 8 x 8-inch baking dish with cooking spray and set aside.

2 Stir together the oats, baking powder, baking soda, cinnamon, salt, and brown sugar in a large mixing bowl. In a separate medium-size bowl, whisk together the milk, melted butter, vanilla, and eggs. Pour the milk mixture into the oats mixture and stir until well mixed. Stir in the peaches.

3 Pour the batter into the prepared dish and bake until set and lightly browned on top, 45 to 50 minutes.

4 Serve warm by itself or with a drizzle of fresh cream or a scoop of ice cream. It is delicious on its own, though. You could make this for breakfast and then heat up the leftovers and serve with ice cream at suppertime!

Baked Peach Oatmeal Pudding is best served warm but will keep, covered in the refrigerator, for up to 2 days.

Overnight Stuffed French Toast with Strawberry Syrup

This is great for company or for those mornings when you just want to make your family feel extra special! It mixes up easily the night before and just has to be popped in the oven to cook the next morning. A simple strawberry syrup is the perfect complement. *Serves 6*

Nonstick cooking spray,
  for coating the baking dish
1 package (8 ounces) cream cheese,
  at room temperature
1 jar (10 ounces) strawberry
  preserves (regular or sugar-free)
1 deli loaf French bread
4 large eggs
1 cup milk
1 teaspoon vanilla extract

1 Lightly coat a 9 x 13-inch baking dish with cooking spray and set aside.

2 Place the cream cheese and 3 tablespoons of the strawberry preserves in a medium-size mixing bowl and beat with an electric mixer at medium speed until well combined and creamy, 1 to 2 minutes. Set aside.

3 Cut the French bread into six 1½- to 2-inch-thick slices. Reserve the end pieces for another use. Cut a pocket into the side of each slice with a bread knife, being careful not to go all the way to the bottom. Stuff each pocket with the cream cheese mixture. Arrange the slices flat in the prepared dish.

4 Beat together the eggs, milk, and vanilla in a medium-size bowl with a whisk until well blended. Pour over the bread slices in the baking dish. Cover and refrigerate for several hours or overnight.

5 Preheat the oven to 350°F. Uncover and bake until golden brown, 30 to 40 minutes.

6 Meanwhile, place 1 cup of the strawberry preserves in a microwave-safe bowl. Microwave at 30-second intervals, stirring between each, until melted and of a pourable consistency. Drizzle over the French toast and serve.

Overnight Stuffed French Toast will keep, covered in the refrigerator, for up to 1 day. (It reheats nicely in the microwave.)

Overnight Stuffed French Toast with Strawberry Syrup, page 205

Sopaipillas

I've been to some great Mexican restaurants in my time, and one of my favorite things to order are warm sopaipillas drizzled with honey. Our dear friends the Maestas family are from New Mexico, and this recipe came from their mother. So simple, yet so delicious! *Makes 12 sopaipillas*

2 1/2 cups all-purpose flour,
   plus extra for rolling out
   the dough
1 teaspoon salt
1 teaspoon baking powder
1 cup granulated sugar
2 tablespoons ground cinnamon
3 tablespoons vegetable oil,
   plus extra for frying
3/4 cup warm water
Honey, for serving

1 Stir together the flour, salt, and baking powder in a large bowl until just blended. In a separate small bowl, stir together the sugar and cinnamon and set aside.

2 Add the vegetable oil and warm water to the flour mixture and stir until a sticky dough forms.

3 Lightly flour a work surface and your hands. Place the dough on the work surface and roll it into a ball, kneading just enough to help it stay together.

4 Pinch off golf ball-size portions of the dough and roll them into balls. Return the balls to the mixing bowl and cover with a towel. Allow to rest for 5 minutes.

5 While the dough balls are resting, fill a medium-size skillet with vegetable oil to a depth of 1 inch. Place over medium-high heat to preheat while you prepare the dough. Line a plate with paper towels and place it next to the stove.

6 Take each ball, one at a time, and roll it out on a floured surface with a rolling pin into an oval about 2 inches wide and 4 inches long. Repeat until all of the dough balls are flattened.

7 Sprinkle a little flour into the hot oil. If it sizzles, the oil is ready. Once the flour sizzles, reduce the heat to medium. Carefully place 2 to 3 sopaipillas at a time into the oil and cook until browned on one side, about 2 minutes. Turn with tongs and brown the other side, about 2 minutes more. Remove the sopaipillas from the oil and place them on the lined plate to drain.

8 While still hot, dip both sides of each sopaipilla into the cinnamon sugar mixture. Repeat the cooking and dipping processes until all of the sopaipillas are done.

9 Serve with a drizzle of honey or with honey on the side for dipping.

Sopaipillas are best served the day they are made.

Funnel Cakes

If you've ever had a funnel cake at a festival or fair, you know the simple crispy deliciousness that is this iconic fried bread. The surprise comes when you realize how easy they are to make at home! They are actually less of a mess to make at home because you don't have the coating of confectioners' sugar on your clothes that you get when eating them in the outdoor breeze. My kids think it's so cool that their mama can make these—and I'll take cool points wherever I can get them. *Makes 4 or 5 funnel cakes*

Corn oil, for frying (see Note)
2 large eggs
2 tablespoons granulated sugar
1 cup milk
2 cups all-purpose flour
1 teaspoon baking powder
1/2 teaspoon salt
1 cup confectioners' sugar,
    for garnish

1 Pour the corn oil in a large, heavy-bottomed skillet to a depth of at least 1 inch. Place over medium-high heat to preheat.

2 Meanwhile, place the eggs, granulated sugar, milk, flour, baking powder, and salt in a large mixing bowl and beat with an electric mixer at medium speed, scraping down the side of the bowl as needed, until well blended and smooth, 1 to 2 minutes.

3 Test the oil by dropping a tiny sprinkling of flour into it. If the flour sizzles, the oil is hot enough. Once it's hot enough, turn the temperature down to medium. Line a plate with paper towels and place it next to the stove.

4 Hold your finger over the opening in the bottom of a funnel and add 1/2 cup of the batter. Hold the funnel over the hot oil and remove your finger, moving the funnel in a swirling pattern and crisscrossing the batter multiple times in order to connect the cake. Continue until the funnel is empty.

5 Cook until lightly browned on the bottom, about 2 minutes. Use tongs to carefully flip the cake over and cook the other side, 2 minutes more. Remove the cake from the oil and place it on the lined plate. Repeat the process until all of the batter is used.

6 Sprinkle the top of the cakes with the confectioners' sugar and enjoy immediately.

NOTE: Vegetable oil can be used to fry these, but I find they have better flavor if fried in corn oil.

Pineapple Fritters

Fruit fritters are one of those fun little treats that you can serve as an appetizer, a breakfast, a side, or just an anytime treat. These golden brown beauties are pretty on their own, or you can dust them with a light coating of confectioners' sugar if you like. For an extra-special touch, serve alongside pineapple preserves or honey, for dipping. *Makes about 24 small fritters*

Vegetable oil, for frying
2 cups self-rising flour
    (see page 276)

½ cup brown sugar (light or dark)
1 teaspoon ground cinnamon
1 cup milk
3 tablespoons melted butter
2 large eggs, lightly beaten
1 can (16 ounces) pineapple tidbits,
    drained
Confectioners' sugar, for garnish
    (optional)
Melted butter, honey, or warmed
    pineapple preserves, for serving

1 Pour the vegetable oil in a medium-size skillet to a depth of 1 inch. Place over medium-high heat to preheat the oil to 350°F while you prepare the batter.

2 Stir together the flour, brown sugar, and cinnamon in a large mixing bowl with a fork. Add the milk, butter, and eggs and stir together with a spoon until well combined. Stir in the pineapple tidbits.

3 Line a plate with paper towels and place it next to the stove. Reduce the heat to medium. Working in batches to avoid crowding the skillet, drop the batter by ⅛ cupfuls into the hot oil and brown on one side, about 2 minutes. Turn with tongs and brown the other side, about 2 minutes more. As the fritters cook, remove them to the lined plate to drain.

4 Dust the fritters with confectioners' sugar, if desired. Serve with melted butter, honey, or warmed pineapple preserves.

Pineapple Fritters are best served soon after they are made.

Feather-Light Chocolate Biscuits

This recipe comes to you courtesy of my sweet little Katy. Chocolate biscuits are one of her favorite treats.

As far back as I can remember and as far back as our family stories go, biscuits have been a staple on our tables. There are as many ways to make them as there are cotton plants in a field, and all of them are wonderful. The great thing is that these recipes have been handed down from one generation to the next, and at some point we've each taken our turn standing in the kitchen while the craft was explained and demonstrated before we stepped in and began making them on our own.

This recipe sprang up out of Katy's love for chocolate, so it isn't a generations-old recipe, but it will become one as soon as Katy Rose starts making them herself. Right now she's beside me, helping with each step along the way. Sometimes I just stand over her shoulder and talk her through it. Soon enough, I'll be off doing something else while Miss Katy works kitchen magic all on her own. And that is what it is all about: cooking up memories together while teaching our kids to cook on their own. Next time you head into the kitchen, take the hand of someone dear to you and invite them along. *Makes about 12 biscuits*

Nonstick cooking spray,
    for coating the baking sheet
2¼ cups self-rising flour
    (see page 276), plus extra
    for rolling out the dough
½ cup (1 stick) cold butter,
    cut into slices
½ cup granulated sugar
1 cup semisweet chocolate chips
1 cup plus 1 tablespoon whole milk,
    plus extra as needed
1 cup confectioners' sugar
1 teaspoon vanilla extract or butter
    flavoring

1 Preheat the oven to 450°F. Lightly coat a baking sheet with cooking spray and set aside.

2 Place the flour and cold butter in a large bowl. Cut the butter into the flour with a fork or pastry cutter until fully incorporated and the mixture resembles lumpy flour. Place the bowl in the refrigerator for 10 minutes.

Feather-Light Chocolate Biscuits

3 Stir the granulated sugar and chocolate chips into the flour mixture until well blended. Add the 1 cup of milk and stir until just moistened (add up to ¼ cup more milk if needed).

4 Turn the dough out onto a lightly floured surface. Dip the palms of your hands in flour and pat the dough into a ½-inch-thick rectangle. Gently fold the right side over onto the middle of the rectangle. Fold the left side over on top of the folded right side, like you are folding a piece of paper to put into an envelope.

5 Pat this out again into a rectangle and repeat the folding process once more, being careful not to roll the dough too thin. It needs to be at least ½-inch thick. This procedure will result in the biscuits being light and layered. Dip the rim of a roughly 2-inch glass or biscuit cutter into flour and use it to cut out the biscuits. Place the biscuits on the prepared baking sheet with their sides touching.

6 Bake until lightly golden on top, 14 to 16 minutes.

7 Meanwhile, prepare the glaze: Stir together the confectioners' sugar, vanilla, and the remaining 1 tablespoon milk in a small bowl until smooth. Brush the glaze over the tops of the warm biscuits while they're still on the baking sheet. Allow to cool for a few minutes before serving.

Feather-Light Chocolate Biscuits are best served the day they are made.

Cherry Rolls

from **VICKI PERFETTI**

"**T**his recipe comes from my maternal grandmother, Velma Blackwell. She was the youngest of nine, and her mother died very young. Her father ran a boarding house, and since she was the youngest, most of her siblings had already left home. So, at the age of eleven, she became the boarding-house cook.

"This is one of my favorite dishes of hers, and I still consider it a real treat when my mom makes these rolls for special occasions. I was only twelve when my grandmother passed away in 1976. She was such a special

CHRISTY'S NOTE: I halved this recipe and used an 8 x 8-inch pan and it came out wonderful. I heated up and ate the rolls for several days all on my own—in the name of research, of course! This is a recipe my family will enjoy for years to come. In fact, my mother has made these once a week since we got this recipe!

person to me and is still the best cook I've ever known." *Serves 12*

Nonstick cooking spray,
   for coating the baking dish
2½ cups granulated sugar
1½ cups plus 1 tablespoon
   all-purpose flour, plus extra
   for rolling out the dough
2 cans (14½ ounces each) tart
   red cherries, drained and juice
   reserved
2 tablespoons butter
2¼ teaspoons baking powder
½ teaspoon salt
2 tablespoons vegetable
   shortening
¾ cup milk

1 Preheat the oven to 350°F. Lightly coat a 9 x 13-inch baking dish with cooking spray.

2 Stir together 1 cup of the sugar and the 1 tablespoon of flour in a medium-size saucepan. Add 2 cups of the cherry juice (supplement with water if you don't have quite 2 cups) and bring to a boil over medium-high heat. Once it reaches a boil, boil for 1 minute and remove from the heat. Stir in the butter and set aside.

3 Sift the remaining 1½ cups flour with the baking powder and salt in a medium-size bowl. Add the shortening and cut together with a long-tined fork or pastry cutter. Stir in the milk and mix with a spoon until a dough forms.

4 Turn out the dough onto a floured board and knead lightly for a few seconds. Roll the dough into a ¼-inch-thick rectangle with a rolling pin. Spread the cherries on top. Sprinkle with ½ cup of the remaining sugar. Starting with a long edge, roll up the dough like a jelly roll and press the edges together to seal.

5 Cut into 1½-inch slices and place cut side down in the prepared baking dish. Pour the cherry juice mixture on top. Sprinkle with the remaining 1 cup sugar.

6 Bake until lightly golden, 25 to 30 minutes. Serve warm.

Cherry Rolls are best served the day they are made.

Almost Famous Orange Rolls

This recipe makes a small and dainty orange roll. My home state of Alabama has a few places that are known for their orange rolls. Surprisingly, I've never been to

Paradise Doesn't Have to Mean Perfect

I'm good at a few things—but housekeeping isn't one of them. I believe we all have different God-given talents. Combined with those are certain obstacles and challenges that we must overcome at the same time. Keeps life interesting.

For me, one of those obstacles is housework. Sure, I'm busy. I use that as an excuse most times. Truth is, with all of the thoughts whizzing around in my head like a box of mismatched fireworks, my brain doesn't see the mess and clutter in my house. But regardless of the multiple reasons, it still comes down to the fact that although my home has been in magazines, it requires two weeks of deep cleaning to be even remotely presentable.

But I still try, and I'm always working on it. Recently, we spent a great deal of time organizing, finding homes for objects that have never had a home beyond being close at hand, and donating things my kids have outgrown. We made huge headway and that felt good.

But something happened last week that really put all of that in perspective for me. My daughter had a friend she wanted to spend some time with, so I picked her up and took them to Katy's favorite restaurant.

When we have these "dates" with her friends, I'm kinda the gray man. I am there, but I'm not. They talk and play and go about their visit as if I'm invisible. Kinda like the chauffeur. The parents reading this know what I'm talking

any of those restaurants! Given the chance to go out to eat or stay home, I generally choose to stay in whenever possible. It's not that I'm a homebody, it's just that I realize how blessed I am to have my home and everyone in it, and I need a few lifetimes in order to enjoy it fully.

Here is my simple take on orange rolls, and I hope you get to try them soon because

they are surprisingly low-fuss and supremely divine! *Makes 24 rolls*

about. I enjoy this because I pretend to be lost in my thoughts while I'm really just listening in and enjoying their excited conversation. Although sometimes I do find my thoughts drifting, only to be called back by something particularly funny or heartwarming.

And so, as I was sitting there looking out the window, Katy's voice called me back. "You have GOT to come to my house soon. You are going to LOVE IT. My house is a complete paradise!"

I did a double blink and looked at her in surprise. Her face was animated and lit up with glee as she smiled with excitement. I was completely taken aback.

Paradise? But the sink is full of dirty dishes. There is Mount Laundry in our living room, and I can't remember the last time someone actually put the toilet paper on the holder. *Paradise?* I looked down in confusion as I recalled that new pink chair Katy picked out for a reading corner in her room. How excited she was to have a birthday party in our house to show off the diner furniture we'd bought, and that big pot of chicken and dumplings she'd fawned over the night before.

I thought of her cuddling up against her dad on the couch as they read books and that big basket she uses to tote her sweet cat around . . . the third- (or fourth-) hand piano I bought her off Craigslist for a hundred dollars that she decorated with a collection of My Little Ponies and pounds away on throughout the week. I thought of that big old pile of shoes in the den that seems to grow daily as everyone comes in and gets comfy—bare feet on their own turf.

Come to think of it, I can't begin to count the hugs, kisses, "I love you"s, and laughter that have taken place in the five years we have lived here. The walls must be nigh on bursting with it at this point. But Paradise? You bet. Mount Laundry and all.

Nonstick cooking spray,
    for coating the muffin tins
1 loaf (1 pound) frozen bread
    dough, completely thawed
All-purpose flour, for rolling
    out the dough
1/2 cup (1 stick) butter,
    at room temperature
1 tablespoon grated orange zest

3 tablespoons orange juice
    concentrate (1 tablespoon
    thawed and 2 tablespoons
    frozen)
2 to 3 tablespoons granulated
    sugar
1/2 cup confectioners' sugar

1 Lightly coat 2 mini muffin tins with cooking spray and set aside.

2 Place the bread dough on a floured surface and roll it out to about a 17 x 6-inch rectangle. It's easier to roll the dough out part way, let it rest for 5 minutes, then finish rolling it out.

3 Place the butter, orange zest, and 1 tablespoon thawed orange juice concentrate in a medium-size mixing bowl and mix with an electric mixer at low speed until well blended, 1 minute.

4 Spread the orange butter mixture over the dough, leaving about a 1/2-inch border around the edges. Sprinkle with the sugar. Starting with a long edge, roll the dough into a log about 6 inches long and 1 1/2 inches thick. Press the seam and ends together to seal.

5 Cut the log into 24 even slices. Place the slices in the cups of the prepared muffin tins. Lightly spray the tops with cooking spray and cover loosely with plastic wrap. Allow to rise in a warm place until the dough has doubled in size, 30 minutes to 1 hour.

6 Preheat the oven to 350°F. Remove the plastic wrap from the rolls and bake until lightly browned, 20 minutes.

7 Place the confectioners' sugar and 2 tablespoons of the frozen orange juice concentrate in a small bowl and stir until smooth and creamy. Brush the mixture over the tops of the rolls while still hot in the muffin tins. Allow the rolls to cool before removing.

Almost Famous Orange Rolls will keep, in an airtight container at room temperature, for 2 to 3 days.

Harvest Stuffed Cinnamon Rolls

This is a deluxe version of your classic cinnamon roll, taken over the top with the addition of dried cranberries, toasted pecans, and a little bit of orange zest. You still have all the goodness of the cinnamon

Harvest Stuffed Cinnamon Rolls

roll and more. I like to get up early from time to time and make these in the wee hours of the morning for my kids to take to school for the staff. This simple recipe uses frozen bread dough as a significant shortcut. Most of the work is just waiting around for them to rise!

One of the great things about this recipe is that it can be made in advance and then frozen to enjoy later. Simply prepare the rolls through step 7, and once cooled, store them in the freezer. To reheat, leave them on the counter in the baking pan to thaw for 1 hour, then place the pan on a rimmed baking sheet, cover it loosely with aluminum foil, and bake in a preheated 200°F oven until heated through, 15 to 20 minutes. Remove from the oven and continue with step 8. They're nearly as good as fresh-baked! *Makes 12 rolls*

Nonstick cooking spray,
   for coating the baking pan
1/2 cup dried cranberries
   (or raisins or dried cherries)
1 loaf (1 pound) frozen white bread
   dough (such as Rhodes brand),
   thawed
All-purpose flour, for rolling out
   the dough
1/2 cup (1 stick) butter or
   margarine, at room temperature
1 cup packed brown sugar
3 tablespoons ground cinnamon
   (or less to taste)
1/2 cup toasted chopped pecans
1 tablespoon grated orange zest
   (or more to taste)
3 ounces cream cheese, at room
   temperature
1 1/2 cups confectioners' sugar
1/2 teaspoon vanilla extract
   (optional; I usually just leave
   it out)
1 to 2 tablespoons milk (optional)

1 Lightly coat a 9 x 13-inch baking pan with cooking spray and set aside.

2 Place the cranberries in a small bowl and cover with 1 cup hot water. Let them sit for 5 minutes to plump, then drain well.

3 Roll out the bread dough into a 9 x 16-inch rectangle on a floured surface. Spread ¼ cup of the butter over the dough.

4 Mix together the brown sugar and cinnamon in a small bowl with a spoon until well blended. Sprinkle over the top of the dough, leaving about a ½-inch border around the edges so it will seal. Sprinkle the pecans, cranberries, and orange zest over the brown sugar mixture.

5 Starting with a long edge, carefully roll the dough into a log, squeezing lightly as you do to seal it. Cut crosswise into 1-inch slices with a serrated knife.

6 Place the slices in the prepared pan and cover with plastic wrap or a clean towel. Place in a warm, draft-free area and allow to rise until the dough doubles in size, 2 to 3 hours.

7 Preheat the oven to 400°F. Remove the plastic wrap and bake until lightly golden on top, about 15 minutes. Allow to cool slightly while you prepare the icing.

8 Mix together the cream cheese, the remaining ¼ cup butter, the confectioners' sugar, and the vanilla extract, if using, in a large mixing bowl with an electric mixer at medium speed, scraping down the side of the bowl as needed, until smooth and creamy, 1 to 2 minutes. If the icing becomes too thick, add 1 or 2 tablespoons of the milk. Spread the icing over the cinnamon rolls.

Harvest Stuffed Cinnamon Rolls will keep, covered at room temperature, for up to 3 days, or individually wrapped in aluminum foil, stored in a zip-top bag, and frozen for up to 2 months.

7

Old-Fashioned Fruit Salads

FRUIT IS ONE of my all-time favorite desserts. It just can't be beat in its simplicity and perfection. While I love just about any fruit on its own, I find that with a little blending and sometimes a light dressing to enhance the flavor, it comes to life on a whole new level.

No gathering would be complete without a congealed salad (also known as a Jell-O salad, for those of you who don't live in the South ☺). The fruit and gelatin combine to form a delicious surprise that goes with almost anything. In the South, we usually eat congealed salads as a side dish, but they are equally good as a light dessert.

Peach Buttermilk Congealed Salad

Buttermilk adds a richness and subtle tang to this old-fashioned salad. You can easily switch up the flavors based on your preference and add some fresh chopped seasonal fruit to further complement it if you like! This is a must at church socials and family reunions. *Serves 4 to 6*

1 can (20 ounces) crushed
    pineapple
2 boxes (3 ounces each) peach
    gelatin (or your favorite flavor)
2 cups buttermilk (store-bought
    is best here)
1 container (8 ounces) frozen
    whipped topping (such as
    Cool Whip), thawed, or 1 cup
    whipped cream (see page 277)

1 Place the crushed pineapple and its juice in a medium-size saucepan over medium heat and bring to a boil. Once boiling, add the gelatin and stir until well mixed. Remove from the heat.

2 Stir in the buttermilk and allow to cool, 20 to 30 minutes. Stir in the whipped topping until fully incorporated.

3 Transfer the mixture to a bowl and cover with plastic wrap. Place in the refrigerator to chill before serving, 3 hours.

Peach Buttermilk Congealed Salad will keep, covered in the refrigerator, for up to 5 days.

Aunt Tina's Dr Pepper Salad

My sister-in-law, Tina, introduced me to this salad while we were visiting a few years ago and it instantly became a dear favorite. If you have any Dr Pepper fans in your house, make their day at the next barbecue by bringing out this little gem. It works really well with Coca-Cola, too! *Serves 6 to 8*

1 can (20 ounces) crushed
    pineapple
2 boxes (3 ounces each)
    cherry gelatin
3/4 cup Dr Pepper (regular or diet)
1 can (21 ounces) cherry pie filling

Aunt Tina's Dr Pepper Salad

1 Drain the pineapple juice from the can into a medium-size saucepan over medium heat. Add 1/2 cup water and bring to a boil.

2 Once boiling, remove from the heat and add the gelatin. Stir until dissolved. Add the Dr Pepper, cherry pie filling, and crushed pineapple and stir until fully incorporated.

3 Pour into a 6-cup heatproof mold or serving bowl and cover with plastic wrap. Refrigerate until chilled and set, about 4 hours. Serve cold.

Aunt Tina's Dr Pepper Salad will keep, in a covered container in the refrigerator, for up to 1 week.

Keep Pedaling

Did you have a bicycle as a kid? I had a pink one with a banana-style seat and the words "powder puff" written on it. It was beautiful, my pride and joy. I put a piece of masking tape down the center of the seat as soon as I got it. I'd get on it and line up the zipper of my brother's hand-me-down jeans with that strip of tape to help me find my balance as I was teaching myself to ride. Once I learned, man I was off! I imagine some folks who didn't know any better might have thought I was just riding a bicycle as I wore ruts into the roads in my neighborhood, but if you were ever in the seat of your own bicycle as a child, you know the truth: I was flying! Every morning I'd get up with the sun, get dressed as quickly as I could, and then head out for a day of pedaling as fast as I could while the wind flew through my hair and I soared through the skies of Huntsville.

Oh, how I remember the joy of that first day when it was warm enough to ride your bike after the winter! I'd ride all day long only to wake up the next day with legs so sore I could hardly walk, but by golly I'd still get on that bike within a day or two and be back to flying again.

You know, so much of life is like that. It starts out fun, then we realize it's hard, but we stick with it and pedal some more and eventually we're rewarded with some good flight time. If we just stick with it. And keep pedaling.

If it feels hard today, if you're a little sore from trying—don't give up. Keep pedaling. You'll fly soon.

Raspberry Salad

from STACEY SLIGH

"This is my granny's Jell-O salad that she makes for church parties and get-togethers, and the bowl is always empty when she leaves. Once, a sweet lady at church even typed up copies for everyone to have because they liked it so much.

"Granny always made sure to take care of me growing up. I would stop by her house for dinner on my way to school, where I was taking night classes. She also taught me how to cook! We have a show pig farm and my granny often tells me the story of when her daddy brought pigs home one day and the pigs had to live upstairs in their house for a couple nights until her daddy built a shelter for them. So she loves hearing our stories when our baby pigs are born! My granny will be ninety this year, and she is the strongest woman I know." *Serves 6 to 8*

1 box (6 ounces) sugar-free
   raspberry gelatin
1 cup boiling water
1 can (14 ounces) cranberry sauce
   with berries
1 can (20 ounces) crushed
   pineapple, with juice
1 cup chopped pecans or walnuts
1 container (16 ounces) frozen
   whipped topping (such as
   Cool Whip), thawed

1 Mix together the raspberry gelatin and boiling water in a large mixing bowl until the gelatin is dissolved. While the mixture is still hot, stir in the cranberry sauce and pineapple. Add the nuts.

2 Cover the bowl with plastic wrap and place in the refrigerator to chill for several hours. Just before serving, spread the whipped topping over the top.

Raspberry Salad will keep, covered in the refrigerator, for up to 5 days.

CHRISTY'S NOTE: I am always on the lookout for congealed salads that can be served with meals as a side dish, like my granny's was in the old days. While this recipe calls for whipped topping for garnish, I think it is great served alongside meat and vegetables without the topping. Either way, it is delicious. I love cranberries and nuts and this has them both. After I tested the recipe, I ended up eating most of it myself over a couple of days!

Apple Salad

It's not often that you see heavy cream in a recipe that doesn't call for you to whip it. Here, you cook that delicious cream along with some sugar and flour as a thickener. The resulting sauce has a rich buttery flavor unlike any other. Tart apples are a perfect complement. If I'm taking this salad somewhere, I like to make the sauce a day ahead of time and store it, covered, in my refrigerator. The morning of the event, I peel and chop my apples, finish the recipe, and return it to the fridge until it's time to leave. *Serves 8 to 10*

What Is a Congealed Salad?

Aside from fresh garden vegetables and sweet tea, nothing says summer gathering to a Southerner like congealed salad. However, outside of the southern United States, most folks refer to them as gelatin or Jell-O salads. *We just like to be different.*

My great-grandmother, who lived the majority of her life as a sharecropper, considered congealed salads to be the ultimate treat. Back in her day, though, it was a treat that could be enjoyed only in the winter due to the fact that they didn't have a refrigerator. The heat of Alabama summers would never allow the gelatin to set up!

My grandmother says that in the wintertime my great-grandmother Lela had an old washtub she kept out in the back of her house. She'd let it fill up with water and as soon as it got cold enough to freeze, off she'd go to mix up a congealed salad in her kitchen and then place it out on top of that ice to set in time for dinner.

By the time I came along, Lela was living a well-deserved, comfortable life in my grandmama and granddaddy's house. She was in her eighties by then and didn't get out much, but once a week she'd put on her good dress and black leather shoes and hook her large black leather purse on her arm for her weekly trip to Kroger with Grandmama. One of the first things she put in her cart every week was a container of gelatin from the deli. She always smiled like a kid taking hold of a lollipop at having such a luxury as store-bought gelatin, available year-round. Even now, something so small still makes my heart smile whenever I see it and think of what joy it gave her. There are so many small pleasures in our life today that it's easy to take them for granted; memories of Lela remind me to open my eyes to them whenever possible.

Fruit Salad from a Can?

What to do when the fruit you crave isn't in season? There are some wonderful fruit salads that can be made entirely of canned fruit, or of canned fruit with a mixture of fresh. Salads like this are often budget-friendly and still have the pop of flavor along with many of the vitamins that fresh fruit salads offer. I always keep a few cans of my favorite fruit cocktail (in juice) in my pantry so I can whip it up with whatever fresh fruit I have on hand and a light dressing (if desired). Refrigerate until cold and have a summer-worthy treat year-round.

1/3 cup all-purpose flour

3/4 cup granulated sugar

2 cups heavy (whipping) cream

1 can (16 ounces) crushed
   pineapple, with juice

1/2 cup maraschino cherries,
   chopped

5 large tart apples, peeled, cored,
   and chopped

1/4 cup (1/2 stick) butter, melted
   and cooled

1 cup chopped nuts

1 Stir together the flour and sugar in a medium-size heavy-bottomed saucepan. Add the heavy cream and pineapple. Place over medium heat and stir constantly until the sugar dissolves and mixture begins to thicken, 10 minutes. Remove from the heat.

2 Pour the cream mixture into a medium-size heatproof bowl and refrigerate until chilled and thickened, about 1 hour.

3 Stir in the cherries, apples, butter, and nuts. Return to the refrigerator and chill until ready to serve.

Apple Salad will keep, in a covered container in the refrigerator, for up to 3 days.

Five-Cup Fruit Salad

from CINDY BURTON

My mother-in-law was hands down the sweetest of sweet little old ladies. When I first met her in 1987, she came waddling through the hallway with the prettiest dimpled grin on her face. I knew right then that we would be good friends.

"Her name was Ruby Helen Reece Burton and she was the mother of seven children with my husband being her 'baby boy.' We used to joke about how both she and Oliver, my father-in-law, were the babies of their families, and Eldon (my husband) and I were the babies of our families. We would always say we are doing pretty good for a bunch of babies!

"Ruby was the queen of making do. She and Oliver were poor throughout their entire fifty-six years together, but you wouldn't be able to tell it by anything Ruby said or did. She never let on like they didn't have money for anything she wanted; she always found a suitable alternative to whatever it was.

"Often you would see Ruby crocheting hand towels or working on some type of sewing project to make a little extra money. Oh, how she loved to craft and bring smiles to people's faces. Another one of her fine traits was her wonderful salesman skills. It has been said that Ruby could sell ice to an Eskimo and make them think they were getting a steal!

"I could go on and on about how special this woman was to me and my family, but with tears rolling down my face while thinking about her, I will end with this special recipe that she was known for, Five-Cup Fruit Salad. Now folks, this is just a basic little fruit salad that I am sure many of you have tasted in some variation, but to our family, it is five layers of love, happiness, joy, family, and faith.

"Ruby passed away a few years ago and our family hasn't been the same since. I still miss her so much and would love to walk into her home and hear that sweet voice say, 'Howdy Doody, Momma Moo.'" *Serves 5 or 6*

1 cup mini marshmallows
  (fruit-flavored or plain)
1 cup canned mandarin oranges,
  drained
1 cup frozen whipped topping
  (such as Cool Whip), thawed
1 cup pineapple chunks, drained
1 cup fruit cocktail, drained

Mix together all of the ingredients in a large mixing bowl. Refrigerate until ready to serve.

Five-Cup Fruit Salad will keep, in an airtight container in the refrigerator, for up to 1 week.

CHRISTY'S NOTE: This salad is just flat-out delicious and it's almost too simple to believe! The wonderful thing about it is that you can substitute whatever is in season or add your favorite fruits to it to make it your own. I fell in love with it right off.

Guilt-Free Orange Dream Salad

Guilt-Free Orange Dream Salad

Most families have some version of this Orange Dream recipe in their files. My mother, who has always held the orange Creamsicle pop in highest regard, loves to whip this up for her and my father as a light dessert.

The "guilt-free" in the title comes from using sugar-free Jell-O and pudding, and light whipped topping. If you are not watching calories or sugar in your diet, this recipe works equally well with the regular ones.

Serves 4 to 6

1 box (3 ounces) sugar-free
    orange gelatin
1 can (11 ounces) mandarin oranges
    in light syrup
1 box (3 ounces) sugar-free vanilla
    instant pudding mix
1 container (8 ounces) light frozen
    whipped topping (such as Cool
    Whip), thawed

1 Place 1 cup water in a small saucepan over medium-high heat and bring to a boil. Once boiling, remove from the heat and stir in the gelatin until dissolved.

2 Drain the syrup from the mandarin oranges into the gelatin and stir. Set the mixture aside to cool to room temperature.

3 Pour the cooled gelatin mixture into a large mixing bowl and add the pudding mix. Beat with an electric mixer at medium speed until smooth and creamy, about 1 minute.

4 Use a large spoon to fold in the whipped topping until well blended. Stir in the mandarin oranges and transfer the salad to a serving bowl. Cover and refrigerate until chilled, 2 hours.

Guilt-Free Orange Dream Salad will keep, covered in the refrigerator, for up to 4 days.

Miss Barbara's Must-Have Grape Salad

If you've never had grape salad before, you're missing out on one of the most refreshing salads of summer! I usually go with Miss Barbara Ingram's grape salad recipe whenever I make some. Hers has stood the test of time and has been served at countless weddings and bridal showers. You don't have to use two different kinds of grapes unless you just want to; they are there to add more color to the final dish.

Old Scrap Iron!

In 2013, my grandmama went to heaven to be with her beloved Jay (my granddaddy). I used to tell her that when she died I was going to tell the story of why she was called "Old Scrap Iron" and she would always laugh and say, "Oh, I don't care if you tell it now, but you better tell it after I die at least because that's a funny story!"

So Grandmama, I'm gonna keep my word. When Grandmama was a girl, they always lived out in the country. Around the time she was fourteen—she was such a gangly thing that you wouldn't have been able to tell her from a boy if not for her skirt—they lived in an old shack house with a raised front porch. Grandmama would go out every spare chance she got to look for pieces of scrap iron to sell to the scrap iron man when he rolled through town.

The problem was that the scrap iron man came only once a month, so if you didn't catch him, you had to wait a whole other month to sell your scrap iron. On the day he happened to come through, Grandmama was in her bedroom taking what we call a "spit bath," which is basically washing with a bowl of water and an old rag. She heard someone call out "Scrap iron man's a-comin'!" and she got so excited thinking of how much she'd found and how much money she would be able to get for it that she took off out of her room, crawling up under the porch to collect all of her pieces before running out to the road to meet the scrap iron man.

She sold her iron and then turned around to find the stern face of her mother (my great-grandmother Lela). Only then did she realize that in her haste and excitement, she had failed to put her shirt on! She said, "Mama whipped me all the way back to the house!" She and Lela laughed whenever they told that story for the rest of their lives. One of Grandmama's brother's friends would call from time to time and say, "Well, hello there, Old Scrap Iron!" And that is how my sweet grandmama Lucille got her nickname!

Lucille "Scrap Iron" Sanders Pockrus as a teenager

This recipe makes a large amount, so feel free to cut it in half. *Serves 8 to 10*

2 pounds seedless green grapes
2 pounds seedless red grapes
1 package (8 ounces) cream cheese, at room temperature
1 container (8 ounces) sour cream
½ cup granulated sugar
1 teaspoon vanilla extract
½ cup chopped pecans

1 Remove the grapes from the stems and place them in a colander. Rinse well with cold water and drain.

2 Mix together the cream cheese, sour cream, sugar, and vanilla in a large bowl with an electric mixer at medium speed until smooth and well mixed, 1 to 2 minutes. Fold in the grapes and stir well until completely coated.

3 Spoon the salad into a large serving bowl and sprinkle with the chopped pecans. Cover and refrigerate until ready to serve.

Must-Have Grape Salad will keep, covered in the refrigerator, for up to 4 days.

Super Fruit

Mama and I have been enjoying this salad for more than twenty years, ever since a friend on a diet passed on the recipe, calling it "Super Fruit." We make ours sugar-free and it ends up counting as a fruit on most diets, but with a lot more flavor and variety than eating a single banana or apple. Feel free to add fresh fruit along with the canned or use fresh fruit entirely. *Serves 4 to 6*

2 cans (14 ounces each) no-sugar-added fruit cocktail
1 can (15 ounces) no-sugar-added mandarin oranges, peaches, or fruit of your choice
1 box (1 ounce) sugar-free vanilla instant pudding mix

1 Drain the juice from the cans of fruit into a medium-size bowl. Add the pudding mix and stir with a wire whisk until smooth.

2 Add the fruit and stir until well combined. Cover with plastic wrap and refrigerate for several hours before serving. Enjoy!

Super Fruit will keep, covered in the refrigerator, for 2 to 3 days.

With Sugar or Without?

I know that there are a lot of folks who have to watch their sugar intake for one reason or another. For that reason I have included several recipes that call for sugar-free ingredients. Those recipes work very well with sugar-free products and have passed my taste test. Of course, feel free to use regular products if you do not have a problem with sugar. All of these recipes will work great with either choice.

Ambrosia

In Greek mythology, ambrosia was known as the food of the gods. One taste of this and it's easy to see that this delicious fruit salad combination was aptly named. This salad has played a key role in family reunions, church potlucks, and summer picnics for as long as I can remember. It's simple to throw together, but don't let the simplicity fool you: This is a heavenly fruit salad that lives up to its name. *Serves 5 or 6*

1 can (20 ounces) pineapple chunks, drained and juice reserved
1 large apple, peeled and chopped
1/2 cup granulated sugar
1/2 cup sour cream

1 can (15 ounces) fruit cocktail, drained
2 cans (15 ounces each) mandarin oranges, drained
1 cup mini marshmallows
1 cup chopped pecans
1 cup sweetened shredded coconut

1 Place the pineapple juice in a small bowl and add the chopped apple. Stir to coat and set aside.

2 Place the sugar and sour cream in a large mixing bowl. Stir together until well combined.

3 Drain the apples, discarding the pineapple juice or saving it for another use, and add them to the sugar mixture. Add the pineapple chunks, fruit cocktail, mandarin oranges,

marshmallows, chopped pecans, and shredded coconut and stir well.

4 Cover and refrigerate until thoroughly chilled before serving.

Ambrosia will keep, covered in the refrigerator, for up to 3 days.

Whoa Horsey Salad

This is a fluffy, creamy fruit salad that's taken over the top by pieces of juicy fruit in every bite. The salad tastes rich and sweet, but we actually make it with low-sugar ingredients (you can go full sugar if you like).

Why the name? Well, my mother developed this recipe while I was recovering from breaking both of my legs in a horse riding accident. We both got a kick out of the name then and still giggle over it now. We've proved time and again that a sense of humor can make any situation better. *Serves 6 to 8*

1 can (8 ounces) pineapple tidbits
1 can (8 ounces) crushed pineapple
1 can (11 ounces) mandarin oranges
1 box (3 ounces) sugar-free vanilla
    instant pudding mix
10 to 12 maraschino cherries
½ cup chopped pecans (optional)
1 container (8 ounces) light or
    regular frozen whipped topping
    (such as Cool Whip), thawed

1 Drain the juices from the pineapple tidbits, crushed pineapple, and mandarin oranges into a large mixing bowl. Whisk the pudding mix into the juices until smooth and creamy.

2 Cut the mandarin oranges and maraschino cherries in half and add them, the pineapple, and the pecans, if using, to the pudding mixture. Stir gently to combine. Fold in the whipped topping.

3 Cover with plastic wrap and refrigerate for several hours before serving.

Whoa Horsey Salad will keep, covered in the refrigerator, for up to 1 week.

8

Simple Candies and Sweet Snacks

THESE ARE THE "special occasion" recipes that we make when there is a party or sporting event or we just want to add a sprinkle of surprise to someone's day! These are the ones that mean holiday to us, like fudge, cloud cookies, and tiger butter. They are also the recipes that Mama has highlighted in the table of contents of her handwritten cookbook, the ones that she makes every Christmas. That is the main reason we save them for special gatherings. These are the recipes that take us back to our childhood and that we hope our children will recall for years to come.

Cream Cheese Mints

These delicious little mints melt in your mouth, are a cinch to make, and disappear quickly. Even better, since they're so easy, you can turn out a whole platter of them for a party or work function in no time flat. If you're making these for a baby or bridal shower, they are easily tinted using just a few drops of food coloring. I like to take tiny stamps and press designs into them for holidays. *Makes 80 mints*

1 package (8 ounces) cream cheese,
    at room temperature
3 tablespoons butter,
    at room temperature
4 to 6 drops peppermint oil
8 cups confectioners' sugar
1 tablespoon milk, if needed

1 Place the cream cheese, butter, and peppermint oil in a large mixing bowl and beat with an electric mixer at medium speed until fluffy, 1 to 2 minutes.

2 Add 7 cups of the confectioners' sugar gradually while beating on medium speed, scraping down the side of the bowl as needed, until it is doughlike in consistency, 1 to 2 minutes (it will seem stiff and dry at first). If it is too dry to form balls after you are done mixing (this is rare), add the milk and mix again.

3 Shape the dough into 1-inch balls and place on waxed paper.

4 Place 1 cup of the confectioners' sugar in a small bowl and roll each ball in it to coat. Flatten each ball slightly with your fingertip, a fork, the back of a spoon, or a tiny stamp. Allow the mints to dry for a few hours before serving or storing.

Cream Cheese Mints will keep, in an airtight container at room temperature, for up to 2 days, or in the refrigerator for up to 5 days.

NOTE: If you want to tint these with food coloring, add 2 to 3 drops when you mix the dough in step 2, before you form the balls.

Cream Cheese Divinity

Cream Cheese Divinity

I love traditional Southern divinity candy and shared our family recipe in my first book; the holidays just aren't the same without it. Divinity is a white, fluffy candy made from egg whites and sugar, which requires perfect weather and lots of mixing. Mama and I both make up batches and divvy it out like gold doubloons among our families and friends. It's just that good.

So here is the thing: This recipe is not traditional divinity. I didn't develop it to be that. I developed it to be an awful lot like it but simple enough for anyone to make and just as good.

Will it remind you of divinity? Definitely. But this is decadently wonderful in its own special way. Think of how good cream cheese frosting tastes, especially when you get a bite that has a big pecan on it, and you have some understanding of what this is going to be like—only a good bit better.

Guess what else, though. This recipe doesn't depend on the weather, or the temperature of your house, or how your pinkie toes are crossed. There is no thermometer needed, no syrup to be made, and nothing hot that will give you a burn. You toss all of the ingredients in a mixing bowl, mix, roll into balls, and press a pecan in the center. That's it. Seriously! *Makes 50 to 60 pieces*

1 package (8 ounces) cream cheese, at room temperature

3 tablespoons butter, at room temperature

1 tablespoon lemon juice

1 teaspoon vanilla extract

7 to 9 cups confectioners' sugar (I buy a 2-pound bag)

50 to 60 pecan halves (optional)

1 Place the cream cheese, butter, and lemon juice in a medium-size mixing bowl and beat with an electric mixer at medium speed until fluffy, 1 to 2 minutes.

2 Add the vanilla and gradually add 7 cups of the confectioners' sugar. Beat at medium speed, scraping down the side of the bowl as needed, until well blended, 2 to 3 minutes. Add up to 1 cup more confectioners' sugar if needed to make a thick cookie-dough consistency.

3 Place 1 cup of the confectioners' sugar in a small bowl. Shape the dough into 1-inch balls and dip the bottoms in the sugar to coat. Place the balls on waxed paper or parchment and press a pecan half into each one, if desired, flattening the ball slightly.

4 Allow the divinity to dry at room temperature until they're no longer sticky, 2 to 3 hours, before serving.

Cream Cheese Divinity will keep, in an airtight container at room temperature, for up to 2 days, or in the refrigerator for up to 2 weeks.

Cornetha's Strawberry Candy

This is a recipe I got from my grandmother Cornetha. She and Papa Reed (Mama's daddy) got married when my mother was fourteen, adding a whole other branch to our family tree. Honestly, at this point we have one of those HUGE oak trees with all of the branches jutting out all over the place (you know I had thirteen living grandparents when I was born, right?).

Cornetha (called Mama Reed by my children) and Papa hosted all of the big Reed family reunions at their farm each summer and she used to let us stay with them during vacation Bible school week so that we could attend it at her church. I loved getting to spend the night there because each morning she'd let me go and gather the eggs from the chicken coop. Of course, there was one drawback to spending the night at the Reed farm—and that was the clothesline. Each morning after breakfast, Cornetha would set out for the line with her basket. You'd hear the clothes snapping as she gave 'em a good shake to get the wrinkles out and then hung them on the line, *just knowing that your underwear was among them.* This wouldn't have been so bad back at home because our clothesline was in the backyard, but out there on the farm Papa had set Cornetha's up in the most convenient spot, just outside the laundry room door with an unobstructed view from the road.

I remember trying to hide my clothes before I went to bed but let me tell you, I've never in all of my born days known anyone more efficient with clothes washing than my grandmother Cornetha! Lo and behold, no matter what avoidance tactic you used (and we tried them all), come early morning that sun would rise on your undies hanging on the line. We survived it, though, and I wouldn't trade those memories for anything in the world. *Makes 36 candies*

1 can (14 ounces) sweetened
   condensed milk
1 cup sweetened flaked coconut
1 cup finely chopped pecans
   (or any nut you prefer)
3 boxes (3 ounces each) strawberry
   gelatin

1 to 2 jars (3 ounces each)
   red sugar crystals (you can get
   by with 1 jar, but I use 1½)
½ cup slivered almonds
   (about 36 pieces)
Green food coloring

1 Combine the milk, coconut, pecans, and gelatin in a medium-size bowl and mix with a large spoon until fully blended. Cover with plastic wrap and refrigerate for 48 hours.

2 Place the red sugar crystals in a large bowl. Form teaspoonfuls of the coconut mixture into the shape of a strawberry and roll the pieces in the red sugar crystals.

3 Place the almonds in a zip-top bag and add a few drops of green food coloring. Seal and shake until well coated. Pour them out onto a paper towel and let them dry slightly. Place one in the end of each strawberry as a stem.

Cornetha's Strawberry Candy will keep, in an airtight container in the refrigerator, for up to 1 week.

Easy Fudge Meltaways

This is yet another product of my daughter and me playing in the kitchen. Inspired by her love of chocolate and one of our favorite truffles, we decided to come up with our own version that features a soft, melty fudge chocolate throughout. These come together surprisingly fast and are an excellent addition to offer on a candy tray or to package and give as gifts. We prefer to keep ours cold. *Makes 50 to 60 candies*

1 package (8 ounces) cream cheese,
   at room temperature
3 tablespoons butter, at room
   temperature
½ cup plus 2 tablespoons
   unsweetened cocoa powder
1 teaspoon vanilla extract
1 tablespoon lemon juice
1 tablespoon milk
6 to 7¼ cups confectioners' sugar

1 Place the cream cheese and butter in a large mixing bowl and beat with an electric mixer at medium speed until smooth and creamy, 1 to 2 minutes. Add the ½ cup of cocoa powder, the vanilla, lemon juice, and milk and beat again until well combined.

2 Add 6 to 7 cups of the confectioners' sugar, 1 cup at a time, and beat well, scraping down the side of the bowl after each addition, until it is thick and very sticky, like cookie dough.

3 Stir together the remaining 2 tablespoons cocoa powder and the remaining ¼ cup confectioners' sugar in a small bowl until there are no lumps.

4 Pinch off small portions of the dough and roll into 1-inch balls. Roll the balls in the sugar mixture to coat. Repeat until all of the dough is used. Store, covered in the refrigerator, until ready to serve.

Easy Fudge Meltaways will keep, in an airtight container in the refrigerator, for up to 2 weeks.

Cinna-bun, Chocolate, or Peanut Butter Fudge

This super-creamy fudge is the hallmark of every holiday for us, and with its many variations, there is a flavor for everyone. Growing up, we had only the chocolate version, but nowadays we enjoy the peanut butter and cinnamon versions just as much (cinnamon chips are fairly new and are sometimes difficult to find except around the holidays). Mama always makes hers with pecans, but my kids prefer it plain and I do, too, because that saves me a lot of money!

You may recall this recipe from another of my cookbooks—I'm offering it here, too, because no celebration would be complete without it. This fudge is a requirement during the holidays. *Makes 3 pounds*

Nonstick cooking spray, for coating
   the baking pan
3 cups granulated sugar
2/3 cup evaporated milk
3/4 cup (1½ sticks) butter or
   margarine
1 package (12 ounces) cinnamon,
   chocolate, or peanut butter
   chips

1½ cups marshmallow cream
   (such as Fluff)
½ teaspoon vanilla extract
½ cup pecans or other nuts,
   chopped (optional)

1 Lightly coat a 9 x 13-inch baking pan with cooking spray and set aside.

2 Combine the sugar, milk, and butter in a medium-size heavy-bottomed saucepan over medium heat and bring to a boil, stirring constantly. Once it reaches a boil, clip a candy or deep-fry thermometer to the side of the pot and continue stirring until it reaches soft-ball stage (238°F), about 5 minutes.

3 Remove from the heat. Add the chips, marshmallow cream, vanilla, and nuts, if using. Stir vigorously with a large spoon until well blended.

4 Pour into the prepared pan and cool completely. Cut into small squares.

The fudge will keep, in an airtight container at room temperature, for up to 1 week, or in the refrigerator for up to 2 weeks.

Chocolate Chip Meringues

My kids call these "cloud cookies," and although they taste like you fussed over them, they are one of my favorite "last-minute" cookies to make. Good thing, too, because Katy has a habit of remembering them right before bedtime on Christmas Eve. You know it's hard to turn down a Christmas Eve request! *Makes 2 dozen cookies*

Nonstick cooking spray, for coating
   the baking sheets
2 large egg whites
Pinch of cream of tartar
¼ teaspoon salt
¾ cup granulated sugar
2 bags (12 ounces each)
   chocolate chips
Colored sugar sprinkles (optional)

1 Preheat the oven to 300°F. Lightly coat 2 large baking sheets with cooking spray and set aside.

2 Beat the egg whites, cream of tartar, and salt in a medium-size mixing bowl with an electric mixer at high speed until soft peaks

241

Guess What? You're Buoyant!

I had the hardest time learning how to swim as a child. People would try to teach me—goodness knows how many hours they spent on that—but I never could quite get it. I'd let go of the side and sink like a lead weight.

Then, in second grade, I checked out a book from the school library that explained the principles of swimming. That book taught me the one thing I hadn't realized before: I was buoyant.

Boy howdee, that was news to me! Once I knew that, I was off to the races, and the very next time I got into a pool I lifted my legs up, lay on my back, and floated. Moments later I was swimming.

Isn't that something? You know, life is full of obstacles that prevent us from thinking we can swim. We get knocked down and dunked and end up gripping the sides of the pool just waiting for the water to drain or hoping it will evaporate. It never does, but so many folks spend their lifetime just clinging to the side. The trick is, when we're dunked, to learn to bob right back to the top the first chance we get.

That longing in your heart to just break the surface . . . that's because you're meant to be on top, not sinking. And you have the ability, too, but you may not realize it. Nothing can keep you down for long.

Know why? You're buoyant.

---

form, 2 to 3 minutes. Add the sugar and beat until stiff peaks form. Gently fold in the chocolate chips.

3 Drop by level tablespoonfuls on the prepared baking sheets. Sprinkle lightly with the sugar sprinkles, if desired.

4 Bake until the meringues are dry and crisp, 20 to 25 minutes. Cool on the baking sheets for 2 minutes, then remove to wire racks to cool completely.

Chocolate Chip Meringues are best the day they are made, but they will keep, in an airtight container at room temperature, for up to 3 days. They do not hold up well in humid or moist environments.

Peanut Butter Cups

I happened upon this treat by accident (or desperation) one summer when my son was going to a pool party and needed to take a snack to share. My first thought was brownies, then cake, then cookies, and I went on down the list until I came up with something that would be really good but not make a lot of mess in the kitchen. So I took a standard peanut butter bar recipe and flipped it into peanut butter cups.

I was not prepared for the reaction. Every speck was snatched up and I received text messages and even emails telling me *how wonderful Mrs. Jordan's homemade peanut butter cups were.* I'll be derned if it didn't put a spring in my step! Just in case you ever need a little extra spring in your step, this is the recipe to do it! *Makes 24 peanut butter cups*

2 cups creamy peanut butter
1/2 cup (1 stick) butter or margarine
1/2 cup packed brown sugar (light or dark)
1 teaspoon vanilla extract
2 1/2 cups confectioners' sugar
1 package (12 ounces) semisweet chocolate chips

1 Line two 12-cup muffin tins with muffin papers.

2 Place the peanut butter, butter, and brown sugar in a large microwave-safe bowl. Microwave at 30-second intervals until the butter and peanut butter are melted, 1 to 2 minutes.

3 Add the vanilla and confectioners' sugar and stir with a large spoon until they form a dough that pulls away from the side of the bowl and forms a ball.

4 Pinch off pieces of the dough and roll them into 1 1/2-inch balls. Place one ball in each muffin paper. Press the dough flat into the papers with your fingers and set aside.

5 Place the chocolate chips in a microwave-safe bowl and microwave at 30-second intervals, stirring after each, until completely melted. Spoon over the top of the peanut butter pats and spread evenly.

Tiger Butter

6 Allow to cool completely at room temperature until the chocolate hardens, or place the tins in the refrigerator to speed up the process. Enjoy!

Peanut Butter Cups will keep, in an airtight container at room temperature, for up to 1 week.

Tiger Butter

I can't even begin to tell you how many batches of Tiger Butter I've made over the years. This is the one candy my children request the most around Christmastime because they want to give it to all of their teachers and friends. I am doubly grateful that it is so easy to make! Once Christmas draws near, I just make sure I have plenty of the simple ingredients on hand because it never fails that one of my children will say they need a batch for the following day just before they go to bed! This is a creamy, fudgelike confection that is sure to please the chocolate and peanut butter lovers in your life. *Makes about 2 pounds*

1 package (24 ounces) white almond bark (see Note)
1/2 cup crunchy peanut butter
1 cup semisweet chocolate chips (milk chocolate works fine, too)

1 Line a rimmed baking sheet with waxed paper and set aside.

2 Break up the almond bark as best you can in a large microwave-safe mixing bowl. Microwave at 30- to 45-second intervals, stirring after each, until the bark is melted and smooth. Stir in the peanut butter with a large spoon until melted and well blended. Spread the mixture evenly on the prepared pan.

3 Place the chocolate chips in a small microwave-safe bowl and microwave at 30- to 45-second intervals, stirring after each, until smooth and melted. Drop dollops of the melted chocolate onto the peanut butter mixture in the pan and swirl with a knife or a toothpick (a toothpick will create finer lines).

4 Place the baking sheet in the refrigerator until the mixture hardens, or let it cool at room temperature until completely hardened. Break into pieces with your hands.

Tiger Butter will keep, in an airtight container at room temperature, for 2 to 3 weeks.

NOTE: Almond bark is a confectionary coating usually found near the chocolate chips. Despite the name, there are no nuts in the ingredients. It's just a less expensive form of white chocolate (minus the chocolate).

Cinnamon Cashews

These taste like the roasted cinnamon nuts we like to buy while out and about during the holidays, the nuts that smell so amazing when you enter the shop and you try to get by with just the sample but end up buying a cone of them. This recipe works just as well with any type of nut. *Makes 1 pound*

Nonstick cooking spray, for coating
   the baking sheet
1 large egg white
1 cup granulated sugar
1 teaspoon salt
2 teaspoons ground cinnamon
1 pound cashew halves or pieces
   (about 2 cups)

1 Preheat the oven to 300°F. Lightly coat a large rimmed baking sheet with cooking spray and set aside.

2 Place the egg white and 1 tablespoon of water in a small mixing bowl and beat with an electric mixer at medium speed until frothy, about 1 minute. In a separate small bowl, stir together the sugar, salt, and cinnamon until well blended.

3 Pour the cashews into the frothed egg white and stir to coat well. Take a handful of cashews at a time and gently toss them in the sugar mixture with your hands to coat.

4 Place the cashews on the prepared baking sheet and bake, stirring every 10 minutes, until lightly browned and smelling delicious, 30 to 40 minutes. Remove from the oven and stir once more. Allow to cool, then remove from the baking sheet.

Cinnamon Cashews will keep, in an airtight container at room temperature, for 2 to 3 weeks.

Candied Peanuts

I make this recipe far more often than I do the Cinnamon Cashews (page 246), mainly because peanuts are so much more affordable than other nuts. This also has a distinctly different taste to it that takes me back to my childhood and a candy I loved called Boston Baked Beans. They are little peanuts covered in a very thick candy coating that has been dyed a deep red color. These nuts taste like the homemade (and better) version of those! *Makes 2 cups*

1 cup granulated sugar
2 cups raw peanuts (skins on)

1 Preheat the oven to 300°F.

2 Combine the sugar and 1/2 cup of water in a medium-size saucepan. Place over medium heat and stir just until the sugar dissolves.

3 Add the peanuts to the sugar water and continue to cook over medium heat, stirring constantly, until the peanuts are completely coated with sugar and no sugar syrup remains, about 30 minutes.

4 Pour the peanuts onto an ungreased rimmed baking sheet and spread them out a bit with a spatula or spoon. Bake, stirring every 10 minutes, until dry and lightly browned, about 30 minutes. Cool on the baking sheet.

Candied Peanuts will keep, in an airtight container at room temperature, for 2 to 3 weeks.

Everyone's Favorite Cereal Bars

A few years back, I misread the classic recipe for Rice Krispie Treats (again, where are my glasses?) and ended up doubling the marshmallow cream and

The Only Air-Conditioned Bicycle in Madison County

My maternal grandfather, Papa Reed, was born in 1927 in Madison County, Alabama. He was a wiz at innovation from an early age. Papa was always scouring trash piles and discarded items for something that could be useful to one of his inventions.

Once, during the hottest part of the summer, someone threw out an old fan and Papa mounted it on the handlebars of his bicycle so that when he rode the wind blew into the blades and created the only air-conditioned bicycle in the neighborhood. In addition to being inventive, he was also very self-reliant. When you are one of ten kids with hardworking parents, you pretty quickly learn to fend for yourself. When Papa Reed was eleven years old, the family moved to a large farm more than thirty miles away from the neighborhood where he had grown up. He decided that he wanted to go visit his friends and cousins in the old neighborhood, so he asked his mama if he could ride his bicycle to see them. She gave her permission and Papa set off, with no water or food whatsoever. Can you imagine?

Papa Reed enjoying a breeze on his bicycle—see the fan tied to the handlebars?

He rode for quite some time and started getting pretty hungry. Eventually, he came upon a house with a heavily laden apple tree so he stopped, knocked on the door, and asked the lady if he could have some water and apples to take with him. She obliged, he ate a few, and then he set off again!

Things sure were different in those times. I can't help but smile every time I see an apple tree as I recall the gumption of a scrawny little boy with an air-conditioned bicycle!

1 Lightly coat a 9 x 13-inch baking dish with cooking spray and set aside.

2 Place the butter and marshmallow cream in a large, microwave-safe bowl. Microwave at 45-second intervals, stirring after each, until melted and well blended. Add the cereal and stir well to coat.

3 Turn out the mixture into the prepared baking dish and allow to cool before cutting, or eat warm and enjoy it anyway!

Everyone's Favorite Cereal Bars will keep, in an airtight container at room temperature, for up to 3 days.

NOTE: If you can find only 8-ounce containers, that will be just fine.

adding a bit of extra butter. The result was FANTASTIC. I immediately applied it to these cereal bars and couldn't stop eating them. If you want to take your classic cereal treat bar up a notch (or ten), try this. The result is a whole other animal! *Serves 12*

Nonstick cooking spray, for coating
the baking dish
1/2 cup (1 stick) butter
3 containers (7 ounces each)
marshmallow cream
(such as Fluff; see Note)
10 cups cereal of your choice
(such as Golden Grahams,
Fruity Pebbles, or Rice Krispies)

9

Sweet Sippins

THERE IS SOMETHING ABOUT having an icy cold or soothing warm drink in hand that encourages folks to sit back, slow down, and enjoy life. Where I'm from, sweet tea is a daily staple.

Every recipe in this chapter is suitable for the whole family (meaning there's no alcohol whatsoever), so young and old can enjoy relaxing with a glass of something sweet to sip on while we all push the pause button on the busyness of life.

Daddy's Milkshakes

This recipe was an integral part of my childhood. Growing up, we usually had these milkshakes on Sunday night right before bedtime because my dad worked the second shift and he was off on Sunday and Monday. Therefore, Sunday was the first night that he was able to make them for us. We always had him add whatever extras we wanted: chocolate chips, peanut butter, and so on. To this day, I've not tasted a finer milkshake. *Serves 1*

1½ cups vanilla ice cream
²/₃ cup milk
½ teaspoon granulated sugar
2 to 3 tablespoons chocolate chips, chocolate-coated candy, peanut butter, or other add-ins of your choice

Place the ice cream, milk, sugar, and desired add-ins in a blender or milkshake maker and blend until creamy. Pour into a glass and enjoy!

Popa's Coke Floats

from MELISSA HAYDON

"When I was a little girl I spent a lot of my summers with my grandma and popa. We spent the long summer days in the garden, visited the post office daily, and stopped at the grocery store on the way home.

"There were two things we were sure to find when we visited: homemade vanilla ice cream and Coca-Cola. Like most grandparents, they always fixed us a treat to make us feel special. Popa would whip us all up a bowl of vanilla ice cream and pour Coca-Cola over the top. Instant joy came over us.

"Some of my fondest memories are of those days with my grandparents. By the time I was twelve, my grandmother had become ill and had to be placed in a nursing home for care. This was very hard on Popa, though he would never admit that he was lonely. I spent my last summer there with him that year keeping him company. We did our daily trips to the store and to the post office. We tended

Popa's Coke Floats

to the garden during the early hours of the day before it became too hot. We snapped beans and shelled peas under the big tree in the backyard while enjoying an ice-cold Coca-Cola. I was full of questions and he was so eager to answer them. That summer was the best one of my childhood. A few months later he became the angel I always knew he was. My heart overflows." *Serves 1*

2 to 3 scoops vanilla ice cream
12 ounces Coca-Cola, chilled

Place the ice cream in a glass. Pour the Coca-Cola over the ice cream. (The amount of Coca-Cola varies depending on the glass size and how much ice cream you use.) Enjoy!

CHRISTY'S NOTE: This old-fashioned treat can be changed simply by using a different flavor of cola (aka soda). Orange is wonderful with vanilla ice cream, but Coca-Cola is still my favorite of all. It reminds me of hot summer days sitting on the porch and enjoying good conversation and cool breezes.

Old-Fashioned Egg Cream

Taste-wise, an egg cream is somewhat like a milkshake, only not as thick and it actually quenches your thirst rather than inducing it. They have just a bit of milk in them, although they taste much milkier than they are. When you taste one you'll be surprised, given the light richness, that there isn't more involved and that eggs or cream aren't used.

Why is it called an egg cream if it doesn't have eggs or cream? Many people have speculated over the title, and the reason that makes the most sense to me is that during the height of soda fountains, it was popular to add a raw egg and cream to drinks for flavor, thickness, and richness. Since this miraculously tastes like it may indeed have an egg and cream in it, the name was sort of a marketing ploy to help sell an inexpensive drink. Regardless of the mystery, these drinks are simple as can be and a great treat any day! *Serves 1*

2 tablespoons chocolate,
    strawberry, or caramel syrup
    (regular or sugar-free)
1/3 cup whole milk
3/4 to 1 cup club soda or seltzer,
    chilled

Sip and Savor

When I was a little girl, summers seemed to stretch out far longer than the rest of the year. Each morning my sister and I would rise with the sun (our older brother slept in) and rush to get dressed so we could get out and enjoy the early-morning coolness. Mama would make us hold still long enough to have a quick breakfast and to put our hair into ponytails, and then we were out the door like rockets!

The day would be spent swinging, playing freeze tag, riding bicycles, picking wild flowers, drinking from the "hose pipe," and tending to our "zoo" of butter tubs filled with dirt and whatever bug we had dug up that day. At the end of those wondrous days we'd come in sporting a "dirt necklace" and Mama would send us off to get a bath before supper.

As I've gotten older, summers seem to have gotten shorter. Maybe it's because my attention is on my to-do list rather than on finding the best roly-poly for my butter-tub zoo. Maybe it's because I've aged and forgotten the fun to be had just beyond my back door. Maybe it's because I work too much and play too little. Maybe it's all of these things and more.

I often hear folks talk about kids these days and how they don't enjoy summer or playing outside like we used to. When this happens, though, I can't help but think that the children are only following our example when we're indoors sitting in front of our computers and televisions.

When was the last time you rode a bicycle, blew bubbles, or played hopscotch? You know we're never too old to look for four-leaf clovers or lie in the cool grass and search the clouds for familiar shapes. Regardless of your birth date, your youth is still there waiting for you to enjoy it. As a matter of fact, I don't think we get old because of age. I think we get old because we forget to be young.

The good news is that summer still offers the same treasures to be discovered that it did during our childhoods. Turns out, I just happen to have two wonderful tour guides who don't have any plans other than to hang out with me until school starts back up. Summers are still slow—we just have to grab a glass of iced tea, kick off our shoes, and join in.

Sip and savor, folks. Sip and savor. That's the sweetness.

Pour the syrup into the bottom of a tall drinking glass. Add the milk and stir vigorously to combine. Add the club soda slowly, leaving room for it to fizz at the top. Insert a straw and enjoy!

Orange Juice Special

My husband, Ricky, says this smoothie tastes like one of the Orange Julius drinks, but I think it tastes more like a Creamsicle. Concentrated orange juice is the secret to its burst of flavor, while the milk and vanilla make it nice and creamy. Although Ricky and I disagree on what it tastes like most, we both agree that it is worth making whenever we get a chance! *Serves 4*

1 cup frozen orange juice
　　concentrate
1 cup milk (I use whole)
1 teaspoon vanilla extract
1/2 cup granulated sugar, or to taste
Ice, for serving

Place the orange juice concentrate, milk, vanilla, and sugar in a blender and mix until frothy. Pour into a glass over ice and serve immediately.

Fresh Strawberry-ade

Most of us have folks in our families who can't tolerate sugar like they used to (*raises her hand*). They usually end up being left out in the cold when it comes to serving up treats. This drink changes all of that for sugar-intolerant folks but also impresses everyone else as well—in a big way. The most difficult part of making and serving this is going to be convincing everyone it doesn't have added sugar in it. Honestly, even though I'm the one making it, sometimes I still find myself feeling guilty for drinking it— it tastes that good. This is the most delicious drink, sugar-free or otherwise, that I have ever had. *Makes 2 quarts*

2 cups fresh strawberries, washed
　　and hulled (see Note)
1 packet (2-quart size) pink
　　lemonade mix (such as Crystal
　　Light)
Ice, for serving

1 Place the strawberries in a blender and puree until fully liquefied.

Hey, Honey!

Honey is one of my favorite sweeteners and I tend to use it a lot in beverages, especially if they have fruit in them, as it's a great complement to the natural sweetness of fruit. However, if you see honey in a recipe in this chapter and either don't want to use honey or don't have any on hand, you can easily substitute sugar for it. Hint: The lighter the honey, the milder the flavor. I prefer dark honeys, but your family may prefer light.

2 Fill a 2-quart pitcher halfway with water. Stir in the pink lemonade mix. Add the strawberry puree and fill the rest of the way with cold water. Stir well. Serve cold over ice.

Fresh Strawberry-ade will keep, covered in the refrigerator, for 1 to 2 days. Stir it before serving.

NOTE: If the strawberries aren't sweet enough, add ¼ cup Splenda, or to taste. (I've never had to add Splenda!)

Watermelon-ade

I have a difficult time making recipes with watermelon because I feel like watermelon by itself is about as perfect as it can get. Just hand me a salt shaker and knife and get out of my way! But this recipe is an exception, because it is basically watermelon that you can drink. No knife, no stickiness, just sit back with a straw and drink the whole melon if the mood hits ya. I add just enough "extra" stuff to enhance the flavor, being careful not to detract from it. So next time you go to get a watermelon, get two instead. Eat one, drink the other. You can't go wrong! *Serves 2 to 4*

5 to 6 cups cubed watermelon,
    black seeds removed
¼ cup lime juice
¼ cup honey
Pinch of salt (optional, but I
    wouldn't consider watermelon
    without it!)
Crushed ice, for serving
Lime slices and fresh mint leaves,
    for garnish (optional)

Place the watermelon, lime juice, honey, and salt in a blender and blend on high speed until completely liquefied. Serve immediately

Watermelon-ade

over crushed ice and garnish with lime and mint, if you like.

Fresh Peach-ade

This is a twist on lemonade that takes it to a whole new level. The combination of lemonade and peaches gives it a sweet citrusy flavor, perfect for summertime. You want to use peaches that are sweet and in season for this. If that isn't possible, there is nothing wrong with grabbing a 29-ounce can of peaches in light syrup and draining them well. *Makes 2 quarts*

3 to 4 medium-size fresh peaches
    (or one 29-ounce can peaches
    in light syrup, drained)
1 packet (2-quart size) lemonade
    mix (such as Crystal Light)
Ice, for serving

Peel and dice the peaches into bite-size pieces. Place in a blender and puree until liquefied. Fill a 2-quart pitcher halfway with cold water. Stir in the lemonade mix until it's dissolved. Add the peach puree and fill the pitcher to the top with cold water. Stir well. Serve over ice.

Grow Your Own Tea

Years ago, I took a trip to a garden store and purchased an assortment of herbs for a kitchen herb garden. Like I do when choosing herbs to add to dishes, I smelled each one to decide if it was coming home with me. Lemon balm immediately took a place in my basket! Little did I know, that day was the beginning of a very long relationship. All of the other herbs died rather rapidly but lemon balm took over with wild abandon and has come back bigger and stronger each year. I now have an herb garden consisting entirely of lemon balm, and I'm perfectly fine with that. I break off leaves and toss a few in my pot when brewing summer tea to add a light note of flavor to it. It tastes as if someone has tossed a piece of lemon drop candy into my tea pitcher! I also dry it and make tea exclusively of dried lemon balm leaves. It is fun to experiment with herbs this way, and there are endless varieties that make excellent tea. Try your hand at growing your own!

Fresh Peach-ade will keep, covered in the refrigerator, for 1 day.

French Mint Tea

Mama always enjoyed this with her sister when they visited a little restaurant in Decatur, Alabama. Sadly, it is no longer in business. She bought their cookbook years ago and modified this recipe. You can substitute artificial sweetener if desired and it still tastes wonderful. As kids, we used to tease Mama and call this her swamp water because of its cloudy appearance. *Makes 1 gallon*

8 standard-size orange pekoe tea bags
2 tablespoons dried mint leaves
1 can (12 ounces) frozen pulp-free orange juice concentrate
8 tablespoons lemon juice or the juice of 4 lemons
2 cups granulated sugar

❶ Place the tea bags and mint in a medium-size saucepan and add enough water to generously cover. Bring to a boil over medium-high heat. Once it reaches a boil, remove from the heat, cover, and let steep for 30 minutes.

❷ Remove the tea bags. Add the orange juice concentrate, lemon juice, and sugar. Stir to dissolve the sugar and orange juice. Strain into a 1-gallon pitcher, add enough water to fill to the top, and refrigerate.

French Mint Tea will keep, covered in the refrigerator, for up to 1 week.

Southern Sweet Tea

I've seen lots of recipes lauding a simple syrup to sweeten tea, but when making tea is as simple as this, that just seems to be adding a lot more work into what began as a simple process. I think simple syrup is useful if you want to serve your tea unsweetened and let folks sweeten it themselves, the reason being that once the tea has cooled or been poured over ice, getting sugar to dissolve is not an easy task. In my family, though, we drink so much tea that whenever we have a gathering we just make both sweet and unsweet. No need to fuss with a syrup when you can just add it directly to the pitcher. Whenever you can in life, keep it simple. *Makes 2 quarts*

5 standard-size orange pekoe tea
   bags (or 2 family-size bags)
¾ cup granulated sugar (see Note)
Ice, for serving

1 Place the tea bags in a small saucepan. Fill with water to a depth of about 3 inches and bring just to a boil over medium heat. As soon as the tea comes to a boil, remove from the heat and set aside.

2 Fill a 2-quart pitcher halfway with cool water and add the sugar. Stir. Add the hot tea and stir. Add more water, if necessary, to make 2 quarts. Serve over ice.

Southern Sweet Tea is best served the same day but will keep, covered in the refrigerator, for 1 day.

NOTE: Never pour hot tea directly over sugar. Always add the sugar to the cold water first. Pouring hot tea directly over sugar scorches it and adds a bitter flavor to your tea.

The Secret to Uncloudy Tea

*T*here are all sorts of hints and tips on the internet about how to keep your iced tea from being cloudy. I've never once made cloudy tea, but from what I've seen from folks who have, it involves letting their tea bags sit for far too long before mixing the tea up. I think the key is to bring your tea to a boil, let it sit for just a minute or two, and then mix it up. There is no sense in dillydallying when making sweet tea anyway.

Tropical Pink

My son and I love to experiment with fun drinks in the kitchen. Even though I don't personally drink alcohol, I love to pick up nonalcoholic mixers and see what we can dream up. This drink was the result of a sunny Saturday afternoon and my son's request for "something kind of tropical-tasting that involves Sprite." Tropical Pink has become one of my favorites! *Serves 1*

The Difference Between an Ordinary Life and an Extraordinary Life

The difference between an ordinary life and an extraordinary life is finding extraordinary things in an ordinary life. Everyone wants to change the world, don't they? The problem is that we tend to want to do it in big, sweeping gestures. We feel too small to be able to have the impact we want to have. But I've got news for you: That little part of the world around you reaches further than you think! Fact is, you ARE changing the world, every minute and every day. People are looking forward to and even relying on the kindness you think no one notices. Every day you impact the lives of people who impact the lives of people who impact the lives of people. So please don't think you're small; you're so much bigger than you realize. If only you could see how your smile changes the world.

Crushed ice, for serving

1/2 tablespoon grenadine

2 tablespoons liquid piña
   colada mix

1 can (12 ounces) regular or diet
   lemon-lime soda

1 Fill a large glass at least halfway with crushed ice. Add the grenadine, piña colada mix, and one third of the soda. Stir to mix.

2 Add the remaining soda and serve immediately.

Bananaritas

I've been making these ever since my son was little, and I often whip them up for morning breakfast smoothies. When he was in kindergarten, he got on a smoothie kick and requested this particular one several times a week. Back then, I didn't really give much thought to calling them banana margaritas. Fortunately for me, his kindergarten teacher knew me pretty well by the time he walked into school one morning

Family-Friendly Drink Bar

I had the pleasure of going on a mission trip with Operation Christmas Child a few years back, where I met fellow volunteers Buddy and Carol Smith. As adoring grandparents, they had an instant connection with all of the children we visited and they were just a delight to be around. Carol told me about something she does whenever her grandchildren visit. She said every afternoon, she sets up fun drinks and snacks and they have what they call "family happy hour," where they all have drinks and visit with one another.

Typically we think of "happy hour" or "bars" as things that are to be experienced by adults only, but there are so many fun beverages you can make that can be enjoyed by the entire family. Some favorites:

EGG CREAMS
My children love these. They have a flavor reminiscent of a milkshake, with a nice bubble and less richness. This old-fashioned fountain drink is simple to mix up and customize one at a time and contains no egg, despite the name. See my recipe on page 253.

FRUIT-ADES
All you need for an array of spritzers are cut-up fresh fruit, fruit juices, and seltzer water!

HOT COCOA BAR
It is amazing how many variations for hot cocoa there are. Just add a teaspoon of your favorite flavoring syrup—we like caramel—when adding the water to the cocoa and stir to combine. We call it hot chocolate where I'm from, but whatever you call it, you're sure to make everyone happy!

and proudly announced to the class that he'd had a margarita for breakfast! *Serves 2*

Ice
4 medium-size bananas
1/2 cup milk
1/4 cup granulated sugar
1/2 cup lime juice
Lime zest, for garnish (optional)

Fill a blender halfway with ice. Add the bananas, milk, sugar, and lime juice and blend until frothy. Serve immediately.

Bananaritas

Sunrise OJ

This is similar to a Shirley Temple. I always made it as a special treat for my son, Brady, when he was little. Brady has been drinking this since he was knee-high to a grasshopper, and it's still one of his favorite breakfast drinks. *Serves 1*

1 cup orange juice
2 tablespoons grenadine
2 maraschino cherries

Pour the orange juice into a glass and add the grenadine and cherries. Do not stir. The grenadine will sink to the bottom and form a sunrise at the top of the glass. Serve immediately.

Angel Sangria

A traditional sangria involves wine, fruit, and sometimes seltzer water. I make family-friendly versions of drinks for all of us to enjoy and add "angel" to the name so folks know they are nonalcoholic, since we don't drink alcohol. My angel version of sangria uses regular (Concord) grape or muscadine grape juice and I extend the shelf life by adding fruit-flavored juices instead of the actual fruit. This allows the sangria to keep in the refrigerator for much longer than it would with fresh fruit.

However, to make it more fun to serve, you can fill glasses with ice, add a few slices of apple or orange, and then pour the juice over them if you like. *Makes about 1 quart; serves 4*

3 cups Concord or muscadine
    grape juice
1 cup orange juice
1/2 cup apple juice
Ice, for serving
Fresh apple or orange slices,
    for garnish

Stir together the juices in a 2-quart container and place in the refrigerator until thoroughly chilled. Fill 4 glasses with ice. To serve, dip the fresh apple slices in the drink mixture (to prevent browning) and then press down to mount them on the sides of the ice-filled glasses. Fill each glass with sangria and enjoy!

Angel Sangria will keep, covered in the refrigerator, for up to 1 week (omit the fresh fruit if storing).

We Can Always Be More

We can always be a little nicer. We can smile a little bigger and more often. Instead of passing folks on the street quietly we can greet them with "good mornin'." We can be the bigger, nicer person to the persistent grump at work. In time, you'll be amazed at the people you can soften through the simplest kindnesses, but you'll be even more amazed to find that each act of kindness you perform makes you feel better as the day goes on.

Apple Juice Brew

We had a version of this drink on a family trip to Disney World and my kids and husband immediately gave me the task of coming up with a recipe for it. My son, Brady, and I took the challenge, and this was our winner. It's great to serve this drink in chilled glass mugs. *Serves 4*

3 cups ice
3 cups unsweetened apple juice
1/2 cup butterscotch syrup,
   plus extra for serving
1 cup marshmallow cream
   (such as Fluff)
Whipped cream (see page 277),
   for serving

Place the ice, apple juice, butterscotch syrup, and marshmallow cream in a blender and puree until smooth and frothy and the marshmallow cream is fully incorporated. Pour into 4 glasses and top each with the whipped cream and a drizzle of butterscotch syrup. Enjoy immediately.

Blushing Apple Juleps

When was the last time you sat outside and sipped on something? When I was little, that was what folks did during their downtime. They'd drag a chair underneath a shade tree, pour a big glass of iced tea or lemonade, and sit and sip as they visited.

Mixing up these delicious concoctions is as simple as pouring the juice and stirring, so you can have them ready to go in about the time it takes folks to assemble chairs over by the shade tree. *Makes 2 quarts*

4 cups apple juice
1 cup orange juice
1 cup pineapple juice
1/4 cup lemon juice
1 jar (10 ounces) maraschino
    cherries
Ice, for serving
Mint or lemon balm sprigs, for
    garnish (optional)

Pour all of the juices into a 2-quart pitcher and stir well. Add 3 to 4 tablespoons of juice from the jar of cherries and stir again. Chill until ready to serve. Serve over ice with a cherry in each glass. Garnish with mint or lemon balm, if desired. Or just drink it and leave the plants in the yard!

Blushing Apple Juleps will keep, covered in the refrigerator, for up to 1 week.

Mulled Pineapple Juice

I found the base recipe for this drink written on an index card and tucked inside my grandmama's oldest cookbook. It reminded me of a drink I'd had once with a hint of caramel and, seeing how well caramel and pineapple complement each other, I decided to add just a bit of spice to make an old recipe even better. This is a very comforting drink. Serve it in place of traditional mulled apple cider for a unique twist. *Serves 4 to 6*

1 can (46 ounces) unsweetened
    pineapple juice
2 teaspoons ground cinnamon
1/2 teaspoon ground nutmeg
    (optional)
1/2 teaspoon ground allspice
1/2 cup caramel ice cream topping

The Sweet Memories of a Crisp Fall Day

After our sweltering summers, I can't help but feel a rush of excitement when a cool fall breeze begins to blow. Do you remember being a kid in the fall? I remember my sister and I would rake up every leaf we could find into a huge pile and spend the day jumping in it, burying ourselves in the leaves, and raking them up again once the pile was destroyed from all of our antics. You can sure bet our neighbors didn't have any stray leaves hanging around their yard when we were done!

I always loved the cozy, well-worn flannel shirts handed down from my brother.

I always looked forward to Mama getting out our fall clothes because that meant a fresh crop of my brother's flannel shirts from the year before were handed down to me. I'd rather have an old, worn flannel shirt than a new one any day. The soft flannel and slightly too large size were like being wrapped up in a hug from sunup until we were called back into the house at suppertime. Most of my childhood was spent wearing my brother's old clothes, which I have to laugh at now because I know my daughter would be mortified at the very thought of putting on "boy clothes." But for us, we were just proud to have what we had. I thought my brother had hung the moon, so I was proud to be following in his footsteps, even if it was just because I was wearing his old shirt.

I experienced fall more back then than I do now, because as a child I absolutely *lived* in it. Nowadays, I sit here looking at it through my living room window. But you know what? A ray of sunshine is calling my name and the breeze just floated an orange-red leaf by my window. I think it's time to show the kids how to build a jim-dandy of a leaf pile....

When we're done, we'll come back inside and have a cup of caramel apple cider (see page 269) and toast to memories of the past and all the ones yet to be made.

Why We Love Vintage Things

Why do I seek out, collect, and cherish vintage pieces? It's not about the "things." It's about the memories . . .

My grandmama, granddaddy, and great-grandmama all lived together when I was growing up. When I visited their house, they would always have coffee in the evenings. I was never left out because Grandmama mixed me up a special cup of warm milk, sugar, and just enough coffee to color it.

Grandmama had these china mugs on pedestals and each of us would get to drink out of one. I sat at the table with them, my little hands wrapped around the handle while I gazed at the design of an assortment of little sheep that patterned my grown-up mug with my very own coffee inside. I

loved those mugs for all of the many ways they made me feel special.

That was long ago and I've no idea what happened to them, but I've been looking for one for close to ten years. Recently, I found one online and bought it. The day it came in the mail, I held my breath as I opened the box and felt tears spring to my eyes as I pulled out a mug identical to the one from so long ago.

Logically, I know it's just a cup, but that night as I drank my coffee, I felt just a little bit closer to those three precious grandparents. Even though they're no longer here in the flesh, the four of us were having coffee together again after all those years.

And that is why we treasure our vintage things: because of the vintage memories.

Combine all of the ingredients in a large pot over medium heat and bring just to a boil while stirring. Reduce the heat to low and simmer for 15 minutes. Serve immediately.

Mulled Pineapple Juice will keep, in a pitcher in the refrigerator, for up to 1 week. Reheat, stirring, over medium heat before serving.

Slow Cooker Caramel Apple Cider

This slow-cooked apple cider is the perfect treat at the end of a school day or on a lazy Saturday afternoon. During the colder months, I make a batch on the weekend and store whatever we don't finish in the fridge to quickly heat up after school or for weeknight treats. Don't let the simplicity fool ya, though. This caramel apple cider is definitely party worthy as well! *Serves 8 to 10*

1 bottle (64 ounces) apple juice
1 tablespoon ground cinnamon
1/2 teaspoon ground cloves
1/2 teaspoon ground allspice
1 jar (12 ounces) caramel ice cream
    topping
Whipped cream (see page 277),
    for serving (optional)

1 Place the apple juice in a 5- or 6-quart slow cooker on low heat. Stir in the cinnamon, cloves, allspice, and the caramel (reserve a bit if you want to drizzle some over the cider before serving). Stir well after 1 hour.

2 Continue cooking on low (the house will start to smell really great), 3 more hours.

3 Serve in mugs topped with whipped cream and a drizzle of the reserved caramel, if desired.

Slow Cooker Caramel Apple Cider reheats well. Store leftovers in a pitcher in the refrigerator and reheat individual cups in the microwave until warm.

NOTE: To make this on the stove top, place the apple juice, spices, and caramel in a large pot over medium heat and stir until it comes to a low boil, 2 to 3 minutes. Reduce the heat to low and simmer, stirring often, until the spices infuse the cider, 30 minutes.

Happy Anniversary Punch

Party Punch

My sister-in-law, Tina, is one of those go-to people whenever there is a party or shower that needs to be thrown. This is her delicious punch recipe, which she served at my bridal shower. *Serves 25 to 30*

2 cans (46 ounces each) pineapple juice, chilled

2 bottles (2 liters each) lemon-lime soda, chilled

2 cans (12 ounces each) frozen lemonade concentrate, thawed

Just before serving, stir together all of the ingredients in a large punch bowl. Enjoy!

Happy Anniversary Punch

This is the punch that was served at my parents' twenty-fifth anniversary party. It is easy to transport because we make it up as a concentrated mix and then add the other ingredients just before serving. It is our family's favorite celebration punch and always reminds me of the many weddings and happy events where it's been served.

If you're serving this to a crowd, mix up several pitchers of punch concentrate so that you can add more to the punch bowl as needed. We use gallon jugs for this to make it easier to transport. *Serves 12 to 15*

1 cup granulated sugar

1 quart cranberry juice cocktail

1 can (46 ounces) pineapple juice

2 liters ginger ale

Orange slices, fresh raspberries, and mint leaves, for garnish (optional)

1 Combine the sugar, cranberry juice cocktail, and pineapple juice, stirring until the sugar is dissolved to make a punch concentrate.

2 Pour about 2 cups of the concentrate into a ring-shaped ice mold or ice cube trays and freeze. Refrigerate the remainder of the concentrate and the unopened ginger ale overnight.

3 When ready to serve, mix the refrigerated punch concentrate with the ginger ale in a punch bowl and add the frozen punch concentrate on top. Garnish with the fruit and mint, if you like.

Leaving Joy in Your Wake

I once read an amazing quote from George Washington Carver: "No individual has any right to come into the world and go out of it without leaving behind him distinct and legitimate reasons for having passed through it."

Some might look at my grandmother's life and think she didn't have a distinct reason. She didn't win any big awards, she was never on TV, and paparazzi never followed her around hoping for just one more photo. But to all who knew her, she was an anomaly compared to our world today. Eternally optimistic, it seemed that no matter what life threw at her, she was like a fishing bobber that just bobbed right up to the top. Hard times marred every decade of her existence, but she never let them mar her good nature or loving disposition.

Throughout her life, she taught us so much. When she wanted to decorate a cake but had no fancy cake decorating skills, she just iced it smooth and dipped strings in different colors of food coloring and took turns laying them across the cake until she had a pattern. My mother said it was the prettiest birthday cake she ever saw.

When it came to money, I lost count of how many times she told me, "Always pay your share and a little bit more, then nobody will think ill of you." This, from the woman who grew up in the kind of poverty most of us only read about.

She loved her Jay (my granddaddy) like nobody's business and worked side by side with him tirelessly in whatever endeavors he struck out upon, whether it was gardening during the hottest part of the day or waking up at three in the morning to make breakfast for him and his friends before they went fishing.

Grandmama got up every morning ready for whatever task came her way. She was the only person I could call at 4:30 a.m. and know that she'd answer the phone with a cheery hello and have a chat while we drank coffee together.

She didn't complain. She didn't whine. She took the hand she was given and she focused her energy on making the best of it. And when she left us, although it was a hard blow, she left nothing but joy in her wake. Now that's how you live a life. ☺

Pour the pineapple juice into a punch bowl. Add the Kool-Aid and sugar and stir until dissolved. Pour in the soda and serve immediately.

Sunshine Punch

This sunshiny punch is beautiful in both flavor and appearance, perfect for a spring get-together or a bridal or baby shower. It has a nice light flavor, but the addition of ice cream and sherbet makes it a creamy delight that all will love. *Serves 12 to 15*

1 bottle (24 ounces) pineapple juice
3 cans (12 ounces each) lemon-lime soda
Yellow food coloring (optional)
1 quart vanilla ice cream
1 quart pineapple sherbet

1 Stir together the pineapple juice and lemon-lime soda in a large punch bowl. Add a few drops of yellow food coloring, if desired.

2 Scoop the ice cream and sherbet into the top of the bowl and stir gently until it melts a bit and forms a layer of foam. Serve immediately.

Easy Kool-Aid Fruit Punch

This is a simple and quick punch that can change flavors and colors based on what type of Kool-Aid packets you choose. It is especially perfect for children's birthday parties because you can pick the flavor to match the color scheme of the party. This recipe has been around about as long as Kool-Aid has and it's always a hit! *Serves 12 to 15*

1 can (46 ounces) pineapple juice
2 packets (0.14 ounces each) unsweetened Kool-Aid drink mix
2 cups granulated sugar (or Splenda)
2 liters lemon-lime soda

10

Pantry

THESE ARE THE go-to recipes that form the backbone of many of the desserts in this book. From a reliable cookie crumb crust to homemade whipped cream, you'll find what you need here to make your treats that much more special and delicious.

Cookie Crumb Crust

This is a quick and easy pie crust for those times when you don't want to be bothered with making a traditional pie crust. I especially love this crust with Best Ever Orange Meringue Pie (page 140), but it works great with any filling that does not require additional cooking. It can also be made with chocolate wafer cookies instead of vanilla. And although this crust does not have to be baked at all, it can be if the pie recipe you are using calls for it. *Makes one 9-inch crust*

1 box (11 ounces) vanilla wafers
6 tablespoons (3/4 stick) butter or
    margarine, melted
3 tablespoons granulated sugar

1 Crush half of the wafers and place them in a medium-size mixing bowl. Stir in the butter and sugar until well blended.

2 Pat the dough into the bottom of a 9-inch pie plate. Press the remaining wafers along the side of the pie plate to complete the crust. Fill with your choice of filling.

Mix-in-Pan Pie Crust

This delicious, flaky pie crust mixes right in the pan and is enough for any 9-inch pie. If you are making a deep-dish pie or would like enough dough for a pretty fluted edge, double the recipe. *Makes one 9-inch crust*

1 1/2 cups all-purpose flour
1 teaspoon salt
1 1/2 teaspoons granulated sugar
About 1/2 cup vegetable oil
2 tablespoons milk

1 Preheat the oven to 350°F.

2 Stir together the flour, salt, and sugar in a 9-inch pie plate with a spoon until well blended. Slowly add 1/4 cup of the vegetable oil and the milk while stirring. Add the remaining oil, a little at a time, until a rough "ball" of dough forms. (You may not need all of the oil.)

3 Set the spoon aside and mix with a fork. Pat the dough out with your hands to cover the bottom and side of the plate. Crimp the edges with your fingers, if desired.

4 Bake until lightly browned, about 10 minutes. Set on a wire rack to cool.

Meringue

Meringue is a wonderful fluffy topping on any pie, pudding, or custard. It is also good on top of cakes! The trick to preventing your meringue from "shrinking" is to spread it all the way to the rim of the baking dish, which gives it something to cling to as it bakes.

Before whipping up the meringue, make sure your utensils and bowl are very clean. If there is the least bit of greasy residue, the meringue won't froth as it should. Also, make sure no yolk gets into your whites.

I like to beat the egg whites to soft peaks for topping pies and desserts because this is easier to spread. You can beat yours until stiff peaks form if you prefer. (*What on earth do you mean by soft peaks and stiff peaks?* These stages describe the form of the meringue. When you pull your beaters up out of a soft-peak meringue, it will form a point that will then fall back down. If you are at stiff-peak stage and pull the beaters out, it will form a point that will remain sticking up.)

This recipe makes enough to top a pie with about 1 inch of meringue. If you'd like to cover more area or have a thicker meringue (mile-high is fine!), double or even triple the recipe. *Makes enough to top a 9-inch pie or a pudding in a medium-size bowl*

3 large egg whites
¼ cup granulated sugar

1 Preheat the oven to 325°F.

2 Place the egg whites in a large mixing bowl and beat with an electric mixer at medium speed until foamy, about 1 minute. Add the sugar and continue beating at high speed until soft peaks form.

3 Spread on top of a pie or pudding (such as banana pudding), being sure to spread to the edges to seal well. Bake until the top is golden, 10 minutes.

Desserts with fresh meringue are best if eaten within 2 days. They should be stored, covered, in the refrigerator.

Homemade Self-Rising Flour

I hate getting the urge to make a particular recipe and finding that one of the main ingredients is missing. Nothing takes the wind out of my sails like having to make a trip to the grocery store before getting to play in my kitchen. Having this recipe has saved me a trip numerous times, and it takes only a few minutes to mix up. *Makes 1 cup*

1 cup all-purpose flour
1½ teaspoons baking powder
½ teaspoon salt

Stir together all of the ingredients. This mixture will keep, stored in an airtight container at room temperature, for several months.

Homemade Whipped Cream

While frozen whipped topping is definitely a time-saver, some recipes just taste so much more decadent when served with homemade whipped cream. It takes only a few extra minutes to make, and the taste is out of this world. Serve it over cakes, pies, puddings, fruit salads, or drinks of your choice. *Makes 3 to 4 cups*

1 to 2 cups heavy (whipping) cream
2 to 4 tablespoons granulated sugar

Place the whipping cream in a large, chilled mixing bowl and add the sugar to taste (I suggest starting with 2 tablespoons). Mix with an electric beater on high speed until soft peaks and ripples form, about 2 minutes.

Homemade Whipped Cream will keep, covered in the refrigerator, for 1 to 2 days.

Homemade Buttermilk

My grandmother referred to buttermilk as soured milk—and this recipe explains why. Homemade buttermilk can be made in just a few minutes by the addition of lemon juice or vinegar, which causes the milk to sour. It will yield the same results as store-bought buttermilk. *Makes 1 cup*

1 cup milk
1 tablespoon lemon juice or
   white vinegar

Stir together the milk and lemon juice in a small bowl, and let sit at room temperature to thicken, 5 to 10 minutes.

Any leftovers can be stored, covered in the refrigerator, for 1 to 2 days.

Acknowledgments

SIX SHORT YEARS ago I was writing the acknowledgments for my first printed book, marveling at the tremendous blessing of having a book, and thanking my readers for their kindness in being a part of my little online family.

I never dreamed I'd be doing the same thing for a third time, but time has taught me that I almost always underestimate the grace of God when it comes to my own life.

So here I am once more, and my heart is still singing prayers of thanksgiving for every single person who reads this text. I hope you have found encouragement here. I hope you have felt my heart in the words and my love in the recipes. Most important, I hope you've found a little something that reminds you of the sweetness in your own life.

I always try to remember to give thanks to God first, from whom all blessings flow. But that is followed shortly by thoughts of my precious family, who are my dream come true. I spent the first half of my life thus far hoping for a family of my own, and will spend the rest of my life being thankful for these people whom I love more than words, breath, or ink could ever express. Marrying my husband, Ricky, was the single best decision I ever made in my life. My son, Brady, has become the kind of young man my Granddaddy taught me to appreciate: tall, strong of character, and filled with wisdom. My daughter, Katy, is joy and light; so much beauty and compassion are in her heart that she causes me to be a better person just by knowing her. They are among my greatest gifts and I'm so blessed to see how God shares those gifts with the world.

I wake up each day and make the choice to have a good day—and I really have seen that it is that simple. So many people choose to have bad days without even seeing the decision they have made.

I don't know what God has planned for my future but I sure do hope you are in it. May you be blessed with peace, joy, and the ability to always pick out the roses whenever you happen upon a patch of thorns.

Thank you for being here and for allowing me the honor of being a small part of your precious life.

Conversion Tables

Approximate Equivalents

1 stick butter = 8 tbs = 4 oz = 1/2 cup = 115 g

1 cup all-purpose presifted flour = 4.7 oz

1 cup granulated sugar = 8 oz = 220 g

1 cup (firmly packed) brown sugar = 6 oz = 220 g to 230 g

1 cup confectioners' sugar = 4 1/2 oz = 115 g

1 cup honey or syrup = 12 oz

1 large egg = about 2 oz or about 3 tbs

1 egg yolk = about 1 tbs

1 egg white = about 2 tbs

Please note that all conversions are approximate but close enough to be useful when converting from one system to another.

Weight Conversions

U.S./U.K.	Metric	U.S./U.K.	Metric
1/2 oz	15 g	7 oz	200 g
1 oz	30 g	8 oz	250 g
1 1/2 oz	45 g	9 oz	275 g
2 oz	60 g	10 oz	300 g
2 1/2 oz	75 g	11 oz	325 g
3 oz	90 g	12 oz	350 g
3 1/2 oz	100 g	13 oz	375 g
4 oz	125 g	14 oz	400 g
5 oz	150 g	15 oz	450 g
6 oz	175 g	1 lb	500 g

Liquid Conversions

U.S.	Imperial	Metric
2 tbs	1 fl oz	30 ml
3 tbs	1 1/2 fl oz	45 ml
1/4 cup	2 fl oz	60 ml
1/3 cup	2 1/2 fl oz	75 ml
1/3 cup + 1 tbs	3 fl oz	90 ml
1/3 cup + 2 tbs	3 1/2 fl oz	100 ml
1/2 cup	4 fl oz	125 ml
2/3 cup	5 fl oz	150 ml
3/4 cup	6 fl oz	175 ml
3/4 cup + 2 tbs	7 fl oz	200 ml
1 cup	8 fl oz	250 ml
1 cup + 2 tbs	9 fl oz	275 ml
1 1/4 cups	10 fl oz	300 ml
1 1/3 cups	11 fl oz	325 ml
1 1/2 cups	12 fl oz	350 ml
1 2/3 cups	13 fl oz	375 ml
1 3/4 cups	14 fl oz	400 ml
1 3/4 cups + 2 tbs	15 fl oz	450 ml
2 cups (1 pint)	16 fl oz	500 ml
2 1/2 cups	20 fl oz (1 pint)	600 ml
3 3/4 cups	1 1/2 pints	900 ml
4 cups	1 3/4 pints	1 liter

Oven Temperatures

°F	Gas Mark	°C	°F	Gas Mark	°C
250	1/2	120	400	6	200
275	1	140	425	7	220
300	2	150	450	8	230
325	3	160	475	9	240
350	4	180	500	10	260
375	5	190			

Note: Reduce the temperature by 20°C (68°F) for fan-assisted ovens.

Index

MAKE SOMETHING SWEET FOR SOMEONE WHO DESERVES IT AND SHARE IT WITH CHRISTY USING *#SharetheSweetness*.

SWEETNESS JUST FOR YOU!

to: ______________________

from: ______________________

SWEETNESS JUST FOR YOU!

to: ______________________

from: ______________________

Sweetness Just for You!

to: ______________________

from: ______________________

Sweetness Just for You!

to: ______________________

from: ______________________

Sweetness Just for You!

to: ______________________

from: ______________________

Sweetness Just for You!

to: ______________________

from: ______________________

SWEETNESS JUST FOR YOU!

to: ______________________

from: ______________________

SWEETNESS JUST FOR YOU!

to: ______________________

from: ______________________